22-3

11, 12, 28, 30, 35, 40 sqq

BRITAIN'S INVISIBLE EARNINGS

BRITAIN'S
INVISIBLE EARNINGS

The Report of the Committee on Invisible Exports

Director of the Study: WILLIAM M. CLARKE

PUBLISHED FOR THE FINANCIAL ADVISORY PANEL ON
EXPORTS BY THE BRITISH NATIONAL EXPORT COUNCIL
6-14 DEAN FARRAR STREET, LONDON, S.W.1.

PRINTED BY INTERNATIONAL PRINTERS LTD.
ORBIT HOUSE, NEW FETTER LANE, LONDON, EC4.
DISTRIBUTED BY THOMAS SKINNER & CO. (PUBLISHERS) LTD.,
ST. ALPHAGE HOUSE, FORE STREET, LONDON, EC2,
AND SIR ISAAC PITMAN & SONS LTD.,
LONDON.

CONTENTS

Preface by the Chairman
Sir Thomas Bland

Although the essential nature of the contribution of this country's invisible exports to our balance of payments, on which over the years the maintenance of our standard of living depends, emerges clearly from this Report—and it is interesting to find that the Committee's estimate of the City's earnings is higher in total than any previous estimate—it has not, as our terms of reference show, been the task of this Committee to publicize the value and importance of these exports; to this task, by a happy coincidence, the Lord Mayor, Sir Robert Bellinger, has been devoting much energy, with great effect, throughout his term of office. Rather, it has been our responsibility to examine in detail the whole field of Invisibles and recommend means of further improving the favourable balance on Invisibles account.

We found ourselves at the outset confronted by largely uncharted territory and, as we obviously could achieve little without a reasonably clear picture of the volume and nature of our earnings of foreign currency from invisible exports, the Director of our Study and his Assistants have spent many months, in collaboration with the various national associations and institutions concerned (several of whose leaders have been good enough to serve on this Committee), collecting and collating facts, figures and statistics which had never previously been extracted and analysed. And it is largely from this mass of new material that we have drawn a number of conclusions, on which most of our many recommendations are based. In these recommendations we have deliberately avoided a dogmatic approach; we have no wish to tell either the Authorities or the organizations involved how to do their jobs. We have, however, drawn attention to various aspects of our Invisible trade where we feel our net earnings of foreign currency might be increased by changes in law, custom or procedure and we have, besides, suggested directions in which further and deeper investigation, either by the Authorities or by the associations or institutions directly concerned, seems desirable.

We hope very much that the statistical records we have assembled for the first time will be maintained and published year by year as a matter of routine; much of the work occasioned by our Study would be wasted if it were treated as a once and for all exercise.

We have enjoyed, and are most grateful for, the whole-hearted co-operation of the Treasury, the Board of Trade, the Bank of England, the Central Statistical Office and of many individuals, associations and organizations, too numerous to name, to whom our Inquiry has caused a great deal of work but whose collaboration was essential to the production of this Report. I must, further, mention The Economists Advisory Group, and in particular Professor John H. Dunning and Professor E. Victor Morgan, who have been closely associated with the Director of the Study throughout his investigations.

To the Director himself, Mr. William M. Clarke, the Committee are deeply indebted for the compilation and editing of a Report which breaks new ground and paves the way for further inquiry, but which may also be regarded, in its own right, as a unique work of reference on a remarkably complex sector of our economy.

INTRODUCTION

1.   The Committee on Invisible Exports was appointed by the Financial Advisory Panel on Exports as a Committee of the Panel, which had been invited by the British National Export Council to "examine" our invisible exports, with the following terms of reference:
    1. To examine the "Invisible" element in the Balance of Payments.
    2. To consider means of promoting and stimulating Invisible Exports; and to make recommendations.

2.   The Committee was asked to confine itself to the private sector, excluding Government receipts and expenditure, and also to exclude direct investment overseas, already under study by Mr. W. B. Reddaway on behalf of the Confederation of British Industry.

3.   The Committee appointed Mr. W. M. Clarke as Director of the Study and held its first full meeting on June 27, 1966. It began its detailed investigations in July 1966; they were completed a year later. Members of the Committee, when first appointed, were as follows:

Sir Thomas Bland, T.D., D.L. (*Chairman*)
> *Chairman*, Financial Advisory Panel on Exports
> *Deputy Chairman*, Barclays Bank Limited

C. H. Kleinwort, Esq. (*Deputy Chairman*)
> *Deputy Chairman*, Financial Advisory Panel on Exports
> *Chairman*, Kleinwort Benson Limited

Alex Abel Smith, Esq., T.D.
> *Director*, J. Henry Schroder Wagg & Co. Ltd.

D. W. Beharrell, Esq.
> *Chairman*, British Export Houses Association

F. B. Bolton, Esq., M.C.
> *President*, Chamber of Shipping of the U.K.

Sir George Bolton, K.C.M.G.
> *Chairman*, Bank of London and South America Ltd.

Sir Charles Denman, Bt., M.C.
> *Chairman*, Tennant Guaranty Ltd.

The Right Hon. The Viscount Harcourt, K.C.M.G., O.B.E.
> *Managing Director*, Morgan Grenfell & Co. Ltd.

E. J. W. Hellmuth, Esq.
> *Director and Deputy Chief General Manager* (*International*), Midland Bank Ltd.

The Right Hon. Lord Kilmarnock, M.B.E.
> *Chairman*, The Baltic Exchange

R. E. Liddiard, Esq.
> *Chairman*, British Federation of Commodity Associations

F. E. P. Sandilands, Esq., C.B.E.
> *Chairman*, British Insurance Association

R. W. Sturge, Esq.
> *Chairman*, Lloyd's

P. H. Swan, Esq., D.S.O., D.F.C.
> Member of the Council of the London Stock Exchange

R. L. Wills, Esq., C.B.E., M.C.
> *President*, Association of British Chambers of Commerce

4.   During the course of the past year, the following changes in representation on the Committee have taken place:

Mr. Beharrell was replaced by The Hon. R. D. Campbell, as Chairman, British Export Houses Association;

Mr. Sturge was replaced by Ralph Hiscox, Esq., O.B.E., as Chairman, Lloyd's;

Mr. Bolton was replaced by The Hon. Anthony Cayzer, as President, Chamber of Shipping of the U.K.

CHAPTER I

SCOPE OF THE INQUIRY

5.   The Committee's terms of reference were set out in two parts. It was asked to investigate Britain's invisible earnings and to make recommendations about how to increase them further. This meant that the Committee had to consider both the detailed figures of invisible earnings and the way in which they were earned and ought to be earned. The first became a statistical ground-clearing exercise; the second an assessment of the climate in which invisible earnings fluctuated and of the policies, both Governmental and private, that might lead to sustained growth.

6.   "Invisible" earnings need a word of explanation at the outset. Why are they "invisible" and how do they arise? Basically they are the earnings (whether in foreign currency or sterling) from the provision of services to people living abroad: in direct contrast to "visible" earnings which are derived from the sale of physical goods abroad. Whereas "visible" exports can be seen, touched, weighed, as they pass through Britain's ports (both sea and air), "invisible" exports arise from a variety of activities. The performance of a British play on Broadway, the shipping of foreign goods by a British vessel, accounting advice given to a foreign client, the insurance of a foreign factory, the raising of capital in London by a foreign borrower, the profit on a sale of rubber from Malaya to Russia by a British merchant, the purchase of British industrial "know-how" by a foreign firm: all are "invisible" and all lead to the earning of exchange from foreigners.

7.   This is the broad distinction between visible and invisible exports. But the Committee had to concern itself with the more specific definition of invisible exports used in the official balance of payments figures. These are taken to be the earnings from non-residents of the United Kingdom in exchange for the provision of services, together with income derived from overseas assets. The invisible earnings usually shown in Britain's balance of payments also include two other items: one is described as "private transfers" and includes personal gifts, legacies, migrants' funds etc.: the other is Government receipts and expenditure. Both are non-commercial in character, but while the first (private transfers) falls within the Committee's terms of reference, the second (Government receipts and expenditure) was specifically excluded. In short the Committee was asked to concern itself with Britain's *private* invisible earnings. As the Committee will show, this is an important distinction, for Government expenditure has had a significant effect on the recent trend of Britain's invisible income.

8.   This trend can be seen from TABLE 1 which is based on the first table in the annual publication *United Kingdom Balance of Payments* for 1966 (H.M.S.O.),[1]

1. Most of the statistics used in the report are taken from the 1966 issue; where later estimates have been used, they are indicated in the text.

TABLE 1

£ millions	Imports (f.o.b.)	Exports and Re-exports (f.o.b.)	Visible Balance (net)	Invisible Balance (net)	Current Balance
	A	B	C	D	C + D
1952	3,048	2,769	− 279	+ 442	+ 163
1953	2,927	2,683	− 244	+ 389	+ 145
1954	2,989	2,785	− 204	+ 321	+ 177
1955	3,386	3,073	− 313	+ 158	− 155
1956	3,324	3,377	+ 53	+ 155	+ 208
1957	3,538	3,509	− 29	+ 252	+ 223
1958	3,378	3,407	+ 29	+ 307	+ 336
1959	3,640	3,522	− 118	+ 254	+ 136
1960	4,141	3,733	− 408	+ 133	− 275
1961	4,045	3,892	− 153	+ 148	− 5
1962	4,098	3,994	− 104	+ 205	+ 101
1963	4,370	4,287	− 83	+ 190	+ 107
1964	5,016[1]	4,471	− 545	+ 150	− 395
1965	5,065[1]	4,784	− 281	+ 163	− 118
1966	5,261[1]	5,110	− 151	+ 92	− 59

1. Including payments for U.S. military aircraft.

TABLE 2

£ millions	Invisible Balance (net)	Government Spending (net)	Private Invisible Balance (net)	Private Invisible Receipts	Private Invisible Payments
1952	+ 442	− 61	+ 503	1,544	1,041
1953	+ 389	− 66	+ 455	1,531	1,076
1954	+ 321	− 131	+ 452	1,614	1,162
1955	+ 158	− 138	+ 296	1,643	1,347
1956	+ 155	− 175	+ 330	1,817	1,487
1957	+ 252	− 144	+ 396	1,916	1,520
1958	+ 307	− 219	+ 526	2,036	1,510
1959	+ 254	− 227	+ 481	2,050	1,569
1960	+ 133	− 283	+ 416	2,154	1,738
1961	+ 148	− 333	+ 481	2,225	1,744
1962	+ 205	− 361	+ 566	2,331	1,765
1963	+ 190	− 383	+ 573	2,435	1,862
1964	+ 150	− 433	+ 583	2,625	2,042
1965	+ 163	− 446	+ 609	2,806	2,197
1966	+ 92	− 457	+ 549	2,823	2,274

normally referred to as the Pink Book and issued by the Central Statistical Office. The column showing the "visible balance" has fluctuated sharply over the years shown, reaching small surpluses in 1956 and 1958 and large deficits in 1955, 1960 and 1964. The column showing the "invisible balance," on the other hand, has shown a consistent surplus throughout this period. But the surplus has been declining. It dropped from an annual average of £327 million in 1952-55 to one of £180 million in 1962-65 and to £92 million in 1966. It is the reason for this fall in the annual invisible surplus that must be dealt with first. It has a simple explanation. As already explained, Government receipts and expenditure are included in Britain's total invisible earnings, as normally presented in the official balance of payments. And since Government spending abroad, net, has been rising in recent years, this has naturally left its impact on total invisible earnings. If this governmental element is deducted from the total, quite a different picture emerges. Since the Committee's terms of reference exclude the examination of Government spending, the deduction has been done for the same years in TABLE 2. The net invisible balance is again shown in the first column: net Government spending is shown in the second column. When the second is taken from the first (as in column three), the residual is what can be described as Britain's net private[1] invisible earnings. This shows a more encouraging trend. Instead of a decline in invisible earnings, there is a gradual increase from an annual average of £426 million in 1952-55 to one of £588 million in 1962-65 (with a modest slip back to £549 million in 1966).

9.   One further refinement is needed. In the two official publications which regularly contain Britain's balance of payments statistics (*United Kingdom Balance of Payments* and *Economic Trends*), while visible imports and exports are presented gross in most summary tables, Britain's invisible income is invariably shown net after deducting invisible payments from invisible receipts. This makes it difficult to appreciate the full contribution of invisible exports to the economy. For this reason the Committee felt it necessary at the beginning of its inquiry to stress the gross figures of Britain's private invisible receipts and payments. They are shown in columns four and five of TABLE 2. The figure of private invisible receipts of £2,823 million in 1966, therefore, can be directly compared with visible exports (and re-exports) of £5,110 million; thus private invisible earnings contributed 37 per cent of Britain's total foreign exchange earnings in that year.

10.   In undertaking its inquiry, therefore, the Committee was faced with two problems. One was the potential area of investigation. As these figures show, it was tantamount to conducting a detailed investigation into over a third of Britain's foreign exchange earnings (and payments) and into scores of quite separate industries. To look into every source of these earnings, it was decided, would have been impossible with the time and resources at the disposal of the Committee. The second problem arose from the nature of

---

1. "Private" invisible earnings still include two governmental elements that are difficult to extract. The item "interest, profits and dividends" includes some government interest payments (interest on inter governmental loans, Treasury bills, government stock etc.). Secondly, the earnings of public corporations (B.E.A., B.O.A.C.) are included.

most of these earnings. Each activity is different; each activity is highly complex. This brought its own analytical difficulties; it also produced particular problems in analysing the statistical information available and in any attempts to gather new material.[1]

11.   The Committee, therefore, had to decide how to concentrate its resources most usefully. Since so much of the ground was being covered for the first time, it became clear that to suggest areas for future investigation was as important as attempting to initiate new inquiries at once. As a result both approaches were used both in the statistical analysis and in its policy recommendations.

A. *Statistical analysis:*

Apart from the necessary analysis of invisible earnings as a whole (both historically and internationally as shown in Chapters II and III), it was decided to concentrate on the gaps in our statistical knowledge of individual industries and professions. In some cases new figures have been collected for the first time; in others recommendations have been made about future collection.

B. *Policy recommendations:*

In considering ways of improving future invisible earnings, the Committee decided that it was impossible to investigate each industry with the same degree of attention. Some (e.g. shipping, and some of the professions) were already the subject of specific inquiries and could be treated more lightly than others. In other cases, when the necessary investigations were beyond the Committee's resources, the Committee decided to raise questions even if it could not provide the answers and to point the way towards further inquiries. In general the Committee has provided suggestions for raising Britain's invisible earnings without necessarily suggesting that such action is immediately appropriate. In many cases the time for adopting the suggested measures will depend on the state of the economy, on the state of the pound and, ultimately, on political judgements.

1. Consider the foreign exchange deals of the banks. One isolated deal in the so-called Euro-dollar market can often lead to further complex deals, as other dealers get involved in the "spot" and "forward" markets. It is difficult enough to explain these kind of deals; to make any attempt at recording them provides additional problems—of definition, of the cost in time and energy to the dealers and of the danger of double-counting. (See Chapter IV). Similar difficulties faced the Committee in most of its statistical inquiries.

CHAPTER II

HISTORICAL ANALYSIS

12.   In the post-war period Britain's invisible exports have shared a vital relationship with visible trade. In every post-war year but two (1956 and 1958), visible trade has been in deficit; and in every year, without exception, invisible trade has been in surplus. Thus the Committee felt obliged at the outset of its inquiry to consider how long Britain had been dependent on invisible earnings as a regular contributor to its total foreign income and how long this pattern—of visible deficits and invisible surpluses—had been established. Had invisible earnings always been a major feature of Britain's trading activities and were they likely to remain so? Or were they a more recent phenomenon, a valuable, though declining, aftermath of Britain's industrial and commercial dominance in the 19th century, and thus bound to dwindle with time?

13.   There is no dearth of trade statistics. The difficulty lies in interpreting them. Accordingly the Committee has been forced to rely on the work of a number of historians and statisticians over the past 30 years for its interpretation of British trading and commercial history.[1] Year to year records of visible imports and exports extend back nearly 300 years, to 1697. But their quality varies. There is also a marked and, as recent investigations have shown, significant break in the trend shown by the annual series. From 1697 to 1853 the records show, with only five exceptions, unfailing visible export surpluses; from 1853 until the present day, again with a few minor exceptions, they show repeated deficits. At the time and for many years afterwards the apparent reversal of trend was generally accepted. A view of British economic history took shape, based on these figures and on other considerations. This was that Britain was intrinsically a consistent and indeed heavy net exporter; that in the middle of the 19th century some change occurred in her economic structure and competitive ability which converted her into a net importer; and that her earlier export successes had allowed her to build up investments overseas on the proceeds of which she could continue to balance her payments.

14.   By the 1930s, however, when the events of the previous century were coming under close scrutiny, some economic historians found it increasingly difficult to accept the notion that the entire trading propensity of the nation had been over-turned from one year to another. Researches had begun into the nature of the change recorded in 1853. Although it had been known that

---

1. Chief among the economic historians examining Britain's trade records were Imlah of the United States, Schlote of Germany and Clark of this country. These researches, which were taken up by others, including Rostow, Gayer, Cole, Deane, Schumpeter and Maizels, continued until recently. Some of the essential results were published in B. R. Mitchell & Phyllis Deane's *Abstract of British Historical Statistics*, in 1962. Other works drawn on by the Committee are *Economic Elements in the Pax Britannica* by A. H. Imlah and *British Economic Growth, 1688-1959* by Phyllis Deane and W. A. Cole.

a change took place in 1853 in the official statistical methods its full implications were not realized until the pre-1853 trade figures were put on the same basis as those after 1853. In brief, trade data until then had been based on Government "official values," which in fact grossly over-rated exports and under-rated imports; after that date the records consisted of real values of merchandise, as declared by the shippers, in accordance with the modern practice.[1] Thus by the middle of last century, after over a century and a half of the practice of simply multiplying trading volumes by official "values," the trade totals had become increasingly out of line with true values. By 1853, it has been estimated, the official values over-estimated exports by 120 per cent and re-exports by 60 per cent; the true value of imports on the other hand was 19 per cent more than that recorded. Thus, under the official rating, exports for 1853 were recorded at £242 million, and imports c.i.f. at £123 million, leaving a favourable balance of £119 million. The true state of trade has subsequently been put at: exports £115·7 million; imports c.i.f. £148·5 million; causing a consequent trade deficit of £32·8 million.

15. The task of converting the official records prior to 1853 to true values,[2] by using a variety of statistical methods, thus began. This was, of necessity, a lengthy task. By 1958 Professor Imlah had filled in a number of gaps and had succeeded in completing a series of real import and export values back to 1796. Deane and Cole, covering the same ground in 1962, concurred in his findings. The results were unequivocal. The classical era of British export surpluses was found to be non-existent. Britain's trade balances, so far from showing the expected traditional surpluses, consisted of almost unvarying net deficits. In fact from 1796 to 1913 only five years revealed a trading surplus. They were 1797, 1802, 1816, 1821 and 1822. The next were to appear in 1956 and 1958. Thus, as far back as the statistics could trace, Britain had been a net importing country.

16. The size and persistence of this trading deficit and the way in which it has been financed now need to be examined. Although the trading deficit has persisted throughout the 19th century and since, Britain's trading pattern has gone through several phases. The first third of the 19th century reflected a virtual stagnation in trade—at least in money values. Imports, standing at £50·2 million in 1801-1805, and exports at £51·1 million, had changed to no more than £52·6 million and £48·1 million by 1831-1835. Around the half-way mark in the century, however, these trade streams began to broaden rapidly, and grew even faster in the late 1850s and early 1860s. By 1871-1875 imports *by value*, had risen six times to £316·8 million and exports by an equal measure to £297·5 million. Between then and the end of the century expan-

---

1. The official values discarded in 1853 were essentially those devised 157 years earlier when the first Inspector-General for Imports and Exports took up his appointment and worked out a system for recording trade. He chose to assign to each article imported or exported a unit value—the "official value," to calculate from the latter the total value of each consignment, and thence, the total inflow and outflow, by value, of all merchandise for the country as a whole. William Culliford, the first Inspector-General drew up the scale of unit values after painstaking inquiries among merchants and shippers. He was also conscientious in reviewing and correcting the valuations as time went on. Thereafter, however, few efforts were made to keep the official values in step with current prices. As Professor Imlah has put it: "Year after year, through peace and war, dearth and plenty, high prices and low, the clerks meticulously multiplied their quantities by these unchanging rates."

2. These earlier records are still useful in analysing the volume and prices of overseas trade in this period.

sion on both accounts was slower; imports, again in money terms, moved up to £470 million in 1900, and exports to £354 million. In the one and a half decades to the First World War there was a further sharp rise, import values growing by some 50 per cent to £692 million in 1913, and exports by some 80 per cent to £635 million. In the long focus of this historical series, the inter-war years, and particularly the early 1930s, stand out as an interlude of economic famine, with the value of trade in both directions slipping well below the 1913 level between 1931 and 1933. From the end of the Second World War a further period of very fast growth set in. In the 20 years 1946-1965 imports by value multiplied four and a half times from £1,081 million to £5,059 million, and exports, again by value, increased five times from £905 million to £4,779 million. The post-war period, therefore, stands out as the second fastest phase of trade growth by value, in the last 150 years, and it is worth noting that exports rose somewhat faster than imports. Over the century and a half as a whole, it will be seen that imports and exports moved up very largely in step. Because the absolute quantities magnified tremendously, both by value and by volume, the gap between imports and exports grew impressively in relation to itself. Over the complete span of years, however, exports ran very roughly at 85 per cent of the value of imports. There have been at least two periods, none the less, of marked divergence from this average. The percentage of imports paid for by exports fell to an average of 75 per cent in the closing decade of the 19th, and the first five years of the 20th, centuries, and touched the very low point of 72 per cent in 1896-1900. On the other hand, the coverage has fairly consistently run around 90 per cent throughout the post-Second World War period, sometimes, as in 1956-1959, reaching over 99 per cent. Indeed exports have covered an average 96 per cent of the cost of imports over the last 10 years.

17.   In spite of these continuing deficits on visible trade, Britain has balanced her current overseas payments (excluding Government payments) throughout the period since the beginning of the 19th century. The gap has been filled (as was shown in the introduction) by currency income from other sectors, principally the service trades, shipping, brokerage, merchanting, commission agenting, together with banking, insurance and other financial services—and earnings from investments held overseas. The continuing contribution of these invisible earnings is now beginning to be understood. But the difficulty has not been so much the existence of a lengthy but misleading record as in the case of visible trade, but the absence of any formally collected invisible statistics at all until after the Second World War.

18.   There is, of course, plenty of qualitative evidence of Britain's invisible transactions in the past. There is a record, for instance, of the shipment of bullion to set up the East India Company after the granting of its charter in 1600, a true capital export. A number of other corporations and merchant companies were founded at the same time. The growth of joint stock companies in the 18th century was, in England, strongly tied to investment abroad. The South Sea Bubble was merely a strident echo of a sustained business activity. Shipping, merchanting, brokerage and kindred commerces

17

were clearly well established by the end of the 16th century, as is evident from no more obscure a source than the literature of the time. However for the purposes of the present report statistical records are clearly needed. In the absence of formal records, the invisible balance can only be estimated. This can however be reasonably accurate. There are a number of indications on which the arithmetic can be based. There are taxation pointers to the inflow of investment revenues. A number of authoritative statements of our external asset position were made throughout the period. Figures for merchant shipping employed, freight rate indices, and data for port entries and clearances provide a guide to shipping earnings and to insurance and brokerage receipts. A number of series have been constructed on this basis. As with visible trade the series compiled by Professor Imlah is the most authoritative and the one in standard use. It is both fuller and more internally consistent than the others, and it accords with actual figures wherever these are available for cross-verification. It is reasonably accurate for groups of years taken together, and it is used here.

19. In one important respect, however, Imlah's records are not altogether suitable for the analyses both of the separate development of the invisible items, and of the relationship between them. Imlah shows his merchandise series on the normal trade basis, that is to say, exports are valued f.o.b., but imports are quoted c.i.f. This means that within the figure for visible imports there is an invisible element, representing shipping freights, insurance costs, brokerage, commissions and the like. In drawing up the invisible side of his record, Imlah took this into account, and his figures for shipping, insurance, brokerage and kindred earnings are in fact gross incomes. There is no deduction for freights earned by foreign shipowners carrying British imports, since these are already debited in the visible import figure; no deduction, similarly, is made for British shipowners' earnings from British clients on imports to this country, since this sum is already in the imports figure as a debit, and must be cancelled out. The same is true for the other service earnings. The net balance of payments result is of course unaffected, but the immediate effect is to show visible imports and consequently the trade deficit itself somewhat larger than in reality, and at the same time to show shipping and allied earnings also larger than was the case. Imlah's series have therefore been recalculated to produce a series of f.o.b. trade figures in both directions and the true position on the invisible side. The results are set out in TABLE 3 (a). For convenience, a start was made only at the year 1825, and the table is worked through to Imlah's terminal year, 1913.[1]

20. As to the remainder of the period under consideration, there are of course official records for the 20 years from the present day back to 1945. An official statement was also made for the year 1938, and using this and other relevant data, one reliable authority[2] has compiled a five year average for 1934-1938, and this is used. The 13 years 1920-1933 remain a gap difficult to bridge. No kind of official collection of data was made, but the Board of

1. For a description of the method used for the recalculation of Imlah's data, see Appendix A.
2. cf. The Sterling Area: an American Analysis; E.C.A. Special Mission to the U.K., 1951. Cf. also Cmnd. 7928.

Trade issued yearly estimates. These have been used in conjunction with estimates for total invisibles prepared by the London and Cambridge Economic Service. The details are set out in TABLE 3 (*b*).

21.   In all, these compendia give a continuous look on a reasonably comparable basis at the current account of the balance of payments for the years 1825-1965. In conclusion it should be noted that a new balance of payments item, that of Government receipts and expenditures, emerged as a perceptible magnitude after the First World War, and these figures are included in the accounts from that point onwards.

22.   TABLES 3 (*a*) and 3 (*b*), therefore, set out a continuous series of figures of Britain's visible and invisible trading accounts from 1825-1965. The Committee derives three important conclusions from this reconstruction of Britain's historical trading records. They are:

1. Britain, as far back as the statistical records go and probably even farther, has had a continuing deficit on visible trading account. Only seven out of the past 175 years have shown a trading surplus.

2. Over the same extended period, Britain has had a continuous surplus on her invisible trading accounts. If Government spending abroad is excluded from the figures, this invisible surplus has always been big enough to offset the deficit on visible trade.

3. It is clear, therefore, that Britain is and has been for well over a century and a half as much a commercial and financial nation as a manufacturing nation.

TABLE 3 (a)

BRITAIN'S PAYMENTS 1826–1913

	1826–1830	1831–1835	1836–1840	1841–1845	1846–1850	1851–1855	1856–1860	1861–1865	1866–1870
Visible Trade:					(£ millions)				
Imports f.o.b.	47·5	52·6	72·5	69·3	85·6	115·5	159·1	215·4	254·7
Exports f.o.b.	42·5	48·1	59·3	62·7	71·6	105·3	149·1	190·8	234·7
Net	− 5·0	− 4·5	−13·2	− 6·6	−14·0	−10·2	−10·0	−24·6	−20·0
Invisible Trade: Services									
Payments	1·2	1·4	1·8	2·0	2·5	3·4	5·3	7·1	7·3
Receipts	4·6	5·3	6·6	6·7	8·1	11·9	17·0	22·3	26·0
Net	3·4	3·9	4·8	4·7	5·6	8·5	11·7	15·2	18·7
Shipping: Payments	1·2	1·4	1·0	1·4	2·0	3·0	4·2	5·8	6·2
Receipts	5·9	5·9	7·1	8·7	10·7	13·6	20·2	25·3	33·5
Net	4·7	4·5	6·1	7·3	8·7	10·6	16·0	19·5	27·3
Emigrants and Tourists: Net	− 2·7	− 3·5	− 4·0	− 4·6	− 6·1	− 7·5	− 7·5	− 7·7	− 9·2
Total Invisibles									
Net	5·4	4·9	6·9	7·4	8·2	11·6	20·2	27·0	36·8
Net Trade and Services	+ 0·4	+ 0·4	− 6·3	+ 0·8	− 5·8	+ 1·4	+10·2	+ 2·4	+16·8
Interest and Dividends Net	4·6	5·4	8·0	7·5	9·5	11·7	16·5	21·8	30·8
Balance on Current Account	+ 5·0	+ 5·8	+ 1·7	+ 8·3	− 3·7	+13·1	+26·7	+24·2	+47·6

Table 3 (a)

BRITAIN'S PAYMENTS 1826–1913

1871–1875	1876–1880	1881–1885	1886–1890	1891–1895	1896–1900	1901–1905	1906–1910	1911–1913	
				(£ millions)					Visible Trade:
316·8	336·8	351·6	342·8	371·9	422·1	482·2	566·9	655·2	Imports f.o.b.
297·5	257·9	295·2	298·5	287·5	303·7	367·2	487·8	593·9	Exports f.o.b.
− 19·3	− 78·9	− 56·4	− 44·3	− 84·4	−118·4	−115·0	− 79·1	− 61·3	Net
									Invisible Trade: Services
7·4	7·6	8·1	8·0	7·6	8·5	12·9	12·1	14·2	Payments
32·8	29·3	28·0	27·6	26·9	27·6	25·1	49·0	58·7	Receipts
25·4	21·7	19·9	19·6	19·3	19·1	12·2	36·9	44·5	Net
									Shipping:
5·9	6·2	6·3	6·1	6·2	7·2	10·9	13·1	14·8	Payments
36·9	39·8	45·7	43·1	42·8	45·6	54·9	69·0	77·5	Receipts
31·0	33·6	39·4	37·0	36·6	38·4	44·0	55·9	62·7	Net
									Emigrants and Tourists:
− 11·5	− 9·0	− 11·2	− 11·1	− 10·0	− 10·7	− 13·0	− 17·6	− 22·1	Net
									Total Invisibles
44·9	46·3	48·1	45·5	45·9	46·8	43·2	75·2	85·1	Net
									Net Trade and Services
+ 25·6	− 32·6	− 8·3	+ 1·2	− 38·5	− 71·6	− 71·8	− 3·9	+ 23·8	
50·0	56·3	64·8	84·2	94·0	100·2	113·0	151·4	188·0	Interest and Dividends Net
+ 75·6	+ 23·7	+ 56·5	+ 85·4	+ 55·5	+ 28·6	+ 41·2	+147·5	+211·8	Balance on Current Account

Table 3 (b)

BRITAIN'S PAYMENTS 1920–1965

£ (millions)

		1920–25	1926–30	1931–33	1934–38	1946–51	1952–54	1955–57
Visible trade imports (f.o.b.)		1,163	1,075	680	796	2,022	2,988	3,416
Exports and re-exports (f.o.b.)		997	799	435	531	1,773	2,746	3,320
A. Net		−166	−276	−245	−265	−249	−242	− 96
Invisible Trade:								
Other Services	Payments						(180)	204
	Receipts						(316)	381
Net		(+ 55[1])	(+ 75[1])	+ 40[1]	+ 54	(+174)	(+136)	+177
Transport	Payments				85	(189)	(490)	673
	Receipts				90	(274)	(577)	647
Net		(+170)	(+125)	(+ 70)	+ 5	(+ 85)	(+ 87)	− 26
Travel	Payments				34	(75)	(91)	134
	Receipts				26	(41)	(88)	120
Net					− 8	(− 34)	(− 3)	− 14
B. Total services (net)		(+225)	(+200)	(+110)	+ 51	(+225)	(+220)	(+137)
Interest, Profits and Dividends:								
	Payments				30			
	Receipts				200			
Net		(+210)	(+245)	(+160)	+170	+238	+244	+217
Private Transfers	Payments				—		(64)	100
	Receipts				—		(70)	87
Net					—	(− 14)	(+ 6)	− 13
C. Total Private Invisibles:								
	Payments							
	Receipts							
Net		+314	+327	+197	+221	+307	+470	+341
Net Trade and Services A+B		(+ 59)	(− 76)	(−135)	−214	(− 24)	(− 22)	(+ 41)
Net Trade and Private Invisibles A+C		+149	+ 51	− 48	− 44	+ 58	+228	+245
D. Government (net)		− 13	+ 13	− 4	− 6	−166	− 86	−152
Current Balance A+C+D		+136	+ 64	− 52	− 50	−108	+142	+ 92

[1] Includes travel and private transfers.

Sources: 1920–33—Visible trade, invisible balance, government and current balance—"Key Statistics of the British
Economy." Remainder—Board of Trade (figures have been rounded).
1934–38—"The Sterling Area—An American Analysis."
1946–63—Mainly from the U.K. Balance of Payments "Pink Book" 1966 but some detail of invisibles
(1946–54) from earlier editions of the "Pink Book."

Table 3 (*b*)

BRITAIN'S PAYMENTS 1920–1965

(£ millions)

1958	1959	1960	1961	1962	1963	1964	1965	
3,378	3,640	4,141	4,045	4,098	4,370	5,016	5,065	Visible trade imports (f.o.b.)
3,407	3,522	3,733	3,892	3,994	4,287	4,471	4,784	Exports and re-exports (f.o.b.)
+ 29	−118	−408	−153	−104	− 83	−545	−281	A. Net
								Invisible Trade:
224	239	264	260	264	269	292	323	Other Services Payments
419	444	471	507	518	510	560	583	Receipts
+195	+205	+207	+247	+254	+241	+268	+260	Net
646	670	749	760	762	789	851	881	Transport Payments
697	700	730	747	765	792	844	910	Receipts
+ 51	+ 30	− 19	− 13	+ 3	+ 3	− 7	+ 29	Net
152	164	186	200	210	241	261	290	Travel Payments
134	143	169	176	183	188	190	193	Receipts
− 18	− 21	− 17	− 24	− 27	− 53	− 71	− 97	Net
+228	+214	+171	+210	+230	+191	+190	+192	B. Total services (net)
								Interest, Profits and Dividends:
389	396	438	422	418	435	484	538	Payments
683	663	680	686	754	831	900	989	Receipts
+294	+267	+242	+264	+336	+396	+416	+451	Net
99	100	101	102	111	128	154	165	Private transfers Payments
103	100	104	109	111	114	131	131	Receipts
+ 4	—	+ 3	+ 7	—	− 14	− 23	− 34	Net
								C. Total Private Invisibles:
1,510	1,569	1,738	1,744	1,765	1,862	2,042	2,197	Payments
2,036	2,050	2,154	2,225	2,331	2,435	2,625	2,806	Receipts
+526	+481	+416	+481	+566	+573	+583	+609	Net
+257	+ 96	−237	+ 57	+126	+108	−355	− 89	Net Trade and Services A+B
								Net Trade and Private Invisibles:
+555	+363	+ 8	+328	+462	+490	+ 38	+328	A+C
−219	−227	−283	−333	−361	−383	−433	−446	D. Government (net)
+336	+136	−275	− 5	+101	+107	−395	−118	Current Balance A+C+D

Source: 1964-65—"Economic Trends"—June 1967.
N.B. The data used are the most suitable and up to date available. Inevitably, with the variety of sources used, the sum of the components does not always agree with the total given.

APPENDIX A: CHAPTER II

The conversion of Professor Imlah's series cannot be done with anything approaching the accuracy of the original. Imlah's shipping tables were constructed after precise calculation of international tonnage earnings, entrances and clearances in foreign trade at British ports, and price and freight changes throughout the period. Without similar aids the same order of exactitude cannot be achieved. On the other hand Imlah gave sufficient indications in the body of his book to permit the use of an abbreviated method to give a reliable if approximate series of the type desired.

Imlah has calculated, within close limits, the varying percentage of the total import value which was represented by the c.i.f. element throughout the period. Application of the percentage permits the extraction year by year of this element. This leaves imports and exports on an f.o.b. basis. As will be seen from TABLE 3, the structural deficit is unaffected by this revaluation, although the import margin is smaller.

Taking then the c.i.f. amount itself, application of the ratio of British and foreign shipping entries in the foreign trade at British ports in cargo, will produce a breakdown of c.i.f. costs incurred on the one hand in British bottoms and not therefore constituting a foreign currency charge at all, and, on the other, in foreign bottoms, giving rise to a payment across the exchanges. Using the percentage ratio to imports used by Imlah himself to calculate insurance, brokerage and commission arisings, these can be extracted from each side of the breakdown. The remainder is freights. These components can now be redistributed in their proper places on the invisible side of the account. Freights, insurance, brokerage and commissions earned on imports in British shipping must be deducted from the gross income figures and thus disappear altogether from the account. The figures in respect of foreign shipping, however, now enter in as a payment on the invisible side. Under each item—"shipping" and "services"—in the invisible account, there are now two figures: a true figure for receipts consisting of gross earnings reduced in accordance with the above by the total of freights in British bottoms; and a figure for payments derived as just stated. With these, a net figure for actual foreign exchange returns can be added.

CHAPTER III

WORLD COMPARISON OF INVISIBLES

23.   In recent years tables setting out Britain's position among the world's leading exporters of manufactured goods have been published regularly. The Board of Trade publishes details setting out Britain's share of world trade once a quarter. But nothing comparable is done officially for invisible transactions. Is Britain's share of invisibles a dominant one? Which countries are Britain's main rivals? Is world trade in invisibles rising or falling? The Committee found that no regular international comparisons were available either here or abroad. The most notable attempt to provide some international comparisons was made by Professor Ely Devons seven years ago. The results were published in *Lloyds Bank Review* in March 1961. Basing his estimates on the balance of payments statistics collected and issued by the International Monetary Fund, he calculated that in 1958 world receipts from invisible transactions totalled $33,800 million compared with $87,800 million from merchandise exports. Invisibles thus accounted for 28 per cent of total world trade.

24.   The Committee felt it essential to establish the importance of Britain's role in the world's invisible transactions in recent years and accordingly decided to undertake a new more detailed inquiry. Professor Devons had already completed a preliminary analysis of the figures up to 1963 when the Committee began its own inquiry. He generously offered his work to the Committee and his statistics are acknowledged where used in this report. The Committee also undertook a new extensive analysis of its own. In order to facilitate its work, the Committee decided to concentrate on 31 of the leading nations in invisible transactions. These 31 countries accounted for 87·6 per cent of world trade (visible and invisible) and no less than 94·7 per cent of the world's total invisible transactions in 1964. Since the results of the Committee's inquiry broke important new ground, it was decided to publish as much as possible of the new material. Accordingly, while the facts and conclusions relevant to the Committee's inquiry into Britain's invisible earnings are set out in this chapter, further results and additional tabular material are set out separately in the Appendix to this chapter.

25.   Before the results of the Committee's special inquiry are examined, a word of warning is needed about the comparability of the international statistics used. As already indicated, the figures are taken from the Balance of Payments Yearbooks of the International Monetary Fund. Although the Research and Statistics Department of the I.M.F. is constantly improving both the reliability of the figures received from individual countries as well as

their comparability, some discrepancies remain.[1] Following talks with the I.M.F., however, the Committee was convinced that the broad comparisons undertaken for its inquiry were both valid and significant, provided that the comparisons between individual sectors of invisibles were not pushed too far. Wherever figures in the tables are not on the same basis, the Committee has inserted an accompanying note explaining the discrepancy.

26.   The first task was to establish, over an extended period, the value of world trade in invisible items, to analyse its importance, to assess how it was made up and to discover which countries contributed most to these particular activities. The basic statistics are set out in TABLES 4 and 5. TABLE 4 provides a continuous series of world trade in invisibles, from 1959-64, divided into the main categories. TABLE 5 gives invisible receipts and payments for three separate years (1952, 1958 and 1964) broken down into the leading countries. They show that invisible receipts,[2] rising from $16,583 million in 1952 to $44,794 million in 1964, are a large and increasing element in world trade. Their share of total world trade (visible and invisible) rose from 22·5 per cent in 1952 to 24·1 per cent in 1958 and to 25·0 per cent in 1964. Putting this another way, while invisible trade increased nearly three times by value between 1952 and 1964, total world trade grew by less than two and a half times.

INVISIBLE RECEIPTS

27.   TABLE 5 sets out the first analysis of the 31 nations in invisible trans-actions. This "league table" is dominated by two countries—the United States and the United Kingdom. Invisible items accounted for more than 10 per cent of total trade receipts in 1964 for all countries studied except Venezuela and Turkey. Amongst developed countries Norway, Austria, Switzerland, Italy, U.K. and the U.S. were most dependent on invisible receipts which constituted more than 30 per cent of total trade. (Some developing countries, of course, have an even greater dependence on invisibles, usually due to some special factor such as tourism; e.g. Spain, Greece, Mexico.)

28.   The dominance of the U.S. and U.K., though declining, still remained clear in 1964. In that year the U.S. share was close to double that of the U.K., but the U.K. share was more than double that of Italy, the third ranking country. Nevertheless there is a discernible narrowing of the gap between the top two countries and the rest. In 1952 the U.K. share was four times that of Canada, who then ranked third, while U.S. receipts were seven times the size of Canada's. Between 1952 and 1964 the combined share of the U.K. and the U.S. dropped from 49·6 per cent to 41·3 per cent. Britain's share was 17·7 per cent in 1952. In 1958, an exceptionally favourable

---

1. The main difficulties are outlined in a paper entitled "Asymmetries and Errors in Reported Balance of Payments Statistics" prepared by Mr. John S. Smith of the I.M.F. Research and Statistics Department and published in the July, 1967 issue of *I.M.F. Staff Papers.*

2. The definition of invisible receipts used here excludes both Government and transfer items (items 7, 9 and 10 in the I.M.F. Yearbooks). This definition is used throughout the Committee's analysis of 31 countries. Professor Devons included both Government and transfer items in his original study in *Lloyds Bank Review.*

TABLE 4

WORLD TRADE BY MAIN CATEGORIES 1959-63[1] and 1964

Millions of U.S. Dollars

	1959 Receipts	1959 Payments	1960 Receipts	1960 Payments	1961 Receipts	1961 Payments	1962 Receipts	1962 Payments	1963 Receipts	1963 Payments	1964 Receipts	1964 Payments
TOTAL TRADE[2] (Items 1-10)	119,516	120,801	142,697	142,532	150,150	149,096	160,590	160,935	176,444	176,621	179,463	187,400
Total Trade *exc.* items 7, 9 and 10	112,672	110,721	134,149	131,504	141,301	137,240	151,219	148,483	166,496	163,496	134,669	142,800
VISIBLE TRADE	86,184	84,649	102,756	100,972	107,943	105,224	114,876	113,065	126,855	124,935		
1. Merchandise	85,159	84,502	101,702	100,782	106,840	104,994	113,707	112,810	125,617	124,679		
2. Non-monetary Gold	1,025	147	1,054	190	1,103	238	1,169	255	1,238	256		
INVISIBLE TRADE	26,488	26,073	31,394	30,533	33,358	32,017	36,343	35,417	39,642	38,821	44,794	44,600[3]
3, 4. Transport	8,492	8,925	9,870	10,574	10,295	10,135	11,060	11,747	11,805	12,576	(12,411)	(13,004)[3]
5. Foreign Travel	4,887	5,005	6,121	5,678	6,789	6,510	7,438	7,164	8,336	8,021	(9,199)	(8,249)
6. Investment Income	7,772	7,089	8,781	8,246	9,373	8,824	10,265	9,244	11,227	10,296	(12,245)	(9,075)
8. Miscellaneous	5,337	5,054	6,622	6,035	6,901	6,548	7,580	7,262	8,274	7,928	(8,493)	(7,874)
GOVERNMENT AND TRANSFERS	6,843	10,080	8,548	11,028	8,849	11,856	9,371	12,452	9,948	12,866		
7. Government n.i.e.	3,378	5,069	4,379	5,449	4,332	5,564	4,690	5,952	4,955	6,119		
9. Private Donations	1,883	1,803	2,344	2,109	2,636	2,264	2,919	2,386	3,116	2,737		
10. Official Donations	1,583	3,208	1,825	3,470	1,881	4,028	1,762	4,114	1,877	4,010		
Invisible *Trade*/Total Trade *exc.* items 7, 9 and 10.	23.5%	23.5%	23.4%	23.2%	23.6%	23.3%	24.0%	23.9%	23.8%	23.7%	25.0%	23.8%
Government + Transfers/Total Trade (Items 1-10)	5.7%	8.3%	6.0%	7.7%	5.9%	8.0%	5.8%	7.7%	5.6%	7.3%		
Transport[4]/Invisible Trade	32.1%	34.2%	31.4%	34.6%	30.9%	31.7%	30.4%	33.2%	29.8%	32.4%	(29.3%)	(33.1%)
Foreign Travel[4]/Invisible Trade	18.4%	19.2%	19.5%	18.6%	20.4%	20.3%	20.5%	20.7%	21.0%	20.7%	(21.7%)	(21.0%)
Investment Income[4]/Invisible Trade	29.3%	27.2%	28.0%	27.0%	28.1%	27.6%	28.2%	26.1%	28.3%	26.5%	(28.9%)	(23.1%)
Miscellaneous[4]/Invisible Trade	20.1%	19.4%	21.1%	19.8%	20.7%	20.5%	20.9%	20.5%	20.9%	20.4%	(20.0%)	(20.1%)

Source: I.M.F. Balance of Payments Year Books.

Notes: 1. The figures for 1959-63 are derived from data collected by Professor Ely Devons.

2. Total Trade is in all cases the countries reporting to the I.M.F. These were more than 70 in 1959 and 81 in 1964. The inclusion of extra countries is unlikely to greatly affect the totals since these were all minor trading nations.

3. The figures in brackets are *not comparable*. They relate to the 31 leading countries analysed separately by the Committee. These do, however, account for about 90% of the world total.

4. For definitions of these categories see Appendix.

1964

Millions of U.S. Dollars	Invisible Trade		Invisible Trade as Percentage of Total Trade		Percentage of World Invisible Credits	Percentage of World Invisible Debits
	Receipts	Payments	Receipts	Payments		
WORLD[1]	44,794	44,600	25·0	23·8	100·0	100·0
United States	11,832	6,907	31·9	27·2	26·4	15·5
United Kingdom	6,689	5,200	34·7	27·1	14·9	11·7
Italy	2,907	1,957	33·1	23·3	6·5	4·4
Germany	2,731	4,724	14·4	25·5	6·1	10·6
France (Franc area)	2,638	2,680	23·7	23·8	5·9	6·0
Netherlands	1,920	1,316	25·9	17·5	4·3	3·0
Canada	1,467	2,669	15·3	27·3	3·3	6·0
Norway	1,330	813	50·6	29·6	3·0	1·8
Switzerland	1,305[4]	815[4]	31·1	17·7	2·9	1·8
Spain	1,126	348	52·9	14·3	2·5	0·8
Belgian-Luxembourg	1,116	1,106	18·7	18·6	2·5	2·5
Japan	986	2,078	12·8	24·7	2·2	4·7
Sweden	911	718	19·8	26·2	2·0	1·6
Mexico	743	731	40·9	32·8	1·7	1·6
Austria	697	392	32·8	18·0	1·6	0·9
Denmark	641	465	23·3	15·8	1·4	1·0
Australia[2]	491	1,129	14·4	26·9	1·1	2·5
Greece	343	98	52·7	9·9	0·8	0·2
Ireland	342[5]	146[5]	36·5	13·4	0·8	0·3
Yugoslavia	326	160	26·4	10·7	0·7	0·3
South Africa[3]	293	722	10·3	24·5	0·7	1·6
Portugal (escudo area)	287	184	31·1	18·4	0·6	0·4
Puerto Rico[2]	252	546	20·2	26·6	0·6	1·2
India	245	432	12·5	12·9	0·5	1·0
Israel	243	312	41·0	29·9	0·5	0·7
Panama	120	51	58·7	33·1	0·3	0·1
Venezuela	94	1,062	3·7	46·6	0·2	2·4
Morocco	92	116	17·5	21·0	0·2	0·3
Pakistan	88	235	14·9	20·9	0·2	0·5
Turkey	79	169	3·7	26·2	0·2	0·4
Jordan	64	18	72·4	11·3	0·1	—

1. The World is taken as the 81 countries reporting to the I.M.F. in 1964, 73 in 1958 and 65 in 1952.
2. Figures for Australia are for the fiscal year July 1 to June 30. Most other entries are calendar year figures.
3. Non-monetary gold is considered here as merchandise. It constituted 36·3% of South Africa's total trade in 1964 32·6% in 1958 and 32·3% in 1952.
4. Government transactions combined with Others in Item 8 thus slightly overestimating the invisible component.
5. Transport and Insurance reported net thus underestimating the invisible component on both credit and debit side
6. Other Services reported net thus underestimating the invisible component.
7. Travel and Transportation net; similarly underestimating invisibles.

year, it was up to 19·8 per cent, but by 1964 it was down to 14·9 per cent.
29. Some interesting changes took place among the leading nations over these years. As already noted, the U.S. and the U.K. have the highest invisible receipts throughout the period. Italy, West Germany, France and the Netherlands along with the U.S. and the U.K. made up the top six countries in 1964. These same countries were also the leading ones in 1958 though the positions of West Germany and Italy were reversed. In 1952 Canada was third and Norway fifth. The addition of Canada, Norway, Switzerland, Spain, Belgium-Luxembourg, Japan and Sweden to the top six in 1964, produces 13 countries with invisible credits in excess of $800 million. Although the ranking of this group changes, the top 13 in 1958 and 1952 are essentially the same as in 1964. The main exceptions are Spain, which rose spectacularly from a very low level in 1958 to 10th in 1964 largely on the proceeds of foreign travel, and Mexico (14th in 1964), Denmark (16th in 1964) and India (24th in 1964) all of which were in the top group in earlier years. Apart from Spain the greatest changes in ranking within the top group were Canada (3rd in 1952 and 7th in 1964) and Italy (10th in 1952 and 3rd in 1964).

INVISIBLE BALANCES
30. The analysis so far has been concerned solely with invisible receipts. When invisible payments are taken into account, thus showing invisible balances for individual countries, a different pattern emerges. The changes in the resultant surpluses and deficits are naturally more volatile than those of gross receipts. Yet there is a striking consistency in the deficits and surpluses of different countries. As TABLE 6 shows, all but three countries have persistent deficits or surpluses. This suggests, as was shown in the case of the United Kingdom in Chapter II, that there is some long-run stability in the debtor or creditor position of a number of countries. In addition, while there is more fluctuation in the *size* of balances than in their *signs*, there seems to be a tendency for net creditors to increase their surpluses and for the deficits of net debtors to deteriorate. In 1958 and 1964 the largest surpluses from invisible trade were held by the U.S., the U.K. and Italy. These also had the largest invisible receipts in 1964. Spain's surplus was the fastest growing, having increased 25 times in six years. The most significant changes in the orders shown in TABLES 5 and 6 are those of West Germany, France, Canada and Japan, which, though among the countries with the largest invisible receipts, are also the largest debtors. It is also significant that, with the exception of Puerto Rico and Venezuela, the developing countries do not rank among the chief debtors from invisible transactions.

INVISIBLE SECTORS
31. TABLE 4 along with TABLES 11 to 14[1] in the Appendix, provide an analysis of the changes in the broad categories of invisible receipts. These

1. The totals in Tables 11 to 14 in the Appendix are for the 31 countries, not for all countries reporting to the I.M.F. as in Table 4.

29

TABLE 6

BALANCE OF INVISIBLE, VISIBLE AND TOTAL TRADE

(of 31 leading countries)

Millions of U.S. Dollars	Balance of Invisible Trade[1]			Balance of Visible Trade[2]			Balance of Total Trade (Col. 1 plus Col. 2)		
	1964	1958	1952	1964	1958	1952	1964	1958	1952
31 countries	4,199	2,746	3,654	−841	2,398	−1,772	5,040	5,144	1,882
U.S.	5,025	2,942	3,648	6,669	3,313	1,283	11,694	6,255	4,931
U.K.[1]	1,489	1,308	1,193	−1,433	101	−286	56	1,409	907
Italy	950	575	52	−578	−372	−736	372	203	−684
Germany	−1,993	−722	−163	2,413	1,835	531	420	1,113	368
France	− 42	−294	−193	−104	−211	−619	−146	−505	−812
Netherlands	604	399	160	−719	32	162	−115	431	322
Canada	−1,202	−940	−476	977	37	626	−225	−903	150
Norway	517	341	211	−635	−513	−228	−118	−172	− 17
Switzerland	490	355	267	−901	−135	−296	−411	220	− 29
Spain	778	31	n.a.	−1,077	−303	n.a.	−299	−272	n.a.
Belgium-L'bourg.	10	272	−109	22	90	267	32	362	158
Japan	−1,092	−319	−189	375	376	−404	−717	57	−593
Sweden	193	229	205	−169	−280	−160	24	− 51	45
Mexico	12	188	117	−428	−391	−172	−416	−203	− 55
Austria	305	157	10	−355	−114	−147	− 50	43	−137
Denmark	176	90	31	−374	17	− 15	−198	107	16
Australia	−638	−487	−445	−153	149	−829	−791	−338	−1,274
Greece	245	32	− 3	−574	−236	−136	−339	−204	−139
Ireland	196	127	114	−353	−191	−198	−157	− 64	− 84
Yugoslavia	166	56	19	−435	−236	−140	−269	−180	−121
S. Africa	−429	−360	−207	321	119	24	−108	−241	−183
Portugal	103	59	23	−182	− 86	− 53	− 79	− 27	− 30
Puerto Rico	−294	−112	− 53	−507	−242	−186	−801	−354	−239
India	−187	61	121	−1,210	−1,034	−198	−1,397	−973	− 77
Israel	− 69	− 47	0	−381	−243	−277	−450	−290	−277
Panama	69	21	15	− 86	− 46	− 46	− 17	− 25	− 31
Venezuela	−968	−1,067	−588	1,262	972	638	294	− 95	50
Morocco	− 24	− 59	n.a.	− 3	− 14	n.a.	− 27	− 73	n.a.
Pakistan	−147	− 21	− 55	−385	124	− 7	−532	103	− 62
Turkey	− 90	− 76	− 52	− 42	− 35	−129	−132	−111	−181
Jordan	46	7	1	−114	− 85	− 41	− 68	− 78	− 40

No sign indicates credit; minus sign, debit.
Source: I.M.F. Balance of Payments Year Books.
Notes: 1. Includes I.M.F. items 3, 4, 5, 6 and 8.
     2. Includes I.M.F. items 1 and 2.

categories are as follows: transport and merchandise insurance; travel; investment income; and miscellaneous invisibles.[1]

(a) *Transport and Merchandise Insurance Receipts*[2]

This item is the largest but has grown more slowly than any other invisible item. The increase between 1952-58 was 42·4 per cent while over the longer period it was 130·0 per cent. This is slightly less than the increase in total (visible and invisible) trade. Transport also declined as a proportion of invisible trade. It has become decreasingly important in the invisible trade of all countries except Pakistan, Sweden and the Netherlands. (In fairness to shipping it must be recalled that in the years chosen—1952, 1958 and 1964—freight rates were not high).

The U.S. and the U.K. each have receipts at least double those of the nearest competitor (Italy in 1964 and Norway in 1958 and 1952) but their combined share has fallen from 52 per cent in 1952 to 37·6 per cent in 1964.

(b) *Travel Receipts*

World trade in travel has increased faster than any other invisible item. The value index at 100 in 1952 had reached 215·8 in 1958 and 441·0 in 1964. It has also increased as a proportion of total invisibles. Travel has become a more important source of income to most of the individual countries. Most European countries (except the U.K) have shown strong gains while those of Italy, Spain, Greece and Yugoslavia have been spectacular. The dependence of tourist industries on natural attractions and the proximity of high income regions makes this the least concentrated of all items. The top two countries in 1952 (U.S. and Mexico) accounted for 39·1 per cent of all receipts. In 1964, the U.S. and second ranked Italy received 23·2 per cent of the world's trade. The "league table" for travel receipts shows more ranking changes than other items over the 12 years. The U.S. is consistently the highest. (This is perhaps surprising but the average traveller probably spends more money in America than in other countries. This item also includes business trips and the expenses of foreign students and these are likely to be high.) In 1952 proximity to the U.S. clearly determined the size of other tourist industries since Mexico and Canada were second and third respectively. By 1964 the U.S. was still in the lead but its receipts were only slightly above those of Spain, Italy and France, no doubt reflecting the relative rise in Western European incomes.

(c) *Investment Income Receipts*

These have increased less rapidly than both travel and miscel-

---

1. For fuller definitions of these four categories see the Appendix.

2. These two items are, unfortunately, lumped together but it is possible that they are influenced by the same factors such as the volume of trade. In any case these items are difficult to separate since, of the countries studied, only Germany, India, Israel, Italy, Japan, Morocco, Norway, Panama, Portugal, Spain and Turkey list merchandise insurance separately under I.M.F. item 3(2). Many countries, such as the U.K., list these in item 8 as part of a *net* insurance total. Others, such as the U.S., have no separate data. This is not likely to introduce any great discrepancy since merchandise insurance is a small proportion of transport costs.

laneous services. In 1958 they had increased by 81·1 per cent; between 1952 and 1964 the increase was 201·4 per cent. Their share in total invisible trade grew slightly, remaining around 28-29 per cent of the total. As a proportion of invisible trade, investment income increased for a number of countries; notable amongst these were Germany, U.S. and the U.K. The U.K. and the U.S. have far and away the greatest interest in investment but their combined share fell from 82·9 per cent to 76·0 per cent over the period. The remainder is fairly evenly split between Canada and the Common Market countries. This is the U.K.'s fastest growing item both absolutely and relative to the other countries. It has increased four times since 1952 and is the only item for which the U.K.'s share of total trade has increased.

(d) *Miscellaneous Invisible Credits*

This is the second fastest growing item. It increased in value by over three times between 1952 and 1964. Like investment income, miscellaneous credits did not grow smoothly as a proportion of total invisibles. Between 1952 and 1964 the increase was 11·1 per cent but between 1952 and 1958 the increase was 20·6 per cent. The U.K. and the U.S. had the largest receipts and combined they accounted for 42·7 per cent of the trade in 1952. By 1964 their share had fallen to 34·5 per cent. In 1952 the U.K. had a clear lead over all other countries but her share fell by nearly 10 per cent over the 12 years. By 1964 the U.S. had the largest receipts with the U.K. second and Italy a close third followed by Germany. Italy, Greece, Yugoslavia and Japan all increased their trade substantially.

32.   When allowance is made for the invisible payments under these four categories, the pattern differs little from that shown earlier for total invisible balances. There is a long-run consistency about the sign of the balances and a tendency for them to grow. For example, Australia, Venezuela and Canada have persistent deficits on every single item. Ireland has a surplus on every item for each year. Most countries have some items always in surplus, others always in deficit. Of the countries, such as the U.S. and the U.K., in permanent invisible surplus, investment income contributes far and away the largest amount. Miscellaneous items came second. Similarly the persistent debtors pay out most in interest and dividends (although Germany also has a large travel deficit). Other countries have surpluses according to their national specialities, e.g. Norway in shipping, Spain in travel etc.

33.   Other results from the Committee's special inquiry into world invisibles are set out in the appendices to this chapter. In concentrating its attention on the importance of Britain's invisible earnings, the Committee came to the following conclusions:

1. World trade in invisibles has shown and is showing an encouraging expansion, rising faster than visible trade over the years 1952-64 (from $16,583 million in 1952 to $44,794 million in 1964).
2. The United Kingdom is the second country in the world both in terms of its gross invisible receipts and in terms of its net invisible

surplus. (Its invisible receipts in 1964 were well over double those of the third country—Italy.)

3. The first two countries (U.S. and U.K.) dominate invisible earnings far more than any countries dominate the world's visible exports. (In 1964 they accounted for 41·3 per cent of world invisible receipts.)

4. While the United Kingdom's invisible receipts have grown persistently, her share of the world total has declined (from 17·7 per cent in 1952 to 14·9 per cent in 1964, though the figures are not strictly comparable because of the change in statistical methods in 1958).

5. According to the analysis of the four broad categories of invisibles, the pattern of the U.K.'s earnings do not fit world trends closely. Her receipts from investment income are growing faster than the world total; those from travel not keeping pace.

6. The increasing concentration of invisible receipts among the leading countries (the share of the top 31 countries rose from 86·9 per cent in 1952 to 94·7 per cent in 1964) and the striking consistency of the surpluses and deficits, country by country, strongly suggest that the nature of invisibles (particularly the expertise they require) makes them difficult to copy quickly.

7. Britain's growth rate in invisible transactions is either around the average for the leading nations or below it. (See TABLE 9 in the Appendix). Most of the countries with high growth rates in relation to invisibles, however, are developing countries with relatively small turnovers in invisible transactions or developed countries (such as Germany, France and Japan) with persistent deficits. Italy is the main exception, with the third largest invisible balance, the third largest invisible credits and an above average growth rate.

RECOMMENDATION'

34.   The Committee also makes one recommendation: It recommends that regular analyses of world trade in invisibles, along with Britain's role in it, should be carried out and published by the Central Statistical Office aided by the Bank of England.

APPENDIX A: CHAPTER III

WORLD INVISIBLES PER HEAD OF POPULATION

THE following two tables give (*a*) total invisible credits and the four main items per capita in 1964 and (*b*) the growth of these same variables in index form calculated from a base of 100 in 1952.

TABLE 7 shows the U.K. as having the fifth largest level of credits per capita. The U.K. is the only country in the top 12 of any size. The others all have populations of less than 10 million, while Canada, ranked 13th has less than 20 million. The top group contains all the high income Scandinavian and Benelux countries but also lesser developed countries such as Ireland, Israel, Puerto Rico and Panama. In all items except travel receipts, the U.K. per capita level is about four times the average for the 31 countries.

At the top of TABLE 7 there is little consistency in the rankings of the individual items. None of the top 10 countries in terms of total invisibles per capita shows similar high rankings for each individual item. The Netherlands and Denmark come closest. Netherlands' travel credits are ranked 11th and Denmark's investment credits are 14th. Much more consistency is found at the other end of the table where countries with low total invisibles per capita tend to have a similarly low level for each item.

TABLE 8 suggests that countries with a high level of invisibles per capita have experienced a relatively slow rate of growth in the period. Exceptions to this are Austria and Israel which are high in both tables.

In growth of total credits per capita the U.K. is ranked 16th. In all items except investment income (where it is ranked 12th), it has shown less than average increases. In this, its position is not very different from most of the developed high income countries which populate the middle section of this table. The top of the table contains the low but growing income countries; the bottom contains the low and stagnating income countries.

The rankings in TABLE 8 fit an expected pattern. The developed countries show a relatively poor performance in terms of growth of most items because they are growing from a very large base. None of the top seven countries have per capita incomes above $1,000. France and Germany are the only high income countries in the top group and these are growing from a position in which their concentration on invisibles was less than that of similar western European countries.

TABLE 7

INVISIBLE CREDITS *PER CAPITA* 1964

RANKING IN BRACKETS

Million U.S. Dollars	Total Invisible Credits	Transport Credits	Travel Credits	Investment Income Credits	Miscellaneous Credits
1. Norway	360·4	300·3 (1)	21·1 (9)	7·3 (13)	31·7 (5)
2. Switzerland	222·3	9·4 (19)	10·1 (20)	46·2 (1)	66·3 (1)
3. Netherlands	158·3	56·9 (4)	19·9 (11)	42·5 (3)	39·1 (4)
4. Denmark	135·8	67·6 (3)	35·4 (4)	7·2 (14)	25·6 (7)
5. U.K.	123·9	43·3 (5)	9·8 (21)	44·7 (2)	25·6 (7)
6. Ireland	120·0	8·4 (18)	57·9 (2)	36·5 (4)	17·2 (11)
7. Sweden	118·9	86·0 (2)	11·6 (17)	10·8 (10)	8·9 (18)
8. Belge-Lux.	114·9	29·7 (7)	17·9 (12)	21·0 (6)	46·3 (3)
9. Panama	100·8	10·9 (16)	27·7 (7)	0·84(24)	61·3 (2)
10. Israel	98·0	37·1 (6)	22·2 (8)	11·7 (8)	26·2 (6)
11. Puerto Rico	97·7	20·9 (9)	46·1 (3)	10·5 (11)	19·8 (9)
12. Austria	96·5	5·5 (22)	69·7 (1)	5·1 (15)	16·2 (13)
13. Canada	76·1	13·4 (13)	31·8 (5)	19·4 (7)	11·6 (15)
14. U.S.	61·6	12·1 (15)	5·7 (22)	35·8 (5)	8·0 (19)
15. Italy	57·0	14·5 (12)	20·3 (10)	2·8 (19)	19·1 (10)
16. France	54·5	12·7 (14)	17·5 (14)	7·5 (13)	16·9 (12)
17. Germany	48·8	21·2 (8)	12·2 (16)	4·8 (16)	10·0 (16)
18. Australia	44·1	20·8 (10)	5·1 (23)	11·0 (9)	5·7 (20)
19. Greece	40·3	16·1 (11)	10·7 (19)	1·5 (22)	12·0 (14)
20. Spain	35·9	3·2 (24)	29·3 (6)	0·8 (25)	2·6 (24)
21. Jordan	33·7	—	11·6 (17)	2·6 (20)	1·7 (26)
22. Portugal	31·5	5·7 (21)	13·9 (15)	1·8 (21)	9·9 (17)
23. Mexico	18·7	0·0 (30)	17·8 (13)	—	0·98(28)
24. Yugoslavia	16·9	8·5 (17)	3·6 (25)	0·47(26)	4·5 (23)
25. S. Africa	16·8	5·0 (23)	2·6 (26)	4·1 (17)	5·0 (22)
26. Venezuela	11·2	2·4 (25)	0·71(27)	3·0 (18)	5·1 (21)
27. Japan	10·2	6·1 (20)	0·64(28)	1·4 (23)	1·9 (25)
28. Morocco	7·1	1·2 (26)	4·7 (24)	0·46(27)	0·85(29)
29. Turkey	2·6	0·81(27)	0·26(29)	—	1·5 (27)
30. Pakistan	0·9	0·24(29)	0·0 (30)	0·089(28)	0·54(30)
31. India	0·5	0·27(28)	—	0·0 (29)	0·19(31)
31 countries	31·6	9·3	6·86	9·13	6·3

35

TABLE 8

GROWTH OF INVISIBLE CREDITS *PER CAPITA* 1952-1964 (1952=100)

RANKING IN BRACKETS

Dollars	Index of Growth of Total Invisible Credits	Index of Growth of Transport Credits	Index of Growth of Investment Income Credits	Index of Growth of Travel Credits	Index of Growth of Miscellaneous Credits
1. Austria	1,135	423 (5)	3,643 (2)	1,549 (2)	675 (7)
2. Israel	990	598 (3)	2,089 (4)	1,168 (3)	1,379 (2)
3. Japan	850	678 (2)	2,000 (5)	667 (7)	1,056 (3)
4. Jordan	822	—	—	387 (13)	142 (21)
5. Yugoslavia	676	447 (4)	—	2,000 (1)	2,500 (1)
6. Italy	640	354 (9)	737 (6)	1,015 (4)	796 (6)
7. Greece	552	335 (10)	577 (7)	823 (5)	1,000 (4)
8. Germany	469	385 (7)	3,429 (3)	581 (8)	385 (9)
9. Portugal	409	407 (6)	310 (15)	772 (6)	254 (15)
10. France	398	363 (8)	300 (16)	565 (9)	367 (10)
11. Australia	313	239 (13)	458 (9)	557 (11)	259 (14)
12. Belge-Lux.	243	188 (14)	191 (19)	559 (10)	362 (11)
13. Netherlands	239	320 (11)	317 (14)	143 (22)	145 (20)
14. Denmark	230	148 (20)	450 (10)	513 (12)	533 (8)
15. Ireland	225	1,235 (1)	174 (20)	244 (16)	221 (16)
16. U.K.	212	179 (16)	373 (12)	223 (17)	184 (17)
17. Norway	201	187 (15)	406 (11)	352 (14)	302 (13)
18. U.S.	183	120 (21)	203 (17)	173 (19)	308 (12)
19. S. Africa	177	156 (19)	532 (8)	108 (23)	156 (19)
20. Sweden	159	164 (18)	338 (13)	252 (15)	809 (5)
21. Mexico	156	—	—	165 (21)	89 (25)
22. Canada	149	118 (22)	196 (18)	170 (20)	104 (23)
23. Turkey	144	99 (23)	—	186 (18)	183 (18)
24. Venezuela	138	71 (24)	7,895 (1)	—	109 (22)
25. Pakistan	113	171 (17)	119 (21)	—	93 (24)
26. India	83	270 (12)	—	—	45 (26)
31 Countries Average	226	185	241	354	263

APPENDIX B: CHAPTER III

COMPARATIVE GROWTH OF INVISIBLES

The following two tables show the growth of total invisible credits, the main credit items, visible credits, population and income in index form calculated from a base of 1952 = 100.

As is immediately obvious from TABLE 9 the U.K. has had a well below average increase in invisible credits. Of individual items all but investment income fall into the bottom third of the table. This is matched in TABLE 10 by a similarly low rate of growth of visible credits.

Countries which have experienced a rapid growth in total invisible credits have generally had high increases in each of the main items and in visible trade. The top four countries in growth of total invisibles rank in the top third in the growth of each item.

Most of these countries with high rates of growth in invisibles are, as in TABLE 8, relatively underdeveloped. Once again the only high income countries in the top group are France and Germany. These tables perhaps give unwarranted emphasis to less developed countries whose rates of growth from very low bases to still internationally insignificant levels produce very large indices (e.g. Venezuela's investment income index of 125,000). In the two cases where this was particularly marked the simple arithmetic average was augmented with a weighted average.

In comparing growth rates of trade items with vital statistics in TABLE 10 no clear picture emerges.

The U.K. with a close to average rising national income and a less than average rate of population growth is ranked 10th in growth per capita income.

Nevertheless a significant group of countries, Greece, Japan and Yugoslavia, all amongst the fastest growing invisible trading nations, rank in the top third in terms of growth of per capita income.

TABLE 9

INDEX SHOWING GROWTH OF INVISIBLE CREDITS 1952–1964 (1952=100)

TOP THIRD

Total Invisible Credits		Transport Credits		Investment Income Credits		Travel Credits		Miscellaneous Credits	
1. Israel	1,519	Ireland	1,200	Venezuela	125,000	Yugoslavia	2,300	Yugoslavia	2,867
2. Austria	1,181	Israel	920	Yugoslavia	4,500	Israel	1,833	Israel	2,167
3. Japan	930	Japan	766	Germany	3,857	Austria	1,623	Japan	1,233
4. Yugoslavia	795	Yugoslavia	509	Austria	3,700	Italy	1,125	Greece	1,133
5. Italy	699	Germany	444	Israel	3,222	Greece	910	Italy	857
6. Greece	602	Austria	444	Japan	2,267	Portugal	847	Sweden	850
7. Germany	542	Portugal	433	Italy	806	Japan	775	Austria	688
8. France	452	France	411	—		—		Denmark	576

MIDDLE THIRD

Total Invisible Credits		Transport Credits		Investment Income Credits		Travel Credits		Miscellaneous Credits	
9. Portugal	435	Italy	385	S. Africa	710	Australia	713	Germany	440
10. Australia	403	Netherlands	373	Greece	650	Germany	667	France	419
11. Netherlands	279	Greece	370	Australia	586	France	631	Belg-Lux.	391
12. Belge-Lux.	263	Australia	309	Denmark	486	Belge-Lux.	600	U.S.	383
13. Denmark	250	Pakistan	218	Norway	450	Denmark	557	Australia	337
14. S. Africa	238	S. Africa	212	U.K.	401	Norway	390	Norway	334
15. Mexico	230	Norway	207	Netherlands	371	Sweden	270	Portugal	273
16. U.K.	227	Belge-Lux.	203	Sweden	361	Turkey	267	Turkey	256

BOTTOM THIRD

Total Invisible Credits		Transport Credits		Investment Income Credits		Travel Credits		Miscellaneous Credits	
17. U.S.	224	U.K.	192	France	337	Mexico	242	S. Africa	215
18. Norway	223	Sweden	176	Portugal	320	U.K.	238	Ireland	213
19. Venezuela	219	Denmark	161	Canada	261	Ireland	236	U.K.	197
20. Ireland	218	Canada	156	U.S.	249	Canada	227	Venezuela	172
21. Turkey	203	U.S.	146	Belge-Lux.	206	U.S.	209	Netherlands	170
22. Canada	199	Turkey	139	Ireland	168	Netherlands	167	Canada	139
23. Sweden	170	Venezuela	111	Pakistan	150	S. Africa	148	Mexico	134
24. Pakistan	142	Mexico	9	—		—		Pakistan	117

Simple Average	443		354		6,775		400		607
Weighted Average	—		—		689		—		465

TABLE 10

INDEX OF GROWTH OF VARIABLES 1952–1964 (1952 = 100)

	Total Visible Credits[1]		Population[2]		National Money Income[3]		Per Capita Income	
TOP THIRD								
1.	Israel	795	Venezuela	160	Greece	409	Japan	479
2.	Japan	523	Israel	154	Japan	403	Greece	372
3.	France	418	Mexico	147	Germany	329	Germany	284
4.	Italy	417	Turkey	140	Netherlands	296	Italy	267
5.	Yugoslavia	412	S. Africa	135	Italy	291	Netherlands	253
6.	Germany	405	Canada	134	Mexico	269	Austria	232
7.	Austria	283	Australia	129	Yugoslavia	262	Yugoslavia	228
8.	Greece	269	Pakistan	126	Austria	241[4]	Denmark	213
	—		—		S. Africa	241	—	
MIDDLE THIRD								
9.	Denmark	242	U.S.	122	—		Sweden	207
10.	Sweden	235	Netherlands	117	Denmark	232	U.K.	194
11.	Portugal	232	Germany	116	Sweden	223	France	191
12.	Norway	220	Yugoslavia	115	France	217	Ireland	191
13.	Ireland	213	France	114	Australia	214	Norway	188
14.	S. Africa	213	Japan	113	U.K.	209	Mexico	182
15.	Australia	192	Norway	111	Norway	208	Portugal	180
16.	U.S.	190	Italy	109	Portugal	192	Belge-Lux.	178
17.	Belge-Lux.	190	Greece	109	Belge-Lux.	192	S. Africa	178
	—		Denmark	109	—		—	
BOTTOM THIRD								
18.	U.K.	173	—		Ireland	184	Australia	166
19.	Venezuela	171	U.K.	108	Israel	183[4]	U.S.	145
20.	Canada	167	Belge-Lux.	108	U.S.	177	Canada	127
21.	Mexico	163	Sweden	107	Canada	170	Israel	119
22.	Netherlands	128	Canada	107	Venezuela	165[4]	Pakistan	113
23.	Turkey	119	Austria	104	Turkey	155	Turkey	111
24.	Pakistan	99	Ireland	97	Pakistan	142[5]	Venezuela	103
Simple Average		269		121		234		204

1. Derived from I.M.F. Balance of Payments Yearbooks.
2. Many of these estimates are described by the U.N. as being of "questionable reliability".
3. Some of the National Income estimates are similarly unreliable. They have been converted into dollars using I.M.F. exchanged rates. (See Note 4).
4. In 1952 multiple exchange rates were in operation in these countries making conversion into dollars very difficult.
5. The index for Pakistan refers to the period 1952-63; the national income estimate for 1964 was not available.
Source: Statistical Yearbooks of the United Nations.

APPENDIX C: CHAPTER III

THE MAIN INVISIBLE CATEGORIES

THE subsequent tables analyse the four main categories of invisible items. The following notes based on the Balance of Payments Manual of the I.M.F. (3rd edition), outline the definitions used throughout.

1. TRANSPORT AND MERCHANDISE INSURANCE (items 3 and 4)
   (a) This refers to freight and insurance on international shipments of goods and gold and other forms of transportation.
   (b) Item 3a, covering freight, presents a special problem in that although all exports are recorded f.o.b., some imports are valued c.i.f. To adjust for this the I.M.F. uses some conventional factor, usually 10 per cent. In the shipment of certain goods (timber and refrigerated products) this can be a source of considerable error.
   (c) Item 3b, relates to merchandise insurance. This is a small item for which statistics are scarce. Sometimes this is lumped with 3a. Other countries, notably the U.K., include it in 8(i) with other forms of insurance.
   (d) Item 4, Other Transportation has four sections covering the operations of all vessels, including tankers and aircraft. These are passenger fares, time charters, port disbursements and others, which include coastal traffic.

2. FOREIGN TRAVEL (item 5)
   (a) The expenditure of foreigners in the compiling country and the expenditure of its residents abroad.
   (b) There are five categories according to the purpose of the visit; tourist, business, student, government and other.

3. INVESTMENT INCOME (item 6)
   (a) Credit entries refer to the income of residents from investments abroad and debits to the income received by foreigners from investments in the compiling country.
   (b) Section 1 relates to direct investment income. This includes the earnings of foreign subsidiaries, their undistributed earnings and all dividends whether paid or not. All earnings are reported net of tax payable to the host country. Net losses on foreign investment are entered as negative debits; net losses on the investments of a resident abroad are negative credits. These accounts differ from those of the U.N. and O.E.C.D. by the amount of imputed income accruing from investments in non-commercial real estate and the accumulated interest on savings in the form of life insurance.
   (c) Section 2 is Other Interest: all commitment charges in lieu of interest. Section 3 consists of interest on inter-governmental loans and on those of international organizations.

4. OTHER SERVICES (item 8)
   (a) This item consists of a list of 16 categories which is not comprehensive but does cover the usual types of transactions.

(b) The first four categories cover non-merchandise insurance and re-insurance. As noted earlier, from some countries, merchandise insurance may also be included here, often in a net insurance total.

(c) The other items may be listed as follows:

    (i) Personal Income. Mainly the earnings of residents who are the employees of foreigners (credit) and the earnings of foreigners who are employees of residents (debit). Excluded are the employees of central governments and international organizations. Included are the earnings of foreign crews.

    (ii) Management fees. Management fees and office expenses paid by foreign subsidiaries to parent firms.

    (iii) Underwriters' commissions. Underwriting fees earned on the issue of foreign private securities.

    (iv) Agents' Fees. Fees paid by importers and exporters to agents in the compiling country.

    (v) Construction Activity. Construction contracts performed for foreigners such as roads, dams etc.

    (vi) Communications. International settlements of post, telegraph, telephone and radio accounts.

    (vii) Advertising.

    (viii) Subscriptions to Press.

    (ix) Film Rentals. Hiring of motion pictures.

    (x) Copyright and Patent Royalties.

    (xi) Real Estate Rentals. Gross receipts from lease of property by foreigners other than governments and international organizations.

    (xii) Other. All items not covered elsewhere. Membership dues, workers' expenses, transactions in goods and services otherwise unclassified, commissions on the handling of gold and gains and losses on arbitrage transactions in foreign exchange with foreigners.

TABLES 11 TO 19 WHICH FOLLOW
ANALYSE THE FOUR MAIN CATE-
GORIES OF INVISIBLE ITEMS
OUTLINED ON THE PREVIOUS TWO
PAGES

TABLE 11

TRANSPORT AND MERCHANDISE INSURANCE RECEIPTS

	Transport and Insurance Credits (I.M.F. items 3, 4) (millions of U.S. dollars)			Transport and Insurance Credits as Percentage of Total Invisible Trade			Percentage Share of Total Transport and Insurance Credits		
	1964	1958	1952	1964	1958	1952	1964	1958	1952
31 countries	12,411	7,692	5,400	29·3	30·4	37·5	100·0	100·0	100·0
U.S.	2,317	1,672	1,587	19·6	22·5	30·1	18·7	21·7	29·4
U.K.	2,346	1,487	1,221	35·1	27·9	41·5	18·9	19·3	22·6
Italy	743	401	193	25·6	29·3	46·4	6·0	5·2	3·6
Germany	1,191	735	268	43·6	46·8	53·2	9·6	9·6	5·0
France	613	168	149	23·2	17·7	25·5	4·9	2·2	2·8
Netherlands	690	388	185	35·9	46·4	26·9	5·6	5·0	3·4
Canada	258	177	165	17·6	19·7	23·4	2·1	2·3	3·1
Norway	1,108	765	536	83·3	86·1	89·8	8·9	9·9	9·9
Switzerland	55	29	n.a.	4·2	4·0	—	0·4	0·38	—
Spain	99	35	n.a.	8·8	27·8	—	0·8	0·46	—
Belgium-L'bourg	288	244	142	25·8	28·8	33·4	2·3	3·2	2·6
Japan	590	244	77	59·8	67·8	72·6	4·8	3·2	1·4
Sweden	659	484	374	72·3	63·7	69·9	5·3	6·4	6·9
Mexico	0·2	0·3	2·2	—	—	0·7	—	—	—
Austria	40	13	9	5·7	4·7	15·3	0·3	0·17	0·17
Denmark	319	255	198	49·8	63·9	77·3	2·6	3·3	3·7
Australia	232	166	75	47·3	64·3	61·5	1·9	2·2	1·4
Greece	137	62	37	39·9	51·7	64·9	1·1	0·81	0·69
Ireland	24	6	2	7·0	2·8	1·3	0·2	0·078	0·037
Yugoslavia	163	72	32	50·0	67·3	78·0	1·3	0·94	0·59
S. Africa	87	57	41	29·7	26·8	33·3	0·7	0·74	0·76
Portugal	52	19	12	18·1	14·6	18·2	0·4	0·25	0·22
Puerto Rico	54	31	n.a.	21·4	29·5	—	0·4	0·40	—
India	129	67	38	52·7	32·4	16·4	1·0	0·87	0·70
Israel	92	35	10	37·9	46·7	62·5	0·7	0·46	0·19
Panama	13	9	n.a.	10·8	13·8	—	0·1	0·12	—
Venezuela	20	24	18	21·2	24·2	41·9	0·2	0·31	0·33
Morocco	15	19	n.a.	16·3	33·9	—	0·1	0·25	—
Pakistan	24	15	11	27·3	30·8	17·1	0·2	0·20	0·20
Turkey	25	13	18	31·6	31·0	46·1	0·2	0·17	0·33
Jordan	3·4	—	—	5·3	—	—	—	—	—

Table 12

TRAVEL RECEIPTS

	Travel Credits (I.M.F. item 5) (millions of U.S. dollars)			Travel Credits as Percentage of Total Invisible Trade			Percentage Share of Total Travel Credits		
	1964	1958	1952	1964	1958	1952	1964	1958	1952
31 countries	9,199	4,502	2,086	21·7	17·8	14·5	100·0	100·0	100·0
U.S.	1,095	825	524	9·3	11·1	9·9	11·9	18·3	25·1
U.K.	532	386	224	8·0	7·2	7·6	5·8	8·6	10·7
Italy	1,035	492	92	35·6	35·9	22·1	11·3	10·9	4·4
Germany	687	452	103	25·2	28·8	20·4	7·5	10·0	4·9
France	846	167	134	32·1	17·6	22·9	9·2	3·7	6·4
Netherlands	241	85	144	12·6	8·0	20·9	2·6	1·9	6·9
Canada	612	338	270	41·7	37·6	36·6	6·7	7·5	12·9
Norway	78	41	20	5·9	4·6	3·4	0·8	0·9	1·0
Switzerland	590	296	n.a.	45·2	40·5	—	6·4	6·6	—
Spain	918	72	n.a.	81·5	57·1	—	10·0	1·6	—
Belgium-L'bourg	174	124	29	15·6	14·6	6·8	1·9	2·8	1·4
Japan	62	24	8	6·3	6·7	7·5	0·7	0·5	0·4
Sweden	89	60	33	9·8	7·9	6·2	1·0	1·3	1·6
Mexico	704	542	291	94·8	93·1	90·1	7·7	12·0	14·0
Austria	503	167	31	72·2	60·1	52·5	5·5	3·7	1·5
Denmark	167	80	30	26·1	20·1	11·7	1·8	1·8	1·4
Australia	57	18	8	11·6	7·0	6·6	0·6	0·4	0·4
Greece	91	36	10	26·5	30·0	17·5	1·0	0·8	0·5
Ireland	165	97	70	48·2	45·5	44·6	1·8	2·2	3·5
Yugoslavia	69	10	3	21·2	9·3	7·3	0·8	0·2	0·1
S. Africa	46	31	31	15·7	14·6	25·2	0·5	0·7	1·5
Portugal	127	26	15	44·3	20·0	22·7	1·4	0·6	0·7
Puerto Rico	119	34	—	47·2	32·4	—	1·3	0·8	—
India	5[1]	37	6	2·0	17·9	2·6	—	0·8	0·2
Israel	55	12	3	22·6	16·0	18·6	0·6	0·3	0·1
Panama	33	24	—	27·5	36·9	—	0·4	0·6	—
Venezuela	6	—	—	6·4	—	—	—	—	—
Morocco	61	19	—	66·3	33·9	—	0·7	0·4	—
Pakistan	2	0·6	—	2·3	1·3	—	—	—	—
Turkey	8	3	3	10·1	7·1	7·7	—	—	0·1
Jordan	22	3	4	34·4	21·4	74·1	0·2	—	0·2

1. Preliminary.

TABLE 13

INVESTMENT INCOME RECEIPTS

	Investment Income Credit (I.M.F. item 6) (millions of U.S. dollars)			Investment Income Credits as Percentage of Total Invisible Trade			Percentage Share o Total Investment Income Credits		
	1964	1958	1952	1964	1958	1952	1964	1958	1952
31 countries	12,245	7,359	4,063	28·9	29·0	28·2	100·0	100·0	100·0
U.S.	6,878	3,867	2,762	68·1	52·0	52·3	56·2	52·5	68·0
U.K.	2,425	1,982	605	36·3	37·2	20·5	19·8	26·9	14·9
Italy	145	53	18	5·0	3·9	4·3	1·2	0·7	0·4
Germany	270	101	7	9·9	6·4	1·4	2·2	1·4	0·2
France	361	172	107	13·7	18·1	18·3	2·9	2·3	2·6
Netherlands	515	239	139	26·8	22·4	20·2	4·2	3·2	3·4
Canada	373	232	143	25·4	25·8	19·4	3·0	3·2	3·5
Norway	27	13	6	2·0	1·5	1·0	0·2	0·2	0·2
Switzerland	271	218	n.a.	20·8	24·4	—	2·2	3·0	—
Spain	25	3	n.a.	2·2	2·4	—	0·2	—	—
Belgium-L'bourg	204	150	99	18·3	17·7	23·3	1·7	2·0	2·4
Japan	136	27	6	13·8	7·5	5·7	1·1	0·4	0·2
Sweden	83	46	23	9·1	6·1	4·3	0·7	0·6	0·6
Mexico	—	—	—	—	—	—	—	—	—
Austria	37	12	1	5·3	4·3	1·7	0·3	0·2	—
Denmark	34	15	7	5·3	3·8	2·7	0·3	0·2	0·2
Australia	123	55	21	25·1	21·3	17·2	1·0	0·7	0·6
Greece	13	6	2	3·8	5·0	3·5	0·1	0·1	—
Ireland	104[1]	81[1]	62[1]	30·4	38·0	39·5	0·8	1·1	1·5
Yugoslavia	9	0·6	0·2	2·8	0·6	0·5	—	—	—
S. Africa	71	45	10	24·2	21·1	8·1	0·6	0·6	0·2
Portugal	16	7	5	5·6	5·4	7·6	0·1	0·1	0·1
Puerto Rico	27	9	n.a.	10·7	8·6	—	0·2	0·1	—
India	23	38	34	9·4	18·4	14·8	0·2	0·5	0·8
Israel	29	5	n.a.	11·9	6·7	—	0·2	0·1	—
Panama	1	2	n.a.	0·8	3·1	—	—	—	—
Venezuela	25	8	0·2	26·6	8·1	0·5	0·2	0·1	—
Morocco	6	4	n.a.	6·5	7·1	—	—	—	—
Pakistan	9	6	6	10·2	12·5	—	—	0·1	0·1
Turkey	—	0·3	0·1	—	0·7	0·3	—	—	—
Jordan	5	2	—	7·8	14·3	—	—	—	—

1. Includes some items appropriate to Miscellaneous, item 8.

TABLE 14

MISCELLANEOUS INVISIBLE RECEIPTS

	Miscellaneous Credits (I.M.F. item 8) (millions of U.S. dollars)			Miscellaneous Credits as Percentage of Total Invisible Trade			Percentage Share Total Miscellaneous Credits		
	1964	1958	1952	1964	1958	1952	1964	1958	1952
31 countries	8,493	5,509	2,598	20·0	21·7	18·0	100·0	100·0	100·0
U.S.	1,546	1,074	404	13·1	14·4	7·7	18·2	19·5	15·6
U.K.	1,386	1,190	703[1]	20·7	22·3	23·9	16·3	21·6	27·1
Italy	977	424	114	33·6	31·0	27·4	11·5	7·7	4·4
Germany	559	282	127	20·5	18·0	25·1	6·6	5·1	4·9
France	818	445	195	31·0	46·8	33·4	9·6	8·1	7·5
Netherlands	474	354	279	24·7	37·9	40·6	5·6	6·4	10·7
Canada	224	152	161	15·3	16·9	21·8	2·6	2·8	6·2
Norway	117	69	35	8·8	7·8	5·9	1·4	1·3	1·3
Switzerland	389[2]	227[2]	n.a.	29·8	31·1	—	4·6	4·1	—
Spain	80	16	n.a.	7·1	12·7	—	0·9	0·3	—
Belgium-L'bourg	450	330	115	40·3	38·9	27·1	5·3	6·0	4·4
Japan	185	64	15	18·8	17·8	14·2	2·2	1·2	0·6
Sweden	68	169	8	7·5	22·2	1·5	0·8	3·1	0·3
Mexico	39	40	29[1]	5·2	6·9	9·0	0·5	0·7	1·1
Austria	117	86	17	16·8	30·9	28·8	1·4	1·6	0·7
Denmark	121	50	21	18·9	12·5	8·2	1·4	0·9	0·8
Australia	64	20	19	13·0	7·8	15·6	0·8	0·4	0·8
Greece	102	16	9	29·7	13·3	15·8	1·2	0·3	0·3
Ireland	49	28	23	14·3	13·1	14·6	0·6	0·5	0·9
Yugoslavia	86	24	3	26·4	22·4	7·3	1·0	0·4	0·1
S. Africa	88	80	41	30·0	37·6	33·3	1·0	1·4	1·6
Portugal	90	78	33	31·4	60·0	50·0	1·1	1·4	1·3
Puerto Rico	51	31	n.a.	20·2	29·5	—	0·6	0·6	—
India	88	66	153	35·9	31·9	66·5	1·0	1·2	5·9
Israel	65	22	3	26·7	29·3	18·8	0·8	0·4	0·1
Panama	73	31	n.a.	60·8	47·7	—	0·9	0·6	n.a.
Venezuela	43	67	25	45·7	67·7	58·1	0·5	1·2	1·0
Morocco	11	13	n.a.	12·0	23·2	—	0·1	0·2	n.a.
Pakistan	54	27	46	61·4	56·3	74·2	0·6	0·5	1·8
Turkey	46	26	18	58·2	61·9	—	0·6	0·5	0·7
Jordan	33	8	1·6	51·6	57·1	29·6	0·4	0·2	—

1. Reported net.
2. Includes item 7, Government n.i.e.

46

Table 15

TRANSPORT AND MERCHANDISE INSURANCE DEBITS

	Transport and Insurance Debits (I.M.F. items 3, 4) (millions of U.S. dollars)			Transport and Insurance Debits as Percentage of Total Invisible Payments			Percentage Share of Total Transport and Insurance Payments		
	1964	1958	1952	1964	1958	1952	1964	1958	1952
31 countries	13,004	7,943	5,236	33·1	34·2	47·7	100·0	100·0	100·0
U.S.	2,464	1,636	1,294	35·7	36·4	79·4	18·9	20·6	24·7
U.K.	2,341	1,646	916	45·0	41·0	52·3	18·0	20·7	17·5
Italy	898	437	251	45·9	55·0	69·0	6·9	5·5	4·8
Germany	1,528	823	394	32·3	35·9	59·1	11·8	10·4	7·5
France	641	332	142	23·9	26·7	18·3	4·9	4·2	2·7
Netherlands	373	253	135	28·3	38·0	25·6	2·9	3·2	2·6
Canada	490	290	182	18·4	15·8	15·0	3·8	3·7	3·5
Norway	517	380	305	63·6	69·5	79·0	4·0	4·8	5·8
Switzerland	net	net	net	—	—	—	—	—	—
Spain	137	46	n.a.	39·4	48·4	—	1·1	0·6	—
Belgium-L'bourg	276	188	246	25·0	32·6	46·1	2·1	2·4	4·7
Japan	1,076	416	239	51·8	61·3	81·0	8·3	5·2	4·6
Sweden	339	213[1]	168	47·2	40·1	50·9	2·6	2·7	3·2
Mexico	10	9	6	1·4	2·3	2·9	—	0·1	0·1
Austria	106	16	28	27·0	13·2	57·1	0·8	0·2	0·5
Denmark	241	209	158	51·8	67·6	70·2	1·9	2·6	3·0
Australia	448	289	344	39·7	38·8	60·7	3·4	3·6	6·6
Greece	5	51	41	5·0	58·0	68·3	—	0·6	0·8
Ireland	net	net	net	—	—	—	—	—	—
Yugoslavia	66[1]	25[1]	9[1]	41·3	49·0	40·9	0·5	0·3	0·2
S. Africa	209	167	121	28·9	29·1	36·7	1·6	2·1	2·3
Portugal	57	36	18	31·0	50·7	41·9	0·4	0·5	0·3
Puerto Rico	166	84	n.a.	30·4	38·7	—	1·3	1·1	—
India	65	net	net	15·0	—	—	0·5	—	—
Israel	108	60	3	34·6	49·2	18·8	0·8	0·8	—
Panama	23	17	n.a.	45·1	38·6	—	0·2	0·2	—
Venezuela	178	197	107	16·8	16·9	17·0	1·4	2·5	2·0
Morocco	45	48	n.a.	28·1	41·7	—	0·3	0·6	—
Pakistan	120	31	67	51·1	44·9	57·3	0·9	0·4	1·3
Turkey	75	44	62	44·4	37·3	68·1	0·6	0·6	1·2
Jordan	2	net	—	12·8	—	—	—	—	—

1. Item 3 only net.

TABLE 16

TRAVEL DEBITS

	Travel Debits (I.M.F. item 5) (million U.S. dollars)			Travel Debits as Percentage of Total Invisible Payments			Percentage Share of Total Travel Payments		
	1964	1958	1952	1964	1958	1952	1964	1958	1952
31 countries	8,249	4,222	2,069	21·0	18·2	18·8	100·0	100·0	100·0
U.S.	2,216	1,460	822	32·1	32·5	50·5	26·9	34·6	39·7
U.K.	731	434	230	14·1	10·8	13·1	8·9	10·3	11·1
Italy	209	80	17	10·7	10·1	4·7	2·5	1·9	0·8
Germany	1,171	487	79	24·8	21·2	11·8	14·2	11·5	3·8
France	819	110	110	30·6	8·8	14·2	9·9	2·6	5·3
Netherlands	265	83	36	20·1	12·5	6·8	3·2	2·0	1·7
Canada	659	526	329	24·7	28·6	27·1	8·0	12·5	15·9
Norway	74	48	29	9·1	8·8	7·5	0·9	1·1	1·4
Switzerland	243	118	n.a.	29·8	31·5	—	2·9	2·8	—
Spain	66	2	n.a.	19·0	2·1	—	0·8	—	—
Belgium-L'bourg	242	58	34	21·9	10·1	6·4	2·9	1·4	1·6
Japan	78	16	5	3·8	2·4	1·7	0·9	0·4	0·2
Sweden	169	81	46	23·5	15·3	13·9	2·0	1·9	2·2
Mexico	377	238	113	51·6	60·4	54·9	4·6	5·6	5·5
Austria	118	34	6	30·1	28·1	12·2	1·4	0·8	0·3
Denmark	137	56	34	29·5	18·1	15·1	1·7	1·3	1·6
Australia	127	64	31	11·2	8·6	5·5	1·5	1·5	1·5
Greece	39	15	7	39·8	17·0	11·7	0·5	0·4	0·3
Ireland	72	39	net	49·3	45·3	—	0·9	0·9	—
Yugoslavia	13	6	1	8·1	11·8	6·4	0·2	0·1	—
S. Africa	66	45	34	9·1	7·9	10·3	0·8	1·1	1·6
Portugal	57	13	13	31·0	18·3	30·2	0·7	0·3	0·6
Puerto Rico	76	30	n.a.	13·9	13·8	—	0·9	0·7	—
India	22	16	21	5·1	11·0	19·3	0·3	0·4	1·0
Israel	37	3	4	11·9	2·5	25·0	0·5	0·1	0·2
Panama	10	5	n.a.	19·6	11·4	—	0·1	0·1	—
Venezuela	78	99	42	7·3	8·5	6·7	0·9	2·3	2·0
Morocco	34	29	n.a.	21·3	25·2	—	0·4	0·7	—
Pakistan	12	10	12	5·1	14·5	10·3	0·1	0·2	0·6
Turkey	22	13	10	13·0	11·0	11·0	0·3	0·3	0·5
Jordan	10	4	4	56·7	64·3	92·5	0·1	0·1	0·2

TABLE 17

INVESTMENT INCOME DEBITS

	Investment Income Debits (I.M.F. item 6) (millions of U.S. dollars)			Investment Income Debits as Percentage of Total Invisible Payments			Percentage Share of Total Investment Income Debits		
	1964	1958	1952	1964	1958	1952	1964	1958	1952
31 countries	9,075	5,283	2,749	23·1	22·7	25·0	100·0	100·0	100·0
U.S.	1,731	786	432[1]	25·1	17·5	26·5	19·1	14·9	15·7
U.K.	1,291	1,162	605	24·8	28·9	34·6	14·2	22·0	22·0
Italy	243	88	31	12·4	11·1	8·5	2·7	1·7	1·1
Germany	678	240	2	14·4	10·5	0·3	7·5	4·5	—
France	282	177	126	10·5	14·2	16·2	3·1	3·4	4·6
Netherlands	311	153	79	23·6	23·0	15·0	3·4	2·9	2·9
Canada	1,077	691	405	40·4	37·6	33·4	11·9	13·1	14·7
Norway	92	44	14	11·3	8·0	3·6	1·0	0·8	0·5
Switzerland	59	51	n.a.	7·2	13·6	—	0·7	1·0	—
Spain	46	12	n.a.	13·2	12·6	—	0·5	0·2	—
Belgium-L'bourg	222	100	82	20·1	17·4	15·4	2·4	1·9	3·0
Japan	332	67	11	16·0	9·9	3·7	3·7	1·3	0·4
Sweden	30	17	9	4·2	3·2	2·7	0·3	0·3	0·3
Mexico	324	143	87	44·3	36·3	42·2	3·6	2·7	3·2
Austria	58	16	—	14·8	13·2	—	0·6	0·3	—
Denmark	44	16	17	9·5	5·2	7·6	0·5	0·3	0·6
Australia	409	319	153	36·2	42·8	27·0	4·5	6·0	5·6
Greece	13	4	4	13·3	4·5	6·7	0·1	0·1	0·1
Ireland	67	43	37	45·9	50·0	86·0	0·7	0·8	1·3
Yugoslavia	57	9	5	35·6	17·6	22·7	0·6	0·2	0·1
S. Africa	307	258	141	42·5	45·0	42·7	3·4	4·9	5·1
Portugal	29	6	3	15·8	8·5	7·0	0·3	0·1	0·1
Puerto Rico	239	69	n.a.	43·8	31·8	—	2·6	1·3	—
India	234	70	58	54·2	47·9	53·2	2·6	1·3	2·1
Israel	83	33	9	26·6	27·0	56·3	0·9	0·6	0·3
Panama	9	14	—	17·6	31·8	—	—	0·3	—
Venezuela	678	642	425	63·8	60·5	67·4	7·5	12·2	15·5
Morocco	23	25	n.a.	14·4	21·7	—	0·3	0·5	—
Pakistan	64	10	9	27·2	14·5	7·7	0·7	0·2	0·3
Turkey	42	19	5	24·9	16·1	5·5	0·5	0·4	0·1
Jordan	1·3	0·3	0·3	7·0	4·3	7·5	—	—	—

1. Excluded re-invested earnings of foreign subsidiaries.

TABLE 18

MISCELLANEOUS INVISIBLE DEBITS

	Miscellaneous Debits (I.M.F. item 8) (millions of U.S. dollars)			Miscellaneous Payments as Percentage of Total Invisible Payments			Percentage Share of Total Miscellaneous Payments		
	1964	1958	1952	1964	1958	1952	1964	1958	1952
31 countries	7,874	5,152	1,721	20·1	22·2	15·7	100·0	100·0	100·0
U.S.	396	614	81	5·7	13·7	5·0	5·0	11·9	4·7
U.K.	837	776	net	16·1	19·3	—	10·6	15·1	—
Italy	606	189	66	31·0	23·8	18·1	7·7	3·7	3·8
Germany	1,347	742	192	28·5	32·4	28·8	17·1	14·4	11·2
France	938	626	216	35·0	50·3	27·8	11·9	12·2	12·6
Netherlands	367	176	279	27·9	26·4	52·8	4·7	3·4	16·2
Canada	443	333	299	16·6	18·1	24·6	5·6	6·5	17·4
Norway	130	75	38	16·0	13·7	9·8	1·7	1·5	2·2
Switzerland	513[1]	206[1]	n.a.	62·9	54·9	—	6·5	4·0	—
Spain	99	35	n.a.	28·4	36·8	—	1·3	0·7	—
Belgium-L'bourg	366	230	143	33·1	39·9	26·8	4·7	4·5	8·3
Japan	591	179	40	28·4	26·4	13·6	7·5	3·5	2·3
Sweden	180	219	107	25·1	41·2	32·4	2·3	4·3	6·2
Mexico	21	5	—	2·9	1·3	—	0·3	0·1	—
Austria	110	56	15	28·1	46·3	30·6	1·4	1·1	0·9
Denmark	43	33	10	9·2	10·7	4·4	0·5	0·6	0·6
Australia	148	72	39	13·1	9·7	6·9	1·9	1·4	2·2
Greece	41	18	9	41·8	20·5	15·0	0·5	0·3	0·5
Ireland	7	4	6	4·8	4·7	14·0	0·1	0·1	0·3
Yugoslavia	24	10	4	15·0	19·6	18·2	0·3	0·2	0·2
S. Africa	141	104	34	19·5	18·2	10·3	1·8	2·0	2·0
Portugal	41	16	9	22·3	22·5	20·9	0·5	0·3	0·5
Puerto Rico	65	34	n.a.	11·9	15·7	—	0·8	0·6	—
India	111	61	30	25·7	41·8	27·5	1·4	1·2	1·7
Israel	84	26	5	26·9	21·3	31·3	1·1	0·5	0·3
Panama	9	8	n.a.	17·6	18·2	—	0·1	0·2	—
Venezuela	129	227·	56	12·1	19·5	8·9	1·6	4·4	3·3
Morocco	15	14	n.a.	9·4	12·2	—	0·2	0·3	—
Pakistan	38	19	29	16·2	27·5	24·8	0·5	0·4	1·7
Turkey	30	43	14	17·8	36·4	15·4	0·4	0·8	0·8
Jordan	4	2	0·2	21·7	28·6	5·0	—	—	—

1. Combined with Item 7 Government n.i.e.

TABLE 19

BALANCE OF INDIVIDUAL ITEMS OF INVISIBLE TRADE

Millions of U.S. dollars	Transport and Merchandise Insurance			Foreign Travel			Investment Income			Miscellaneous		
	1964	1958	1952	1964	1958	1952	1964	1958	1952	1964	1958	1952
31 countries	−593	−251	164	950	280	17	3,170	2,076	1,314	619	357	877
U.S.	−147	36	293	−121	−635	−298	5,147	3,081	2,330	1,150	460	323
U.K.	5	−159	305	−199	− 48	− 6	1,134	820	0	549	414	703
Italy	−155	− 36	− 58	826	412	75	− 98	− 35	− 13	371	135	48
Germany	−337	− 88	−126	−484	− 35	24	−408	−139	5	−788	−460	− 65
France	− 28	−164	7	27	57	24	79	− 5	− 19	−120	−181	− 21
Netherlands	317	135	50	− 24	2	108	204	86	60	107	178	0
Canada	−232	−113	− 17	− 47	−188	− 59	−704	−459	−262	−219	−181	−138
Norway	591	385	231	4	− 7	− 9	− 65	− 31	− 8	− 13	− 6	− 3
Switzerland	55	29	80	347	178	83	212	167	78	−124	21	80
Spain	− 38	− 11	n.a.	852	70	n.a.	− 21	− 9	n.a.	− 19	− 19	n.a.
Belgium-L'bourg	12	56	−104	− 68	66	− 5	− 18	50	17	84	100	− 28
Japan	−486	−172	−162	− 16	8	3	−196	− 40	− 5	406	115	− 25
Sweden	320	271	206	− 80	− 21	− 13	53	29	14	−112	− 50	− 99
Mexico	− 9·8	− 8·7	− 3·8	327	304	178	−324	−143	− 87	18	35	29
Austria	− 66	− 3	− 19	385	133	25	− 21	− 4	1	7	30	2
Denmark	78	46	40	30	24	− 4	− 10	− 1	− 10	78	17	11
Australia	−216	−123	−269	− 70	− 46	− 23	−286	−264	−132	− 84	− 52	− 20
Greece	132	11	− 4	52	21	3	0	2	− 2	61	− 2	0
Ireland	24	6	2	93	58	70	37	38	25	42	24	17
Yugoslavia	97	47	23	56	4	2	− 48	− 8·4	− 4·8	62	14	− 1
S. Africa	−122	−110	− 18	− 20	− 14	− 3	−236	−213	−131	− 53	− 24	7
Portugal	− 5	− 17	− 6	70	13	2	− 13	1	2	49	62	24
Puerto Rico	−112	− 53	− 34	43	4	− 4	−212	− 60	− 21	− 14	− 3	5
India	64	67	38	− 17	21	− 15	−211	− 32	− 24	− 23	5	123
Israel	− 16	− 25	7	18	9	− 1	− 54	− 28	− 12	− 19	− 4	− 2
Panama	− 10	− 8	− 8	23	19	21	− 8	− 12	− 11	64	23	13
Venezuela	−158	−173	− 89	− 72	− 99	− 42	−653	−634	−425	− 86	−160	− 31
Morocco	− 30	− 29	n.a.	27	− 10	n.a.	− 17	− 21	n.a.	− 4	− 1	n.a.
Pakistan	− 96	− 16	− 56	− 10	− 9·4	− 12	− 55	− 4	− 3	16	8	17
Turkey	− 50	− 31	− 44	− 14	− 10	− 7	− 42	−18·7	− 4·9	16	− 17	4
Jordan	1·4	—	—	12	− 1	0	3·7	1·7	0·3	29	6	1·4

No sign indicates credit: minus sign debit.

TABLE 20

INVISIBLE RECEIPTS AND PAYMENTS AS SHARE OF TOTAL
TRADE AND OF WORLD TRADE
(For 31 leading countries)

In this table the figures shown in Table 5 are expressed in index numbers
(1952=100)

1964	Invisible Trade		Invisible Trade as Percentage of Total		Share of World Invisible Credits	Share of World Invisible Debits
	Credit	Debit	Credit	Debit		
	(1952=100)					
World	270·1	258·5	111·1	104·4	—	—
U.S.	224·2	424·0	111·9	83·7	83·0	164·9
U.K.	227·3	297·1	128·0	101·9	84·2	115·8
Italy	698·8	537·6	145·2	160·7	260·0	209·5
Germany	541·9	708·2	128·6	158·4	203·3	271·8
France	451·7	344·9	105·8	104·8	168·6	133·3
Netherlands	279·1	249·2	102·0	79·2	104·9	96·8
Canada	198·8	219·9	110·9	116·7	73·3	85·7
Norway	222·8	210·6	58·8	92·5	83·3	81·8
Switzerland[1]	178·8	217·3	101·6	102·3	107·4	128·6[1]
Spain[1]	893·7	366·3	275·5	138·8	500·0	200·0[1]
Belgium-L'bourg	262·6	207·1	131·7	98·4	96·2	80·6
Japan	930·2	704·7	166·2	165·8	366·7	276·5
Sweden	170·3	217·6	88·0	163·8	62·5	84·2
Mexico	230·0	354·9	124·3	164·8	89·5	133·3
Austria	1,181·4	800·0	318·4	257·1	400·0	300·0
Denmark	250·4	206·7	102·2	79·8	93·3	76·9
Australia	402·5	199·1	192·0	137·9	157·1	75·8
Greece	601·8	163·3	159·7	51·6	266·7	66·7
Ireland	217·8	339·5	102·0	163·4	88·9	100·0
Yugoslavia	795·1	727·3	188·6	201·9	350·0	300·0
S. Africa	238·2	218·8	109·6	111·4	100·0	84·2
Portugal	434·8	427·9	160·3	157·3	150·0	133·3
Puerto Rico[1]	240·0	251·6	115·4	117·2	150·0	150·0[1]
India	106·5	396·3	86·2	198·5	35·7	166·7
Israel	1,518·8	1,950·0	153·6	636·2	—	700·0
Panama[1]	184·6	115·9	126·0	123·0	100·0	50·0[1]
Venezuela	218·6	168·3	132·1	106·9	100·0	64·9
Morocco[1]	164·3	139·1	127·7	91·7	100·0	60·0[1]
Pakistan	141·9	200·9	136·7	113·0	50·0	71·4
Turkey	202·6	1,167·0	38·1	298·7	100·0	480·0
Jordan	1,280·0	450·0	151·1	141·3	—	—

1. 1958 = 100; 1952 figures not being available.
Sources: Definitions, etc., as in Table 5.

52

TABLE 20

INVISIBLE RECEIPTS AND PAYMENTS AS SHARE OF TOTAL
TRADE AND OF WORLD TRADE
(For 31 leading countries)

In this table the figures shown in Table 5 are expressed in index numbers
(1952=100)

Invisible Trade		Invisible Trade as Percentage of Total		Share of World Invisible Credits	Share of World Invisible Debits	1958
Credit	Debit	Credit	Debit			
		(1952=100)				
162·4	153·7	107·1	107·5	—	—	World
141·0	276·0	110·1	79·4	86·8	180·9	U.S.
181·0	229·6	132·5	112·8	111·9	149·5	U.K.
329·0	218·1	154·4	148·3	204·0	142·9	Italy
311·7	343·8	135·7	153·4	193·3	220·5	Germany
162·8	160·2	87·9	103·1	100·0	104·4	France
154·8	126·1	99·6	79·6	97·6	80·6	Netherlands
122·0	151·6	108·7	113·7	73·3	98·6	Canada
148·7	141·7	107·5	94·4	91·7	95·5	Norway
n.a.	n.a.	n.a.	n.a.	n.a.	n.a.	Switzerland[1]
n.a.	n.a.	n.a.	n.a.	n.a.	n.a.	Spain[1]
199·5	107·9	165·5	93·1	119·2	71·0	Belgium-L'bourg
399·6	230·2	144·2	143·0	216·7	147·1	Japan
142·1	160·9	104·7	113·8	87·5	110·5	Sweden
180·2	191·3	132·5	129·1	115·8	125·0	Mexico
471·2	246·9	217·5	144·3	250·0	166·7	Austria
155·9	137·3	103·9	99·0	100·0	92·3	Denmark
211·5	131·4	162·7	154·9	142·3	84·8	Australia
210·5	146·7	99·4	80·7	166·7	100·0	Greece
135·7	200·0	107·3	170·0	88·9	100·0	Ireland
261·0	231·8	133·6	126·4	200·0	200·0	Yugoslavia
173·2	173·6	118·1	120·9	114·3	115·8	S. Africa
197·0	165·1	130·4	112·8	125·0	100·0	Portugal
n.a.	n.a.	n.a.	n.a.	n.a.	n.a.	Puerto Rico[1]
90·0	133·9	102·8	95·4	57·1	100·0	India
468·8	762·5	130·7	525·5	—	500·0	Israel
n.a.	n.a.	n.a.	n.a.	n.a.	n.a.	Panama[1]
230·2	184·8	135·7	98·6	200·0	118·9	Venezuela
n.a.	n.a.	n.a.	n.a.	n.a.	n.a.	Morocco[1]
77·4	593·2	129·4	157·3	50·0	371·4	Pakistan
107·7	129·7	148·5	188·5	100·0	100·0	Turkey
280·0	175·0	123·2	71·3	—	100·0	Jordan

CHAPTER IV

THE BANKS

35.   The banking structure is made up of domestic banks, discount houses, merchant banks, British overseas banks and the branches of Commonwealth and foreign banks. Virtually all undertake some foreign business. But they have their own characteristics:

1. THE DOMESTIC BANKS

36.   These domestic banks mainly comprise 11 London clearing banks, which operate about 12,000 branches in England and Wales, five Scottish banks with 1,700 branches and eight Northern Ireland banks (most of which also operate in the Republic of Ireland) with some 400 branches, as well as other institutions such as C.W.S. Bank, Yorkshire Bank, C. Hoare & Co., etc. Foreign business on behalf of customers may be brought in to any branch, and all are equipped to deal with it. A large part of the work arising at branches, however, is commonly passed to one or other of a relatively small number of branches or departments which specialize in handling overseas and foreign business.

37.   In general, the domestic banks do not have branches abroad; their overseas transactions are handled through reciprocal arrangement with a world-wide system of correspondent banks. Some may have a few branches overseas—for instance, Midland has a branch in New York—and some have wholly-owned subsidiaries operating in limited areas overseas—such as Barclays Bank (France), Westminster Bank (Foreign) and Lloyds Bank Europe. Some of the domestic banks have shareholdings in British overseas banks, such as Barclays Bank DCO, Bank of London and South America, National and Grindlays Bank and Standard Bank. In recent years, domestic banks have been tending to develop new overseas connections, by joining, for example, with other foreign banks in establishing new banks in foreign countries, for instance in Spain. Details of the overseas connections of the clearing banks are set out in Appendix A.

2. DISCOUNT HOUSES

38.   The discount market is made up of the 12 members of the London Discount Market Association (who alone have the right of recourse to the Bank of England) and of about a dozen other firms. Their foreign business is largely indirect. Although they provide discount facilities for commercial bills, some of which are for the finance of U.K. exports and some for third country trade, the foreign payments are not received by the discount houses. Such earnings will be part of the total charge for credit made by the bank

concerned and will not accrue specifically to the discount houses, who will generally discount the bills for account of a U.K. resident (either the drawer or acceptor). In the case of multilateral deals (i.e. the operations of merchants or brokers where the goods financed do not touch the U.K.) the discount market provides a facility without which income-earning foreign business might not be done.

39.   Although the greater part of their borrowed funds necessarily comes from the domestic banks, they also obtain a substantial part of their funds from the accepting houses and overseas banks, not necessarily with branches in London. These contacts often enable them to place financial business (e.g. acceptance credits for non-residents) in London which, in their view, might otherwise go elsewhere.

40.   In addition, one house maintains a representative in Paris, and others have participations in companies established to do discount market business in Rhodesia, South Africa and Australia. Recently a number of houses have obtained permission to participate in the small but expanding market in dollar certificates of deposit issued by the London offices of certain U.S. and other banks.

41.   Parallel with the discount market there exist large markets in unsecured funds between banks, and in local authority loans. In these markets several brokers, some of whom have indirect interests in currency deposit broking, operate to match lenders and borrowers. Some discount houses have bought their way into such firms and one house has bought a foreign exchange broking business. So far as foreign earnings are concerned, these brokers earn brokerage fees from dealing done between banks.

3. BRITISH OVERSEAS BANKS

42.   These are banks registered in the United Kingdom, where the central management is located and the capital largely held, but with their main business and branches overseas. Hong Kong and Shanghai, which is registered in and managed from Hong Kong is also usually included. A problem arises, of course, in the case of banks which have specialized in a single overseas country, since they gradually become almost indistinguishable from the indigenous banks. Bank of New Zealand is one such example. Thus the list of British overseas banks usually consists of the following seven: Barclays Bank D.C.O., Bank of London and South America, Chartered Bank, Hong Kong and Shanghai Banking Corporation, National and Grindlays Bank, Ottoman Bank, Standard Bank. To these might be added Australia and New Zealand Bank and English, Scottish and Australian Bank.

43.   The environment in which the British overseas banks operate has changed profoundly during the past decade, both in London and overseas. They have largely operated in the countries of the Commonwealth, and other areas with strong British connections (Bolsa is the main exception), their activities influenced not only by the close ties of trade and investment, but also of sentiment. (See TABLE 21 in Appendix A for full details of their branch networks.) The political transformation of the Commonwealth and

the working out of the concept of sovereignty in the developing world has been of profound importance to the banks, making it necessary for them increasingly to adapt their operations within national boundaries, as well as to diversify their activities in other territories. This has affected their capital structures (establishing separate banking corporations such as Standard Bank of South Africa, Bank of South Arabia); and their management organization, with the pressure for local executive boards and indigenous executives. It has resulted in keener competition from indigenous banks, often Government sponsored (such as Ghana Commercial Bank, Uganda Commercial Bank, Volkskas). It has even led to nationalization (in Burma, Egypt, Iraq, Tanzania).

44. The emphasis on modernisation of the economies and of rapid growth through industrialization has been a dominant theme of the developing world. In this setting the increased opportunities for domestic banking as the economies have evolved beyond a simple import-export structure have also confronted the overseas banks with a number of new problems: exchange control, currency instability, demands for industrial financing and changing trade patterns both as to commodities (capital goods requiring longer credit) and geographically.

4. MERCHANT BANKS

45. The term "merchant bank" is often applied to banking houses which are members of the Accepting Houses Committee[1] but the term is descriptive of many more institutions. These banks rarely have branches, at home or abroad. Foreign business has always been important for the merchant banks, whose activities were originally intimately connected with foreign trade and international capital movements. The nature of this business (once primarily concerned with the financing of foreign trade by means of acceptance credits giving rise to Bills of Exchange—the famous "Bill on London"—and capital raising and servicing operations on behalf of foreign borrowers) has been changing. Until the middle 50s the foreign exchange earnings of the merchant banks had been connected with their operations in sterling. In the last ten years or so, however, merchant banks—as well as other financial institutions in London—have developed a large volume of business in U.S. dollars and other currencies. In first helping to create this type of business and then building it up, merchant banks have been instrumental in the development of the new international money market (Euro-dollar market) and international capital markets (Euro-bond market).

BANKING SERVICES

46. Thus the different sectors have developed and are developing differently. But all (apart from the discount market) undertake certain types of foreign business in common. This includes dealing in foreign currency;

1. At present there are 16 members of the Committee. Their names are shown in Appendix B. The main qualification for membership of the Accepting Houses Committee is that the Bills of Exchange they "accept" should be eligible for rediscount with the Bank of England. This privilege carries with it certain obligations. In particular houses are required to conform to certain rules governing their balance sheets.

the financing of overseas trade; making overseas remittances; taking deposits from overseas, both in sterling and foreign currencies; lending abroad, either by on-lending of foreign currency deposits or in other ways; handling foreign securities; and providing information and advice to facilitate overseas trade.

47. The banks are authorized dealers in foreign exchange[1] (and also in gold[2], though their gold transactions are small). The foreign exchange market is centralized in London, and most dealings are conducted by the specialized foreign branches or departments, who are in touch with each other and with other authorized dealers through brokers, and also by telex and phone with exchange markets overseas. Dealings in foreign coin and notes, mainly for travellers, may be conducted through any branch. Branches also provide other facilities for travellers, such as issuing letters of credit or travellers' cheques.

48. Short-term financing of foreign trade is undertaken by the banks and it may relate to exports, imports or goods passing between third countries. Financing methods are complex and varied and subject to exchange control regulations. The banks accept, discount and collect bills of exchange, and open documentary sight or acceptance credits. Medium- and long-term export credit is also provided in various ways, against E.C.G.D. guarantees. All these transactions involve a considerable volume of overseas remittances, which may be made by such methods as cable, telex, air-mail and mail transfers, and drafts.

49. The banks accept deposits from overseas in foreign currencies as well as in sterling, and may themselves on-lend currency deposits. Thus they participate in the large and growing market in "Eurocurrencies," of which London is now the world's main centre.[3]

50. Transactions in foreign securities are undertaken, these again being substantially limited by exchange control. The banks collect interest and dividend on foreign securities held on behalf of customers, and may themselves act as U.K. paying agents for some foreign securities.

EARNINGS OF BANKING

51. It is clear that the banks not only earn foreign exchange from their own services to non-residents, but also help others to earn exchange too. Whereas the second is important, its contribution to the balance of payments is both indirect and impossible to quantify. The banks' direct earnings, in the view of the Committee, should be capable of measurement. This the Committee has attempted to do for the first time. It has meant a close examination of the balance of payments as well as a special statistical inquiry among the banks.

52. Estimates of banking earnings form part of the estimate of invisible exports in the whole balance of payments. It was important, therefore, that the definition and methods used in this part of our inquiry should be consistent with these estimates. Moreover, in order to have maximum value, it was

1. See Appendix C for details of foreign exchange market.
2. See Appendix D for details of London gold market.
3. See Appendix E for details of Euro-dollar market.

essential that any new information produced by the Committee should be in a form that could be readily related to existing official estimates.

53. The banking sector includes all institutions covered in tables for "U.K. Banking Sector" in the Bank of England "Quarterly Bulletin." They are:

The London Clearing Banks and other domestic banks

The Scottish and Northern Ireland Banks

The Discount Houses

Members of:

The Accepting Houses Committee

The British Overseas and Commonwealth Banks Association

The Foreign Banks and Affiliates Association

The American and Japanese Banks of London

Group of other Banks listed on page 95 of the March, 1966, "Bulletin"

54. No separate figures are at present published for this sector or any part of it, but its earnings are included under the two headings of "interest, profits and dividends" (TABLE 12 of the 1966 Balance of Payments Pink Book) and "other services" (TABLE 11).

55. "Interest, Profits and Dividends" is subdivided into "direct investment," "portfolio investment" and "other investment."

56. Earnings of British banks' overseas branches and subsidiaries are included in "direct investment." They are taken net of local taxes and depreciation, and comprise "interest payments in respect of loans granted and the remitted dividends from subsidiaries, together with the parent companies share of unremitted profits which is retained for re-investment." (Pink Book, p. 45.)

57. Interest on external liabilities and claims in *sterling* is included in "other investment." Interest on advances to non-residents and income from the discount of bills for them is counted under this head. Any earnings by banks from portfolio holdings would be included in "portfolio investment."

58. "Financial and allied services" comprises the service (as distinct from interest) earnings of banks along with those of a number of other institutions including the insurance industry, the Stock Exchange and the commodity markets. The main banking elements are:

Commissions in respect of acceptance business

Earnings from foreign exchange dealing, and

Interest on foreign currency balances

Underwriting commissions on overseas loans are estimated but not split between banks and other institutions. No separate estimate is made for any other banking commissions though a rough allowance is made for them in a figure for "other bank charges and brokerage." All figures in this sub-section are net.

SHORTCOMINGS OF PRESENT FIGURES

59. In the view of the Committee the present figures seem to have the following defects:

58

1. They do not give any idea of the contribution of "the banking industry" to the balance of payments. As already noted the service earnings of bankers are lumped together with those of other very dissimilar institutions. Earnings of overseas branches and subsidiaries are included with those of manufacturing industry; while discounts of sterling bills for foreigners come into the same category as, among other things, the overseas earnings of oil companies. For some types of banking earnings, though not all, separate estimates are prepared by the authorities in the course of producing the overall figures of "interest, profits and dividends" and "financial and allied services."
2. For a number of items the figures are compiled by estimating a total of transactions or of assets and then applying a notional average percentage for commission, profit or interest. The results thus depend for their reliability on the accuracy both of the estimated total and the average rate of return.
3. To a small extent the heading, "financial and allied services" is net, i.e. payments due to foreigners under each item are deducted from the corresponding earnings of British residents. This practice may not give a fair indication of the individual contributions of the various institutions concerned to the balance of payments, or of its growth possibilities.

POSSIBLE ACTION

60. The Committee concluded that the present methods of inquiry had been pressed as far as they reasonably could. Apart from the possibility of publishing some of the estimates now kept for internal use, there seemed little prospect of improving the present figures except by direct inquiry from the banks and other financial institutions. The Committee decided that if such an inquiry was found to be practicable, it would enable the contribution of banking to the balance of payments to be shown separately from that of other activities, and would also provide a series of estimates derived independently of the existing ones and which would, therefore, provide a valuable cross check on the accuracy of both.

61. On this basis discussions were begun with the leading banking associations, with a view to drawing up an agreed questionnaire. The final agreed version is set out in Appendix F. Three problems had to be faced. It was necessary to keep the new definitions in line with the official balance of payments figures. Secondly, it was important to rely on informed estimates in areas (such as parts of the foreign exchange market) where full details had not been kept. Finally, there was the need to avoid double-counting, particularly in connection with the collection of earnings on direct investment overseas, and with the interest earnings of the export houses and commodity traders.

62. The results of this special inquiry are also set out in Appendix F. They show the overseas earnings of the banks on the agreed basis. They also indicate the percentage response of the different banking groups in the City.

In interpreting the true invisible earnings of the banks two further adjust-ments are necessary: (*a*) an allowance must be made for the response rate; and (*b*) some allowance has to be made for deposits held by the banks on behalf of other institutions. Both points are taken into account in Chapter XIII, where the banks' contribution to the City's invisible earnings is analysed.

EFFICIENCY OF FOREIGN BUSINESS

63.   The Committee examined how the services of the banks and their invisible income might be stimulated further. This involved an examination of their current efficiency as well as an appraisal of the conditions under which they are operating. The measurement of their efficiency posed a number of acute problems. There are the well-known difficulties that bedevil all efforts to measure productivity in clerical work. These arise from the fact that in such employment there is no physical end-product by which to measure the volume of output, changes in which could be compared with the trend of costs. The experience of the Prices and Incomes Board in this respect is instructive. With all its resources and its experience in measuring productivity it might perhaps have been expected that its investigation would have yielded some hard results in this field. But in para. 135 of its Report on Bank Charges[1] it concludes that a rigorous analysis of the trend of costs with respect to output in banking is impossible:

"Total operating costs (excluding bad debt provisions) increased by 42 per cent in the case of the London clearing banks and by 41 per cent in the case of the Scottish banks between 1961 and 1965. There is no unique indicator of output against which to set these increases. In terms of volume the main work of the banks consists of providing facilities for making payment, and it is in respect of this that the bulk of operating costs are incurred. But the banks are also engaged in borrowing and lending, and provide a range of ancillary services from financial advice to travel information. However, it is possible neither to associate particular costs with particular services, nor to identify adequate indicators of the output of these services. At the same time the mix of services is liable to change over the years. It was symptomatic of this situation that when we asked the banks individually to submit to us indicators of their activity, we received from them lists of items, varying in composition from bank to bank, and comprising in all some 18 separate indicators. We are therefore resigned to the fact that a rigorous analysis of the trend of costs with respect to output is impossible."

64.   Nevertheless, the Committee felt it was important to gain some idea of the efficiency of the banks' "foreign" operations. Three approaches were, therefore, attempted. First, an attempt was made to make some estimate of the increase in the volume of work handled, and to compare it with an indicator of resources employed. Secondly, the clearing banks' services were

1. National Board for Prices and Incomes; Report No. 34, *Bank Charges*. Cmnd. 3292. H.M.S.O.

examined from the point of view of the customer—and the charges for these compared with those made by banks in competing centres. Thirdly, the Committee investigated the scope for increasing efficiency by adopting modern automated techniques. None of these approaches is wholly satisfactory in itself. None gives a complete picture. But, taken together, the Committee believes that they provide some guide to banking efficiency and at least point the way ahead.

65.   With regard to the first approach the change in the volume of U.K. trade was chosen as a rough indicator of output. The Committee believed that this would be widely accepted to be an important determinant of the volume of work handled in the branches of banks dealing with foreign business. One way or another, the activities of these branches are concerned largely with the finance of foreign trade. Conversely, nearly all the trade that touches Britain's shores (and some that does not) is accompanied by, or reflected in, a transfer of funds in London. We accordingly compiled an index of the volume of UK trade (exports plus imports deflated by the price index), using 1938 as the base date. The results shown in the following table, reveal that the volume more than doubled between 1938 and 1965.

Volume of U.K. Foreign Trade (Visibles)	Foreign Branch Staff (Men and Women)
1938 = 100	1938 = 100
1951 = 207	1951 = 120
1955 = 190	1955 = 126
1961 = 202	1961 = 151
1965 = 224	1965 = 154

66.   It is plain that this index understates the increase in the volume of work. In addition to a marked extension of traditional financing facilities, there has been a development of new types of export finance (notably in medium-term E.C.G.D.-guaranteed finance) and of ancillary services (such as travellers' cheques, etc.) as well as the extra work involved in administering Exchange Control. There has also been a very considerable increase in foreign exchange operations.

67.   To set against the indicator of output, we have also compiled an index of staff employed. This index is subject to an even greater margin of error. It is based on the total staff employed in the chief foreign branch of one of the Big Five banks. If this bank's share in the total has been declining (though that is certainly not the bank's belief) the index would understate the increase in staff employed by all the banks. But a cross-check amongst other big banks suggests that the index gives a fair idea of the order of magnitude involved.

68.   It can be seen that while the volume of U.K. visible trade has more than doubled since 1938, the number of staff employed on this calculation has increased by little more than a half. Moreover, the index of total employees masks a significant change in the composition of the staff: the number of men employed actually fell by 10 per cent whilst the number of women trebled. Overall, and after all the necessary reservations have been made, this rough comparison suggests that the foreign branches of the banks

have handled a large increase in work with a small increase in skilled staff. This has been made possible by the application of mechanization in many fields. The scope for raising productivity further is discussed below.

69.   Before leaving this topic, it is worth putting the matter into perspective. It is estimated that the total numbers engaged full-time in "foreign" banking services in the City is not more than 6,000 for the clearing banks (compared with a total staff employed of 142,000), and, say 10,000-12,000 in all. Even if a saving of 10 per cent or so were possible (and as will be seen, there are grounds for believing that it might be), this would make only a small reduction in the total salary costs of the clearing banks and a negligible contribution towards easing the nation's manpower shortage.

70.   Turning to the second approach outlined above, the services provided by the banks can be conveniently divided for purposes of this inquiry under two headings. First, there are those offered by banks in this country to banks and traders abroad and which therefore earn invisible income directly—such as facilities for documentary credits, collections, security management, etc. Secondly, there are the facilities offered by banks to their own customers at home—such as normal short-term finance, collection of foreign bills, etc.; in so far as these are cheap and flexible compared with those offered to foreign companies by their own banks, they make an indirect contribution towards the country's earnings.

71.   With regard to London's competitiveness in the way of commission charges, etc., to foreign customers, this is a matter which has been kept under review by the Committee of London Clearing Bankers. A detailed study of the subject was made by the Foreign Exchange Committee of the C.L.C.B. in 1962 and, after talks with the C.L.C.B., the Committee understood that, broadly speaking, the results still applied.

72.   This study examined, among other things, the principal services provided by the large commercial banks in each of the Common Market countries. It found that while in the main each provided similar types of service, charges were by no means uniform. The inquiry therefore surveyed charges applied to foreign customers by banks in the Common Market and in the United Kingdom under the following headings:

Documentary Credits, Collections, Securities

A. Documentary Credits

The work under this heading may be sub-divided into the following operations: advising, confirming, payment, amendment, acceptance. The costs in the United Kingdom appear to compare quite favourably with those in the Six. The following table ranks the countries *in order of cheapness*.

Table A

Advising	*Confirming*	*Payment*	*Acceptance*	*Amendment*[1]
Italy	Germany	Belgium	Belgium	Germany ⎫
Belgium	*United Kingdom*	*United Kingdom*	Germany	Netherlands ⎬
United Kingdom	Netherlands	Germany	*United Kingdom*	Italy
Germany	Belgium	France	Netherlands	France
Netherlands	Italy	Netherlands	Italy	Belgium
France	France	Italy	France	*United Kingdom*

1. In spite of the U.K.'s position, U.K. bank charges for this item are so small that the position is not significant.

B. COLLECTIONS

TABLE B

Clean	Documentary
Italy	United Kingdom
United Kingdom	Italy
France	France
Belgium	Belgium
Germany	Germany
Netherlands	Netherlands

C. SECURITIES

No proper comparison between banks in the United Kingdom and in other countries can be made as regards charges for *buying* and *selling* securities. On the London Stock Exchange, all transactions are passed through brokers and the bank, where it is involved at all, acts merely as an intermediary. In most Continental countries, on the other hand, the banks themselves deal in stocks and shares (with the United States somewhere between the two, in as much as many, but not all, transactions are passed through brokers). Consequently, it is the London *Brokers'* Commission which should be compared with the overseas *Banks'* charges. Such a comparison reveals London as an expensive centre for dealing, but tells us nothing about the competitiveness of United Kingdom banks. (See Chapter VII for a comparison of dealing costs in European centres.) Although the London bank makes no charge to the customer, it receives from the broker, by way of return commission, one quarter of the scale charge. It is remarkable that this return commission, though received merely for introducing the business, is in some cases more than the foreign banks' charges for actually executing the transaction.

It appears, however, that apart from buying and selling, the charges made by the clearing banks compare unfavourably with those of foreign banks. The clearing banks are used in a substantial way as custodians for securities held for customers outside the United Kingdom. Both for this and for processing the securities the banks make specific charges under various headings, under a schedule agreed amongst the clearing banks. In cases where large blocks of securities are involved, there seems little doubt that charges here do not compare favourably, particularly with regard to the receipt and delivery of securities.

TABLE C

Holding Charges	Receipt and Delivery	Collection of Drawn or Matured Bonds
Italy	Italy ⎱	United Kingdom
Germany	Germany ⎰	Netherlands
United Kingdom	Netherlands	Belgium[1]
Netherlands	Belgium	
Belgium	France	
France	United Kingdom	

73.   It is to be noted that the U.K. tariffs discussed above are those applied by the clearing banks, by agreement amongst themselves, for carrying out business on behalf of customers resident outside the United Kingdom. The agreed schedule has been subject to only a few, minor amendments since it was originally drawn up in 1948, after very considerable labour extending over many years. The clearing banks adhere strictly to it. However, the other banking groups in London, such as the merchant banks, foreign banks, overseas banks, etc., do not strictly conform to it, though they may take it as a guide. There is no agreed schedule of charges in respect of foreign business undertaken for the banks' domestic customers.

1. Figures for France, Germany and Italy were not available.

74.   At a time when inter-bank agreements are being challenged, it may be necessary to give some thought to the agreed tariff of charges to non-residents. Certainly, there seems little doubt that some overseas banks in London are now undercutting the clearing banks' charges on documentary credits, etc., and that profitable work is being lost as a result, though it is not, of course, necessarily being lost to the City. It is up to the clearing banks to decide whether they are content to see their share in this particular type of work decline. Clearing bankers point out that competition has already driven their charges down to the minimum fixed by the schedule, and that at this level many types of work (with the major exception of documentary credits) are unprofitable for them—notably collections, mail transfers (where no charge is made for inter-bank transfers) and security work. Even if the agreement were abolished, therefore, there would appear to be little scope for further reductions in charges.

75.   As for the borrowing facilities provided by banks to their domestic customers, the fullest study available is that conducted by Glyn Mills & Co., the London clearing bank, and published in *The Banker* in May, 1967. The Committee, therefore, has taken the comparative figures and added corresponding rates for the United States, all of which are set out in Appendix G. An examination[1] of this revised list of comparative rates suggests strongly that, at least in terms of flexibility and simplicity, the facilities provided by British clearing banks in this respect compare very favourably with those of any other banking system. This arises largely from the unique predominance in Britain of the overdraft system. Under this system, the customer is charged only on the net daily overdrawn *balance* standing in his current account or accounts. Moreover, because overdraft rates vary in accordance with Bank rate (at a predetermined margin above it), potential borrowers know what their interest charge will be (for any given level of Bank rate). They know also that that will be the only charge they have to face; and any negotiation takes place about the basic rate. By comparison, the short-term borrowing facilities employed both on the Continent and the United States appear to be relatively inflexible and, by the same token, expensive (relatively to any given level of money rates). In many Continental countries, bill discounting remains a common method, with all the paper work that it entails. Where overdraft facilities are available, they would seem to differ in several respects from U.K. practices: in particular, a variety of commitment fees and other commissions are usually charged in addition to the basic rate. In the United States, most short-term advances are made by way of loan, under which the full amount granted is drawn and charged for from the outset (with the additional complication, in the United States, of compensating balances).

76.   The Committee did not think it appropriate to make an extensive investigation of export credit facilities themselves. This is largely because, in all countries, such facilities are closely tied to Government policy and

1. It must be stressed that, although the rates quoted relate to March 1967, their importance lies in the margin between one country and another.

the availability of credit insurance guarantees from Government agencies. It would therefore hardly be fair to attribute all the increased earnings of foreign exchange resulting from improvements in such facilities to the efforts of the banks alone. In Britain, for instance, there has been the development of fixed-rate medium-term finance and of facilities for making short-term finance available at Bank rate. But in both cases this has been made possible only by extensions in the scope of facilities provided by the Export Credit Guarantees Department. Suffice it to say the E.C.G.D. believes that credit insurance facilities offered by this country are fully competitive with, and usually superior to, any available elsewhere in the world.

77.   Turning now to the third issue raised above, the large clearing banks seem to be close to a much wider application of computers to foreign business. Bankers told the Committee that before long they will be able to computerize almost all the usual processes involved in foreign branches—international payments by mail transfer, exchange transactions and book-keeping (with the different currencies and types of account, all of which have to be reconciled one with another), the processing of incoming payments to be made in the United Kingdom on behalf of banks abroad, travellers cheques and so forth. One leading clearing bank has already put a considerable number of these processes on to computer. Another bank is due to install a computer for its foreign business early in 1968. The key technical problem now, the Committee was told, apart from the normal problems of handling the switch-over to computer operations, is to devise a method of putting instructions directly into the computer. The great variety of instructions received from customers in foreign business has always been processed by hand. A good deal of the secondary processing work can now be done by the computers. But it is still necessary to have the customer's original instructions put into a form that the computer can handle, by special staff. The really big savings will come when one piece of information is handled only once.

78.   The principal short-run advantage is of course the savings in staff that will be made possible and the ability to absorb an ever increasing volume of work without a rise in staff. One bank estimates that when the change-over is completed staff savings may amount to as much as 10 per cent. This will be realized even from the relatively limited application of computer techniques that is immediately envisaged at the present. Yet not all clearing banks are so far ahead and not all banks have the kind of foreign business that lends itself to computers.

79.   In the longer run, perhaps equally important results can be expected to result from the increase in the quality of management information that computerization brings. This will enable the banks to determine more exactly than is possible at present the costs and benefits to them of the various services that they offer. For instance, inter-bank transfers of funds are at present not charged: what does this service cost the clearing banks? What compensating benefits accrue? The computer can be used to calculate both the costs and the true profitability of specific processes for the first time.

It is to be expected that this should lead banks to make a more scientific assessment of the charges they should apply to customers.

80.   Each of the three approaches to the problem of the banks' efficiency adopted in this chapter has thrown its own, partial, light on the central issue involved. The first seemed to suggest that banks have financed a very large increase in the nation's trade whilst employing only a little over one half per cent of the nation's manpower. The second has shown that the services they offer are fully competitive with those available in other financial centres —with one or two exceptions, to which the banks should give further thought. The third suggested that the banks might reap important benefits from the application of computerized techniques in the foreign field.

RECOMMENDATION

81.   The Committee recommends that the leading banking associations arrange an inquiry into the operations of the banks' overseas business and into the comparative rates and facilities offered by Britain and other nations.

STIMULATING BANK EARNINGS

82.   The banking sector makes three contributions to the balance of payments:

1. Its services in helping other exporters (visible and invisible) to earn foreign exchange.
2. Its net overseas earnings.
3. The facility it provides for overseas holders of sterling to retain their balances in the form of London bank deposits. (If this were restricted, holders would convert sterling into gold, dollars and other currencies.)

The second and third of these roles (as an earner and as an attractor of sterling balances) are often at odds with each other and in considering ways of increasing invisible earnings the Committee has had to balance one against the other. Interest payments on balances, for example, represent a cost when calculating the banking sector's overseas earnings. At the same time sterling lendings by the banks to overseas borrowers produce a gain in earnings yet also represent an outflow of capital. This is well recognized by the authorities who exercise a rigid control over lendings with the result that they are small in relation to overseas deposits. Thus interest earnings on overseas account are correspondingly small in relation to interest payments.

83.   These points have to be borne in mind in any recommendations relating to the expansion of banking earnings. Thus the Committee has been conscious that a complete freeing of overseas lending might lead to too great an outflow of capital and to undue pressure on the pound. It has, however, considered what might be done without undermining the strength of sterling and has concluded that more flexibility could be introduced into exchange control regulations.

84.   When the 105 per cent ceiling was imposed on bank advances with

the primary objective of reducing domestic demand, it was extended to cover sterling advances to overseas residents. The Committee feels that the greater freedom previously permitted might now be restored as soon as possible unless there is a specific balance of payments danger in such a restoration. Such sterling credits should be available not only for financing U.K. trade but also for transacting business between third countries. The Committee also believes that further study should be given to the effects of extending the normal 180-day limit on sterling credits to overseas residents. Procedures for obtaining an extension might be made plain and the impact of permitting advances of up to 360 days rather than the present maximum of 180 days might be carefully considered to see what adverse effects, if any, would be likely.

85.   In order to make full use of the extremely advanced international money market in London, the Committee also considers it desirable to re-examine most outstanding exchange control restrictions and to remove those which provide no particular defence to the balance of payments and the pound.

86.   It is also proposed that the accepting houses, other major banks, the discount market and the Bank of England might examine ways in which the dollar (or other currency) acceptance market could be built up in London. Such acceptances should only be used against the genuine movement of goods. It seems likely that a developed market of this sort would provide a further source of foreign exchange earnings for the London market.

87.   It has been strongly represented to the Committee, particularly by the British overseas banks, that Government departments and Government agencies do not pass business through the overseas branches of such banks on every occasion possible. In some cases, it has been alleged, loans have been placed with the bank of the recipient country in London rather than with a British bank with branches in the territory concerned. In other instances, Government or semi-official funds abroad have been placed with local domestic banks rather than with the branch of a local British bank. There is clear evidence of American banks taking loan business from British overseas banks through their possession of counterpart funds to U.S. Government loans. In short if full use were made of the British overseas banks by the British Government wherever possible, for the deposit of funds and for remittances and other business usually associated with information and other services, further invisible earnings would accrue. The same would be true if Britain's large industrial firms, operating abroad, did the same.

RECOMMENDATIONS

88.   1. The Committee recommends that the Bank of England and the leading banking associations examine exchange control regulations with the specific purpose of removing restrictions which are hindering the banks' role as major parts of an international financial market and whose removal would not undermine the pound.

2. The Committee also recommends that the Treasury and the Bank

of England consider whether Government departments make enough use of Britain's overseas banking network.

3. The Committee recommends that the Confederation of British Industry and the Association of British Chambers of Commerce be asked whether member firms operating overseas, make full use of British banking facilities abroad and, if not, why not.

APPENDIX A (1): CHAPTER IV

1. OVERSEAS BRANCHES AND REPRESENTATIVE OFFICES OF THE CLEARING BANKS

Barclays	Pacific representative
	New York representative
	European representative in Zurich
	Representative for Belgium and Luxembourg
	Beirut representative
District	New York representative
Glyn Mills	New York representative office (in conjunction with Royal Bank of Scotland and Williams Deacon's)
Lloyds	New York representative office
Martins	European representative (in Paris)
Midland	Branch in New York
National Provincial	New York representative
Westminster	New York representative

2. WHOLLY-OWNED SUBSIDIARIES OF CLEARING BANKS OPERATING OUTSIDE THE UNITED KINGDOM

Barclays
(a) Barclays Bank (France)—Branches in France (13), Algeria (2) and Monaco (1).
(b) Barclays Bank of California (Barclays has 25 per cent interest and Barclays D.C.O. 75 per cent)—Branches in San Francisco and Los Angeles.

Lloyds
(a) Lloyds Bank Europe—Branches in France (9), Netherlands (2), Switzerland (2) and Monaco.
Subsidiaries: Lloyds Bank (Cannes)—1 branch in Cannes.
Lloyds Bank (Belgium)—2 branches in Belgium.
Bax' Bank N.V.—1 branch in Netherlands.
(b) National Bank of New Zealand—Branches in New Zealand.

Midland
Northern Bank—Branches in Irish Republic.

Westminster
Westminster Bank (Foreign)—Branches in France (5) and Belgium (2).
Ulster Bank Ltd.—113 branches in Eire (112 branches in Northern Ireland).

3. CLEARING BANK STOCKHOLDINGS IN BRITISH OVERSEAS BANKS

		Proportion of Equity
Barclays	Barclays D.C.O.	55%
	Barclays Overseas Development Corporation (owned by Barclays D.C.O.)	100%
Lloyds	Bank of London and South America	22·5%
	National and Grindlays Bank	25%
Midland	Midland and International Banks	45%
	Standard Bank	5%
National Provincial	Standard Bank	5%
	National and Grindlays Bank (see Lloyds Bank entry)	10%
Westminster	Standard Bank	5%

4. CLEARING BANKS' OVERSEAS CONNECTIONS

Barclays   Associated banks (shareholdings not known):
       Banque de Bruxelles S.A.
       Banco del Desarrollo Economico Espanol
       Canadian Imperial Bank of Commerce
With Bank of America; Algemene Bank Nederland; Banca Nazionale del Lavoro; Banque Nationale de Paris; and Dresdner Bank, Barclays formed two companies:
       Société Financière Européene (Luxembourg) and
       Société Financière Européene (Paris)

Midland   Bank of Bermuda (9 per cent of equity)

Interest in European Enterprises Development (other participants include Continental and U.S. banking groups).
Equity participation in Industrial Mining and Development Bank in Teheran.
Associated in European Advisory Committee with
       Amsterdam-Rotterdam Bank; Deutsche Bank; and Société Générale de Banque (formerly Banque de la Société Générale de Belgique).
Associated with 5 French, 1 United States and 1 Italian banks in one of three consortia which is offering to finance Channel Tunnel project.
Banque Européenne de Crédit à Moyen Terme (21·7 per cent of equity).

Westminster   Roy West Banking Corporation (25 per cent of equity).
Banco de Financiacion Industrial (Spain).
       (Other participants—6 European and 1 U.S. banks.)
International Commercial Bank (22·2 per cent of equity).
Financiere Espanola de Inversiones S.A. (Spain).

Martins   Compagnie Internationale de Crédit à Moyen Terme (10 per cent of equity); (14 other banks participate—2 American and 12 European).

(Several of the clearing banks are associated with European banks through consortia set up by hire-purchase subsidiaries.)

APPENDIX A (2): CHAPTER IV

TABLE 21

BRANCHES OF BRITISH OVERSEAS BANKS

Countries	Australia and New Zealand Bank	Barclays D.C.O.	Bolsa	The Chartered Bank	English Scottish and Australian Bank	Hong Kong and Shanghai Banking Corp.	National and Grindlays	Ottoman Bank	The Standard Bank Group	Countries
Abu Dhabi	—	—	—	—	—	—	—	2	—	Abu Dhabi
Aden	—	—	—	5[1]	—	1[8]	10	—	—	Aden
Angola	—	—	—	—	—	—	—	—	4	Angola
Argentine	—	—	22	—	—	—	—	—	—	Argentine
Australia	909	—	—	—	536	—	—	—	—	Australia
Bahrain/Qatar	—	11	—	3[1]	—	3[8]	—	1	—	Bahrain/Qatar
Botswana	—	—	—	—	—	—	—	—	10	Botswana
Brazil	—	—	14	—	—	—	—	—	—	Brazil
Brunei	—	—	—	2	—	3	—	—	—	Brunei
Cambodia	—	—	—	1*	—	—	—	—	—	Cambodia
Cameroons	—	7	—	—	—	—	—	—	2	Cameroons
Caribbean	—	146	—	—	—	—	5*	—	—	Caribbean
Ceylon	—	—	—	2[1]	—	6[5]	—	—	—	Ceylon
Chile	—	—	7	1	—	1	—	—	—	Chile
China	—	—	—	6	—	1	—	—	—	China
Cyprus	—	9	—	—	—	—	—	14	—	Cyprus
Fiji	4	—	1	—	—	—	—	—	1*	Fiji
France	—	—	—	—	—	1	—	2	1*	France
Gambia	—	1	—	—	—	—	—	1	1	Gambia
Germany	—	—	—	1	—	1	—	—	—	Germany
Ghana	—	60	—	—	—	—	—	1	29	Ghana
Gibraltar	—	4	—	—	—	—	—	—	—	Gibraltar
Hadaramaut	—	—	—	2[1]	—	—	—	—	—	Hadaramaut
Hong Kong	—	—	—	17	—	65[6,6]	—	—	—	Hong Kong
India	—	—	—	129[1,2]	—	17[5,7]	53	—	—	India
Iran	—	34	—	10[3]	—	6[9]	—	—	—	Iran
Israel	—	—	—	—	—	—	—	—	1*	Israel
Italy	—	—	—	4	—	5[5]	—	—	1*	Italy
Japan	—	—	—	—	—	2[8]	—	12	1*	Japan
Jordan	—	—	—	—	—	—	—	12	—	Jordan
Kenya	—	86	—	—	—	—	50	3	41	Kenya
Kuwait	—	—	—	1[1]	—	6[8]	—	—	—	Kuwait
Lebanon	—	7	—	—	—	5[8]	—	17[11]	—	Lebanon
Lesotho	—	—	—	—	—	—	—	—	12	Lesotho
Libya	—	16	—	3[4]	—	2[10]	—	—	—	Libya
Malawi	—	17	—	—	—	—	—	—	33	Malawi

	Mauritius	Moçambique	Morocco	Muscat/Oman	New Guinea	New Zealand	Nigeria	Pakistan	Papua	Paraguay	Peru	Philippines	Portugal	Rhodesia	Saudi Arabia	Seychelles	Sierra Leone	Singapore	Solomon Islands	Somalia	South Africa	Spain	Sudan	Swaziland	Switzerland	Thailand	Trucial States	Tunisia	Turkey	Uganda	United Kingdom	United States	Uruguay	Viet-Nam	Zambia	Sterling Area	Non-Sterling Area	Total
Moçambique	—	—	—	—	—	—	—	2	1	—	—	69	—	—	—	85	—	11	—	—	816	—	15	—	—	—	—	—	—	13	8*	1	—	—	35	1,089+4*	98	1,191
Morocco	—	—	—	—	—	—	—	—	—	—	—	—	—	—	—	1	—	—	—	—	—	10	1	—	—	—	50	2	1	—	—	—	—	36	64+17[11]	117	
Muscat/Oman	—	—	—	—	—	—	—	21	—	—	—	12	—	—	—	—	2	—	—	—	—	—	—	—	—	33	2	—	—	8	194	2	196				
New Guinea	—	—	2[8]	3[8]	—	4[5]	—	2	—	3[8]	—	10[5]	—	—	—	—	4[5]	6[8]	1[8]	—	4[5,8]	4	1	—	—	—	167	40	207									
New Zealand	—	—	—	—	—	7[1]	—	3	—	19[1]	—	—	—	—	—	—	5[1]	5[12]	3	—	537	—	537															
Nigeria	5	—	—	80	—	2	—	3	2	3	101	2	13	1	831	23	14	—	29	7	3	12	45	238	32	270												
Pakistan	—	5	—	—	217	—	—	—	—	4	1	12	—	69	73	1,593																						
Sterling Area	1,142	—	1,519	74	4	69	1,142																															
Non-Sterling Area	—	—	—																																			
Total	1,142	1,593	73																																			

* Includes representative office.
1. Includes Eastern Bank (20 branches in all).
2. Includes Eastern Bank and 111 branches of Allahabad Bank.
3. Irano British Bank.
4. Commercial Bank S.A.L.
5. Includes Mercantile Bank (51 branches in all).

6. Includes Mercantile Bank and 11 branches of Hang Seng Bank.
7. Includes Mercantile Bank and one branch of British Bank of Middle East.
8. British Bank of the Middle East.
9. Bank of Iran and Middle East.
10. Bank of North Africa.
11. Societe Nouvelle de la Banque de Syrie et du Liban S.A.L.
12. Includes Chartered Bank of London.

71

APPENDIX A(3): CHAPTER IV
HOLDINGS OF BRITISH OVERSEAS BANKS.

AUSTRALIA AND NEW ZEALAND BANK LIMITED

BANKS *Subsidiaries*

Australia and New Zealand Savings Bank Limited	(100% owned)
A.N.Z. Savings Bank (New Zealand) Limited	(100% owned)

OTHER

Australian Banks Export Refinance Corporation Limited.	(small interest)
A.N.Z. Investments Ltd.	(100% owned)

BARCLAYS BANK D.C.O.
Subsidiaries and Associates

BANKS

Barclays Bank of California (owned with Barclays Bank Ltd., 25%)	(75% owned)	1965
National Bank Development and Investment Corporation	(100% owned)	
Credit Congolais S.R.C.L.	(100% owned sub.)	
Bank of London and Montreal (owned with B.O.L.S.A. 33⅓% and Bank of Montreal 33⅓%)	(33⅓% owned)	1965
Bahamas International Trust	(26% owned)	

OTHER

Barclays Export Finance Co., Limited	(20% owned)	1964
Barclays Overseas Development Corp. Limited	(100% owned sub.)	

BANK OF LONDON AND SOUTH AMERICA
Subsidiaries and Associates

Bank of London and Montreal Ltd.	(33⅓% owned)
Balfour Williamson Inc.	(100% owned)
Balfour Williamson & Co., Ltd. (Holding company)	(100% owned)
Balfour Williamson Investment Co. Ltd. (Investment company)	(47% owned)
Cia. Financiera de Londres S.A. (Finance Company)	(99·87% owned)
S.A. Comercial Anglo Ecuatoriana	(100% owned)

THE CHARTERED BANK
Subsidiaries and Associates

BANKS

The Eastern Bank Limited	(100% owned)	
The Chartered Bank of London	(100% owned)	1965
Arbuthnot Latham & Co.	(11% owned)	1967
Allahabad Bank Limited	(over 90% owned)	
The Irano British Bank	(49% owned)	
The Commercial Bank S.A.L.	(49% owned)	1965
Conrad Hinrich Donner (limited partnership taken January 1, 1966)		
Bank of South Arabia Limited	(25% owned)	
Amsterdamse Crediet Maatschappij N.V.	(14% owned)	

HIRE PURCHASE FINANCE COMPANIES

Credit Corporation (Malaysia) Limited	(41% owned)	
The Mutual Acceptance Co., Limited (Australia)	(40% owned)	1965
The Chartered Finance Co., Limited (Singapore)	(100% owned)	
Financings Ltd.	(24% owned)	
Chartered Finance (Hong Kong) Ltd.	(100% owned)	

OTHER

Hatton Court Pty Ltd. (Australia) (Holding company)	(100% owned)
The C.B.I. Development Corporation Ltd.	(100% owned)

The Chartered Bank (Malaya) Trustee Limited	(100% owned)	
The Chartered Bank Hong Kong Trustee Limited	(51% owned)	

ENGLISH, SCOTTISH AND AUSTRALIAN BANK
Subsidiaries

E. S. & A. Savings Bank Limited		1961
Esanda Limited	{ H.P. leasing	
Esanda (Wholesale) (Pty) Limited	{ Instalment finance	
E. S. & A. Managed Investments Ltd.	Unit Trust managements	
Melbourne Safe Deposit Proprietary Ltd.		
Britannia Investment Co., Pty, Ltd.	Property owner	
E. S. & A. Holdings Ltd. (U.K. Company)	Property owning	
E. S. & A. (Security) Proprietary Ltd.	Trustee	
Esanda Nominees	Nominee	

HONG KONG AND SHANGHAI BANKING CORPORATION
Subsidiaries and Associates

BANKS

Mercantile Bank Limited	(100% owned)	1959
British Bank of the Middle East Ltd.	(100% owned)	1960
The Hong Kong & Shanghai Banking Corp. of California	(100% owned)	
British Bank of the Middle East (Morocco) (S.A.)	(100% owned)	
Hang Seng Bank Limited (H.K.)	(51% owned)	1965
Bank of Iran and the Middle East (Iran)	(49% owned)	
Bank of North Africa (Libya)	(49% owned)	1964
Mees & Hope (Bankierscompagnie N.V.)	(small holding)	1964

HIRE PURCHASE FINANCE COMPANIES

Wayfoong Finance Limited (H.K.)	(100% owned)	1960
Malaysian Australian Finance Co. Ltd.	(100% owned)	
Wayfoong Finance (Malaysia) Ltd.	(100% owned)	1960
Hong Kong Finance Ltd. (Australia)	(100% owned)	1964
Mercantile Credits Ltd. (Australia)	(40% owned)	1964
Bowmaker (C.A.) (Pvt) Ltd. (Rhodesia)		
Bowmaker Finance Ltd. (Zambia)		

OTHER

Exporters Refinance Corp. Ltd. (London)	(Finance for exporters)	1961
Roy West Banking Corporation Ltd.	(Financing Corp.)	1965
Trust Corporation of the Bahamas Ltd.	(100% owned)	1965
Wardley Corporation (California) (Property owning company. Owns the bank's buildings in California)		
Wardley Australia (Pty) Ltd. (Investment company)	(100% owned)	1964

NATIONAL AND GRINDLAYS BANK
Subsidiaries and Associates

BANKS

Wm. Brandt's Sons & Co., Ltd.	(66⅔% owned)	1965
Addis Ababa Bank S.C.	(49% owned)	1964
Bank of South Arabia Limited		1966
National Bank of Dubai		1966

OTHER

National & Grindlays Finance & Development Corporation Ltd.		1948
Exporters Refinance Corporation Ltd.	(25% owned)	1961

HIRE PURCHASE COMPANIES

Credit Finance Corporation, Nairobi	(Minority interest)	
Mercantile Credit Ltd., Colombo	(Minority interest)	

OTTOMAN BANK
Subsidiaries and Associaties

Societe Nouvelle de la Banque de Syrie et du Liban S.A.L.	(50% owned)	1963
Worms et Cie (Maroc)	(minority interest)	1966
Ottoman Bank Finance Co., Limited	(100% owned)	1966

THE STANDARD BANK
Subsidiaries and Associates

BANKS

Standard Bank of South Africa Ltd.	(100% owned)	1962
Standard Bank of West Africa Ltd.	(100% owned)	1965
City Merchant Bank	(30% owned)	1964
Midland & International Banks Ltd.	(19% owned)	1964
Banco Standard—Totta de Moçambique	(35% owned)	1966
Banco Totta—Standard de Angola	(35% owned)	1966

OTHER

Standard Bank Finance and Development Corp. Ltd.	(100% owned)	1947
National Industrial Credit Corp. Ltd. (H.P. Finance)	(40% owned)	1959
Standard Bank Finance and Development Corporation of South Africa	(100% owned)	1964
Diners Club, Africa	(100% owned)	1966
Diners Club South Africa (Pty.)	(51% owned)	

APPENDIX B: CHAPTER IV

MEMBERS OF THE ACCEPTING HOUSES COMMITTEE

Baring Brothers & Co. Limited
Brown, Shipley & Co. Limited
Arbuthnot Latham & Co. Limited
Hill, Samuel & Co. Limited
Wm. Brandt's Sons & Co. Limited
Antony Gibbs & Sons Limited
Samuel Montagu & Co. Limited
Hambros Bank Limited
Morgan Grenfell & Co. Limited
Charterhouse Japhet & Thomasson Limited
Lazard Brothers & Co. Limited
Kleinwort, Benson Limited
Guinness Mahon & Co. Limited
J. Henry Schroder Wagg & Co. Limited
N. M. Rothschild & Sons
S. G. Warburg & Co. Limited
(incorporating Seligman Brothers)

APPENDIX C: CHAPTER IV

LONDON'S FOREIGN EXCHANGE MARKET

London believes it has the world's most important Foreign Exchange Market. It is made by banks, dealing among themselves through brokers and also directly with banks abroad. In order to participate in the market a bank needs authority under the Exchange Control Act to buy and sell foreign currencies and to hold balances in such currencies; about 160 banks so authorized operate in the market.

The market has no written constitution. Both banks and brokers have representative committees where matters of common interest are discussed, and rules for good order are established. Deals between parties in London are done over direct telephone lines; and the spoken word is binding.

The function of the brokers is to bring together buyers and sellers among the London banks. The brokers do not run positions in foreign currencies but act purely as middlemen and make their profit by charging both banks brokerage on a fixed scale. There are nine firms, all of which quote for U.S. dollars; and each specializes in two or three other leading currencies in such a way that each of these is handled by at least two brokers. The brokers do not disclose the identities of their buyers and sellers until a deal is about to be clinched, when it is necessary to ensure that the names of the parties are mutually acceptable. Once the names of the parties have been exchanged through the broker, arrangements for settlement are made directly between the banks.

Transactions by the banks are concluded also for domestic customers such as importers and exporters, and with overseas residents, principally banks.

Foreign exchange transactions take various forms (Bills of Exchange, bank notes, etc.) but dealings in the market concentrate almost entirely on the purchase and sale of bank balances. These may be for spot or forward delivery.

A forward transaction is the purchase or sale of foreign currency for future delivery at a rate fixed irrevocably when the deal is done. This facility enables traders to avoid losses which might otherwise arise through changes in spot rates between the initiation of the commercial transaction and its settlement.

In the U.K. a limit is set under the Exchange Control regulations on the extent to which a bank's position, spot and forward combined, may deviate from balance. The amount of net spot exchange which a bank may hold in cover of its net forward commitments is also restricted. Limits are agreed individually with the banks to apply to all currencies collectively.

APPENDIX D: CHAPTER IV

THE LONDON GOLD MARKET

The Market, consisting of a representative from each of five firms[1], meets at Rothschilds at 10.30 a.m. each weekday except Market holidays and Saturdays. Rothschilds act as chairman of the market. Although all authorized banks under the Exchange Control Act of 1947 are authorized to deal in gold, in practice most of the dealings are done by the five firms mentioned.

The meeting, referred to as the "fixing," establishes the price of fine gold in sterling per ounce troy for deals concluded during the session. A commission of $\frac{1}{4}$ per mille (minimum 10s.) is charged on all deals at the "fixing."

The standard unit dealt in is a bar conforming to the specification given in what is termed "the good delivery list," but members are prepared to deal in smaller quantities. Transactions effected either before or after the "fixing" are a matter of negotiation and may be dealt at net prices (inclusive of commission). The London market was reopened (it had been closed in September, 1939) in 1954 and quickly attracted a large part of the world's dealings in gold. Ten years later the Bank of England claimed in its *Quarterly Bulletin* (March, 1964) that London was the "largest and most important gold market in the world."

APPENDIX E: CHAPTER IV

EURO-DOLLAR MARKET

Euro-dollars are essentially deposits of U.S. dollars with commercial banks outside the U.S.A. The Euro-dollar market is made up of banks situated mainly in London and other European centres (including the overseas branches of U.S. banks) which bid for U.S. dollar deposits and offer loans in U.S. dollars. These banks are able to compete with U.S. banks because, in this business, they work on comparatively small margins. They offer higher rates of interest on deposits than banks in the U.S.A., whose deposit rates are subject to restrictions; they also pay interest on very short-term money which U.S. banks are precluded from doing. The rates they charge for loans are, generally speaking, lower than the effective U.S. lending rates. In effect, they operate a wholesale market in dollars, dealing only in large amounts.

Similar markets exist in certain European currencies in centres other than those of the currency concerned, notably in sterling, Deutschemarks and Swiss francs. For example, there is a market in sterling deposits among Continental banks, particularly in Paris, which is known as the Euro-sterling

---

1. Johnson, Matthey (Bankers) Limited; Mocatta & Goldsmid Ltd.; Samuel Montagu & Co. Ltd.; N. M. Rothschild & Sons and Sharps, Pixley & Company.

market. International rates for these other Euro-currencies normally reflect the rate for Euro-dollars and the dollar forward exchange margin against these currencies. But business in these currencies is small compared with that in U.S. dollars. Sometimes the term "Euro-dollar market" is used loosely to comprise also these other Euro-currency markets.

While much of the dealing is between banks, the real significance of the Euro-dollar market lies in the fact that it originally draws its funds from non-bank suppliers and ultimately lends them to non-bank users. These will mostly be commercial customers of the banks and they will pay rates outside those quoted in inter-bank transactions. What the rates are will depend on the amount of the deal and the credit-standing of the customer. Some of the funds supplied to the market will come from central banks, who may also, although to a lesser extent, be borrowers.

The market came into existence (in the late 1950s) for a number of reasons. Foreign banks were able to do dollar business on narrower margins than U.S. banks and had the advantage of being able to offer interest on very short-term money. They were able to lend at rates which compared favourably with those in other money markets. Stable exchange rates, the return of convertibility and the relaxation of official controls on capital movements and on the banks' foreign exchange operations no doubt also helped. From quite early on the East European countries have preferred to hold dollars through West European banks and these funds were being supplemented as dollar surpluses began to be earned, particularly by countries in Western Europe. Another important factor in the early stages was the restriction put on sterling acceptance credits in 1957.

Since then the continuing U.S. deficits have greatly added to the rest of the world's dollar holdings, which have increasingly found their way into the Euro-dollar market. But the market as now established is not necessarily dependent for its existence on the U.S.A. remaining in deficit. It has become an integrated international money market providing its own specialized service and has already shown considerable powers of survival.

It is difficult to make an accurate assessment of the total size of the Euro-dollar market. Figures collected by the Bank for International Settlements show that at the end of 1966 the main eight European centres (United Kingdom, Switzerland, France, Belgium, Netherlands, Italy, West Germany and Sweden) had foreign currency liabilities to non-residents of $18,000 million and foreign currency claims on non-residents of $20,000 million. Of these amounts $14,500 million and $16,000 million respectively were in U.S. dollars—some 80 per cent of the total. These figures are an indication of the gross size of the European market. United Kingdom banks account for almost half of the total with liabilities and claims of over $8,000 million (see TABLE 20 of March issue of the Bank of England *Quarterly Bulletin*). Re-depositing of dollars between banks is a characteristic of the market and the figures are much inflated as a result. The latest available estimates by the Bank for International Settlements put the net amount of Euro-dollars passing through the European market at $13,000 million in December, 1966.

APPENDIX F: CHAPTER IV

THE BANKING INQUIRY

1. THE QUESTIONNAIRE

The questionnaire sent out to the banks on behalf of the Committee took the following form:

"Information is desired from all members of the banking sector in respect of business with non-residents of the U.K. (i.e. with residents of the rest of the Sterling Area and of the non-Sterling Area).

Amounts should be stated in sterling to the nearest £000 (or whatever lowest unit you think necessary). Earnings + /Expenditure —. Where conversion from an overseas currency is involved, please use the same rate of exchange as in your bank's own accounts. Total earnings below £1,000 can be ignored and the questionnaire returned.

1. LENDING AND BORROWING IN STERLING
   (a) Interest earned from
       (i) Overdrafts and short-term loans;
       (ii) Medium-term loans;
           N.B.—Earnings on credit to U.K. exporters not to be included.
       (iii) Discounts;
   (b) Interest paid or credited on sterling deposits and current accounts, i.e. sterling lodgments.

2. LENDING AND BORROWING IN FOREIGN CURRENCY
   (a) Interest earned from
       (i) Loans and overdrafts to non-residents;
       (ii) Other investment income from overseas but see paragraph (7).
   (b) Interest paid on currency deposits and current accounts;

3. CREDIT AND BILL TRANSACTIONS
   (a) Commissions earned for advising, opening and confirming documentary credits, and for payments and acceptances arising thereunder;
   (b) Earnings on collection of bills, clear credits, endorsements and reimbursement credits, etc.

4. FOREIGN EXCHANGE DEALING
   Net earnings on deals with non-residents of the U.K.
   N.B.—It is realized that this item will be difficult to arrive at accurately. Estimates will be acceptable. One suggested method, for example, is that a proportion of the overall earnings on exchange dealing be calculated in a ratio similar to that which the total of dealing with non-residents bears to the total of overall dealing.

5. NEW ISSUES OF OVERSEAS SECURITIES
Net earnings from non-residents of U.K.

6. MISCELLANEOUS RECEIPTS
To include earnings in respect of such items as commitment fees, guarantees, portfolio management, current account operations, security transactions, executor and trustee services, etc.

7. The following *additional* information is desired from those members of the banking sector to whom the following is applicable:
Banks having branches or subsidiaries or associates or Head Offices outside the U.K.[1]:
(*a*) *From United Kingdom incorporated banks which are not subsidiaries or associates of overseas-incorporated companies and which have overseas branches or overseas incorporated companies which are either their subsidiaries owned wholly or in part, or their associates.*
Loan interest and remittances of profits received plus retentions for reinvestment overseas:
(*b*) *From branches in the U.K. (i.e. London Offices) of overseas incorporated banks or banks incorporated in the U.K. which are either subsidiaries, owned wholly or in part, or associates of, overseas-incorporated companies.*
Loan interest paid and remittance of profits abroad plus retentions.
N.B.—The information given in Sections 7 (*a*) or 7 (*b*) should correspond with the information provided in the following sections of Form ODR/A or Form ODR/B respectively in the Overseas Direct Investment Inquiry for the year 1965:
Part II, Section 4 (current transactions).
Part III, Section 7 (current transactions)."

2. THE RESULTS

Summary of replies received from banks

	£000's		
	Credits	Debits	Net
1. LENDING AND BORROWING IN STERLING			
(*a*) Interest earned from:			
(i) overdrafts and short-term loans	12,390		
(ii) medium-term loans	6,831		
(iii) discounts	13,097		

1. For the purpose of this questionnaire:
   (*a*) A "branch" means a "permanent establishment" as defined for the purpose of United Kingdom tax (see Statutory Instruments relating to Income Tax, Double Taxation Relief), other agencies in the United Kingdom of overseas companies being ignored.
   (*b*) The definition applied to a "subsidiary" is that given in Section 154 of the Companies Act, 1948.
   (*c*) An "associate" means a company which, though not a subsidiary as defined in the Companies Act, 1948, is linked to another company by the second company's holding of a "trade investment" in the first company. Holdings of "marketable securities" as portfolio investment should not be regarded as constituting a link for the purposes of this inquiry.
   (*d*) "United Kingdom" is used to include Great Britain, Northern Ireland, the Isle of Man and the Channel Islands.

	Credits	Debits	Net
(b) Interest paid on sterling deposits and current accounts		47,957	
			—15,639

2. LENDING AND BORROWING IN FOREIGN CURRENCY

	Credits	Debits	Net
(a) (i) Interest earned from loans and overdrafts	71,270		
(ii) Other investment income	2,179		
(b) Interest paid on currency deposits and current accounts		77,861	
			—4,412

3. CREDIT AND BILL TRANSACTIONS

	Credits	Debits	Net
(a) Commissions earned	4,070		
(b) Earnings from collection of bills, etc.	2,649		
			+ 6,719
4. Net earnings from foreign exchange dealing			+ 5,366
5. Net earnings from new issues of overseas securities			+ 647
6. Miscellaneous receipts			+ 4,872

7. EARNINGS FROM DIRECT INVESTMENT

	Credits	Debits	Net
(a) Outward investment	34,138		
(b) Inward investment		7,951	
			+ 26,187
TOTAL			+ 23,740

Analysis of The Response from Banks

Response to inquiry according to balances in sterling held on current and deposit accounts with U.K. banks at end-1965

GROUP OF BANKS	%
American banks	99
British Overseas and Commonwealth Banks Association	89
Foreign Banks and Affiliates Association	79
Other overseas banks	86
Discount Market Association	—
Other banks (including Clearing Banks, Scottish, Irish and Japanese banks)	100
Other Financial Institutions	85
OVERALL COVERAGE	89

APPENDIX G: CHAPTER IV

SHORT-TERM LENDING TO INDUSTRIAL CUSTOMERS

Methods and Costs, March, 1967

The following comparisons of lending costs and methods are based on a survey undertaken by Glyn, Mills & Co., the London clearing bank, and published in the May, 1967, issue of *The Banker*. The Committee has condensed some of the descriptive material to fit its purpose and has added details of the United States.

The rates quoted in the report are, unless otherwise stated, *average* figures. Clearly, first-class industrial borrowers will be able to negotiate finer rates. The table is designed to show European and American short-term borrowing costs in comparative form. The table should be read in conjunction with the notes which follow, describing the different borrowing methods. For example, it would be misleading to compare overdraft rates in France with those obtaining in this country since it is something of a euphemism to call the French arrangement "an overdraft" in our understanding of the term, as the notes show. In the attempt to compress so wide a subject into a few pages it is only possible to include the minimum of detail. The survey is not intended to be exhaustive. Its purpose is to give a broad picture of general practices and rates.

LENDING RATES COMPARED

MARCH, 1967

Country	Bank Rate %	Overdrafts	Loans	Commercial Paper	Finance Paper, etc.
U.K.	6	$6\frac{1}{2}$ to 8%	$6\frac{1}{2}$ to 8	Bank Paper 5 11/16% up to 120 days. Trade Paper 7 to $7\frac{1}{2}$% for 90 days, 7 to $7\frac{3}{4}$% for 120 days, $7\frac{1}{4}$ to 8% for 180 days.	
U.S.	4		$5\frac{1}{2}$–$6\frac{1}{2}$	$5\frac{1}{4}$%	$4\frac{3}{4}$ to 5%
Austria	$4\frac{1}{2}$	6 to $7\frac{1}{2}$%	6 to $7\frac{1}{2}$	$5\frac{1}{2}$ to 7%	
Belgium	$4\frac{3}{4}$	$7\frac{1}{2}$% minimum plus a commission of $\frac{1}{4}$ of 1% per quarter on limit of the facility.		$4\frac{3}{4}$% plus a $\frac{1}{4}$ to 1% for 120 day bills.	6 to 7%

Country	Bank Rate %	Overdrafts	Loans	Commercial Paper	Finance Paper, etc.
Denmark	$6\frac{1}{2}$	$8\frac{1}{2}$% plus a commission of $\frac{1}{4}$ of 1% per quarter on the limit of the facility plus establishment commission of $\frac{1}{2}$ to $1\frac{1}{2}$% flat.		$8\frac{1}{2}$% plus a $\frac{1}{4}$ of 1% commission for 90-day bills.	
Finland	6	8%	$7\frac{1}{2}$ to 8	7% for 90-day bills, $7\frac{1}{2}$% for 180-day bills.	$8\frac{1}{2}$%
France	$3\frac{1}{2}$	5·65% plus a commission of 1/20% per month on the highest debit balance in the month. 4·40% Credit Mobilisable (see note).		4% for 90-day bills.	4·40% for 90-day paper.
Italy	$3\frac{1}{2}$	7% plus a charge of $\frac{1}{8}$ of 1% per quarter on the highest figure in the quarter.		6 to 7% for 120-day bills.	
Luxembourg	$4\frac{3}{4}$	6% plus a commission of $\frac{1}{8}$ of 1% per quarter on the limit of the facility.		5% for 120-day bills, $5\frac{3}{4}$% for 121 to 360-day bills.	
The Netherlands	$4\frac{1}{2}$	$6\frac{1}{2}$ to 7%. Usually a commission of $\frac{1}{2}$ to 1% is added based on the limit of the facility but see note.			
Norway	$3\frac{1}{2}$	5% plus a commission of $\frac{1}{4}$ of 1% per quarter based on the limit of the facility but see note.		$5\frac{1}{2}$% for 90-day bills, $6\frac{1}{2}$% for 91 days and over.	
Portugal	$2\frac{1}{2}$	$5\frac{1}{2}$ to 7%	$5\frac{1}{2}$ to 7	$4\frac{1}{2}$% for bills up to 180 days.	

Country	Bank Rate %	Overdrafts	Loans	Commercial Paper	Finance Paper, etc.
Sweden	5	$6\frac{1}{2}$% plus a commission of 1% p.a. based on the limit of the facility.	6 to $8\frac{1}{4}$%	$6\frac{1}{4}$ to $8\frac{1}{4}$% for 90-day bills.	$7\frac{3}{4}$ to $8\frac{1}{4}$% for 90-day bills.
Switzerland	$3\frac{1}{2}$	$6\frac{1}{4}$ to $7\frac{1}{2}$% unsecured. $5\frac{3}{4}$ to $6\frac{1}{2}$% secured. See note *re* commission.	$5\frac{3}{4}$ unsecured $5\frac{1}{2}$ secured	$4\frac{1}{4}$ to $5\frac{1}{4}$% for 90-day bills.	
West Germany	4	$8\frac{1}{2}$%. See notes *re* commission.		6 to 7%	$8\frac{1}{2}$%

Where no figures are shown in a particular column it should not be assumed that the particular method is **never** used. It is rather an indication that it is rarely practised by the commercial banks or is not applicable to short term lending.

2. METHODS COMPARED

The methods are varied and highly complex.

FRANCE (Bank rate $3\frac{1}{2}$ per cent)

(*a*) OVERDRAFTS.—Simple forms: (*a*) Facilité de Caisse (cash facility).

(*b*) Découvert (uncovered advance).

These are granted only to highly credit-worthy customers for short periods, say up to three months. Here there is no underlying paper. The purpose of the Facilité de Caisse is to assist at a time of temporary lack of cash and the arrangement is very short in duration, often a matter of days or weeks. The Découvert arrangement can be for a period of up to three months and is usually permitted only in anticipation of the receipt of funds from a particular transaction. There is a further form of overdraft facility used principally for financing stocks of manufacturers in seasonal businesses. This facility is again of short duration. Though in some cases it may be extended over a year, the overdraft is "funded" at, say, one- to three-month intervals, by a bill rediscountable at the Banque de France under the system known as "Credit Mobilisable." The transaction must have the prior approval of the Banque de France.

Cost to the Borrower.—The cost of overdraft facilities to first class borrowers is 5·65 per cent p.a. To this figure must be added a commission of 1/20 per cent per month on the highest figure in the month. In the case of overdraft arrangements where bills are drawn which are rediscountable at the Banque de France under the "Credit Mobilisable" system the cost to the borrower is 4·40 per cent.

(*b*) DISCOUNTING OF BILLS AND PROMISSORY NOTES.—Each bank has a set rediscount ceiling (Plafond) at the Banque de France and this may be adjusted up or down for each individual bank by negotiation. This ceiling is not, however, absolute and it is possible for the commercial banks to rediscount further paper up to 10 per cent above the ceiling figure but at a penal rate of 1 per cent above Bank rate. Further assistance beyond the 10 per cent concession is available but at an even higher rate, i.e. 2½ per cent above Bank rate. (The first margin is known as "Enfer" (Hell) and the second "Super-Enfer."). The arrangements are further complicated as the banks themselves seem to have set internal limits based on the commodity and industry involved in the transaction.

Bills.—Bills rediscountable at the Banque de France must have the acceptance of a bona fide purchaser of goods, have a maximum tenor of 90 days and bear three signatures, i.e. drawer, drawee and the bank presenting for rediscount.

Cost to the Borrower.—The cost is stated to be 4 per cent p.a. (prime rate 3·60 per cent plus an endorsement commission of 0·40 per cent).

(c) PROMISSORY NOTES.—A further method of short-term lending involves the drawing by a customer of promissory notes in favour of his bank which discounts them. They must be for 90 days or less and bear three signatures, as in the case of bills. This paper may then be rediscounted at the Banque de France but only if prior approval of the transaction has been obtained.

Cost to the Borrower.—The cost is said to be a minimum of 4·40 per cent p.a. made up as follows:

	per cent
Discount at Prime Rate ..	3·60
Engagement commission ..	0·40
Endorsement commission ..	0·40
	4·40

It must be emphasized that the figures quoted in this report *are the absolute minimum costs to first class commercial customers the loss of whose business would be serious to the bank.* It is difficult to elicit closer estimates of the true rates charged. One guess was that the average rates might be about 6 per cent p.a. for short-term money, taking into account all commission charges.

It will be readily seen that much time and energy is spent in processing this paper. Much of it is for small sums. Recently there has been official encouragement for the wider use of overdraft arrangements in preference to short-term bill financing.

N.B.—Bank charges and interest are subject to a service tax of 9·29 per cent paid by the borrower, but this may be offset against the borrower's own tax liability. The tax is due to be repealed with effect from January 1, 1968. But some similar form of tax will almost certainly replace it.

ITALY (Bank rate 3½ per cent)

It has long been the practice for the larger industrial concerns in Italy to have several bankers, since the Banking Law of 1926 laid down that any one customer may not borrow from any one bank more than 20 per cent of that bank's capital and general reserves. This, perhaps, explains the apparent flexibility in the attitude of Italian bankers to lending propositions. There is, however, an inter-bank agreement regulating both charges and minimum lending and deposit rates.

The commercial banks do not arrange advances beyond 12 months and thus each is renegotiated at the end of this time subject to the approval of the Bank of Italy's Banking Supervisory Office.

(a) OVERDRAFTS.—This is the most common form and closely follows British practice.

Cost to the borrower.—The basic rate is 3½ per cent over Bank rate. Since Bank rate, at 3½ per cent, has not moved since 1959 it is this percentage over Bank rate which is changed as circumstances require. In addition to interest at 7 per cent, there is a commission charge of ⅛ of 1 per cent per quarter on the highest figure. The difference between secured and unsecured lending rates is marginal in the context of lending to first-class names.

(b) DISCOUNTING OF BILLS, PROMISSORY NOTES, ETC.—The great majority of smaller commercial transactions are financed by paper of this kind and discounting by the banks is widely practised.

The paper is usually drawn for no longer than 120 days, and, technically, may be rediscounted at the Bank of Italy. It is, however, unusual for these rediscount facilities to be used, particularly in times of ample liquidity. When longer-term bills are drawn they become eligible for rediscounting within 120 days of maturity. Finance against promissory notes, given by buyer to seller, is also common practice.

Discounting is never undertaken without recourse.

Cost to the Borrower.—The costs seem to vary between 2 and 3½ per cent above Bank rate, depending on the names involved and the underlying transaction but in the main it appeared that 4 month paper would be discounted at about 6 to 7 per cent.

SWITZERLAND (Bank rate 3½ per cent)

The figures quoted below apply only to the Canton of Zurich. Rates elsewhere in the country may vary by ¼ to ¾ per cent plus or minus, but since Zurich is the financial centre the variations may be ignored for practical purposes. It should also be noted that each Canton has a Cantonal Bank which normally quotes rates about ½ per cent below the larger commercial banks.

(a) OVERDRAFTS.—Short-term advances are generally in the form of overdrafts and are usually granted for one year or less. Longer periods are entertained but subject to the advance being self-liquidating. Unsecured advances are made to good names. Mortgages and debentures tend to be regarded by the commercial banks as a security of last resort. There are, in fact, Mortgage Banks specializing in advances against such security.

Cost to the Borrower.—Unsecured. 6¼ to 7½ per cent p.a. including ¼ per cent per quarter commission calculated on the highest figure or on the average use of the facility in the case of important names. Secured. Slightly cheaper being 5¾ to 6½ per cent p.a. including ⅛ per cent per quarter commission assessed as above.

(b) FIXED LOANS.—This type of advance is more common in medium-term arrangements but is sometimes applied to short-term propositions usually for a minimum of 6 months. It is essentially a loan for an agreed period on which interest is charged on the principal for the entire period. No minimum balance is required to be kept on current account and no commissions are added. Should the loan not be repaid within the agreed time it may be renewed or switched to an overdraft facility which is dearer.

Cost to the Borrower.—Six month loan. Unsecured: Minimum 5¾ per cent flat. Secured: Minimum 5½ per cent flat.

(c) DISCOUNTING BILLS.—This is also a common form of short-term borrowing. The paper is usually for 90 days or less and must be genuine trade paper. Finance paper and acceptances have no market.

Cost to the Borrower.—For a 90-day bill, with recourse, 4¼ to 5¼ per cent p.a. is the present rate. Stamp duty of ½ per mille per half year is payable.

Whilst there is technically a rediscount facility with the central bank it is not generally used.

WEST GERMANY (Bank rate 4 per cent)

The commercial banks have faced considerable demands for credit in the post-war reconstruction period and in the time of the remarkable economic expansion which followed. There has, therefore, been a tendency for the commercial banks to limit their lending to the shorter term, leaving certain specialized institutions to undertake longer-term arrangements. Short-term lending is by definition up to six months and medium-term, still undertaken by the commercial banks when necessary, up to five years.

(a) OVERDRAFTS.—This is the most common form of lending and corresponds fairly closely to the British system although, in practice, there seem to be rather fewer "on position" (unsecured) advances than we are used to. Security is often taken by assignment of accounts receivable.

Cost to the Borrower.—The normal rate is 1½ per cent over Bank rate. In addition a commission of 3 per cent p.a. is added based upon the limit of the facility but, in the case of large first-class commercial borrowers, this commission may be assessed upon the highest overdraft figure rather than on the limit of the facility. When an account passes into debit it is often the custom to charge a turnover commission of ⅛ of 1 per cent on the credits to the account. The total cost to the borrower is thus 8½ per cent p.a. plus. Although there may be a shading of the rate for first-class borrowers it can only be marginal particularly when credit is short, and lending rates are closely tied to the market rates which are not always reflected in the current Bank rate figure.

In the case of smaller companies who overdraw without authority the rate charged is 10 per cent p.a. including a commission of $1\frac{1}{2}$ per cent p.a.

(b) DISCOUNTING OF BILLS OF EXCHANGE.—The discounting of trade bills and finance paper is common. Each commercial bank has a rediscounting limit with the Deutsche Bundesbank. This facility is generally available only for commercial paper and while, in certain circumstances, finance paper may be rediscounted, this is unusual. More often finance bills are held in portfolio. To be eligible for rediscounting at the Deutsche Bundesbank the bills must have a maximum maturity of 90 days and bear three good names, i.e. drawer, drawee and the bank presenting for rediscount. Although the rediscount limit at the Central Bank is fairly rigid first-class paper has a further outlet in the primary acceptance market established in Frankfurt. This market is controlled by the Privatdiskont A.G. and their rates for rediscount are frequently lower than those quoted by the Deutsche Bundesbank.

Cost to the Borrower.—The minimum cost to first-class names is between 6 and 7 per cent p.a. for trade bills but the average rate is about $6\frac{1}{2}$ per cent p.a. Finance paper not eligible for rediscounting at the Bundesbank costs about $8\frac{1}{4}$ per cent p.a. There is a stamp duty on all bills of $1\frac{1}{4}$ per mille—0·6 per cent p.a.

(c) DISCOUNTING OF ACCEPTANCES.—This method of financing is not widely used and is most usually concerned with import/export transactions. The amount of each transaction must be in excess of DM50,000. The paper may be rediscounted at the Deutsche Bundesbank within the limits set down for each bank.

Cost to the Borrower.—For a first-class commercial customer the total charge is approximately 7 per cent p.a. to which must be added a stamp duty of 0·6 of 1 per cent p.a. When money is in short supply the discounting of acceptances is made more costly forcing the borrower to ask for overdraft facilities.

UNITED STATES (Discount rate 4 per cent)

(a) OVERDRAFT AND LOANS.—There are in general no overdraft facilities granted by American banks. The normal procedure is for loans to be granted, and interest is charged on the full amount drawn. This method may well raise the cost to the borrower compared with the overdraft method in which interest is charged on a fluctuating daily balance. Moreover, the system of compensating balances amounting to 10 to 20 per cent of the facility required also adds to the cost.

Cost to the Borrower.—The prime rate in the United States, i.e. the most favourable rate granted to borrowers, is $5\frac{1}{2}$ per cent. During the first part of 1967 the prime rate was falling, but during this time there was a tendency for bank customers to be reclassified according to their borrowing status, i.e. there was a "re-assessment of criteria." In practice this has meant that the mass of borrowers were paying more for bank accommodation than movements in the prime rate would suggest. At the present time the average borrower from U.S. banks is probably paying around 6½ per cent. First-class borrowers are paying 5½-6 per cent. As already mentioned, however, the U.S. method of granting loans rather than overdrafts and the practice of requiring compensating balances leads to a higher charge to the customer at any given level of interest rates.

(*b*) Discounting of Bills.—This method is also employed to some extent. The rates charged on prime commercial paper, finance company paper and bankers' acceptances are 5¼ per cent, 4¾ per cent and 5 per cent.

United Kingdom (Bank rate 6 per cent)

The U.K. clearing banks operate a broad range of short-term borrowing facilities, based on the predominance of the overdraft system.

(*a*) Overdrafts.—Though some advances are still made by way of loan (where the full amount granted is drawn and charged for from the outset, though on the same terms as overdrafts), this system has increasingly been replaced since World War II by the more flexible overdraft system. Despite this, the British clearing banks do not usually charge commitment fees or commissions on the amount lent to commercial short-term borrowers (though there may be a charge to cover the cost of operating the account whether in debit or credit).

Cost to the Borrower.—The interest charge varies with Bank rate, at a predetermined margin above it. For advances to "blue-chip" borrowers (the very biggest and best of the banks' industrial customers) this is fixed, by convention, at ½ per cent above Bank rate; for the vast majority of other industrial and commercial customers it is 1 or 1½ per cent above. Thus potential borrowers know to within a fraction what their interest charge will be (for any given level of Bank rate), they know that that will be the only charge they have to face, and any negotiation takes place about the basic rate. Furthermore, the overdraft system as practised in Britain operates on the customer's normal current account. Thus the U.K. customer is charged only on the net daily overdrawn balance standing in his current account or accounts.

(*b*) Discounting of Bills.—By comparison with overdrafts, the discounting of bills has been a marginal source of finance for domestic purposes ever since the emergence of Britain's large clearing banks with their nationwide spread of branches early this century. (Domestic bill financing amounts to about 8 per cent, one-thirteenth of the total of bank advances in this country.) It has, however, played a significant part in a few trades, and for certain purposes (notably the finance of stocks) and at certain periods (notably during periods when bank advances were curtailed by direct fiat of the authorities, without a corresponding limitation on bill finance).

CHAPTER V

THE EXPORT HOUSES

89. Export houses provide one of the most direct links between the visible and invisible trades. They are directly concerned with Britain's visible exports; they also earn invisible income for their efforts. They can be segregated in several different ways: those who trade as principals from those as agents; those who serve the buyer from those serving the seller; those who trade in U.K. goods from those who trade in foreign goods; those who promote the sale from those who service a sale already made; and those who finance and/or take the credit risk from those who do not.

90. Export houses include all permutations of these simple divisions and in many cases a house acts in more than one way, such as trading in both U.K. and foreign goods. But the most generally accepted definitions are:

1. The Merchant—he serves neither manufacturer nor buyer; he acts as a principal, buying in the best market and reselling in the best market, accepting the risk of loss as well as the hope of profit.
2. The Manufacturer's Agent—holding sole rights from a manufacturer for the promotion of the sale of some of his goods in one or more markets, usually on an agency basis.
3. The Export Manager; a firm acting as the complete export department of one or more manufacturers, usually on an agency basis.
4. The Factor—a service operation on behalf of the manufacturer, commencing after delivery has been made by the manufacturer; financing, probably taking the credit risk, and possibly doing the invoicing, book-keeping and debt collecting.
5. The Buying Agent—serving the overseas buyer, receiving open orders with wide discretion where to buy and at what price, usually as an agent but sometimes buying as a principal on a back-to-back contract basis.
6. The Indent Agent—a variation from the buying agent, usually only placing indents as an agent with specified manufacturers, but sometimes as a principal on a back·to back contract basis.
7. The Confirming House—probably the biggest category of all; serving the overseas buyer by confirming orders already placed; primarily a financing and credit giving service.
8. The Export Finance House—whose main role is providing medium term finance for large individual capital goods contracts; they mainly serve the buyer and receive from him payment of their charges and interest separately from the payment of the goods.

91. In attempting to assess the foreign earnings of the export houses, it was

necessary to consider the source of the earnings. There are basically four: profit i.e. the difference between purchase and sale prices when trading as a principal; commission i.e. a charge added for a service rendered, either as an agent or in some other capacity, such as guarantor; interest; and the recovery of expenses incurred in the United Kingdom. They can be taken separately:

1. *Profit.* By its nature (that is, the difference between purchase and sale prices) this is usually included in the invoiced price of goods. If they are U.K. goods, it will therefore be included in the "visible" trade returns; if they are foreign goods, it can only be worked out from the merchant's annual accounts, being the total profit from all overseas transactions.

   As far as U.K. goods are concerned, it is impossible to say whether they realize a higher price when sold by a Merchant, and therefore whether they bring additional foreign exchange earnings over and above what the manufacturer would have earned by a direct export sale. Except for the credit insurance premium and the interest element (covered respectively under commissions and interest below), they probably do not.

2. *Commissions.* It is probably true to say that those export houses serving the manufacturer, i.e. the Manufacturer's Agent, the Export Manager, and the Factor, do not earn their commission in foreign exchange, i.e. over and above the price of the goods, as recorded in the visible trade returns, since they are probably paid for their services by the manufacturer out of his own margin; but unlike many manufacturers, they do obtain payment from the overseas buyer for the credit risk, and for interest, over and above the price of the goods.

   It is the export houses serving the buyer who are the major earners of invisibles, in that their services are paid for by the buyer over and above the price for the goods. Their commission covers two distinct services, the work done in handling the goods or the documents, and the risk taken in giving the credit. It can vary from 10 per cent down to 1 per cent on invoice value, but over the great bulk handled probably averages $2\frac{1}{2}$ per cent.

3. *Interest.* It is on this score that the additional invisible earnings created by export houses are, not fully recognized. Whenever an export house gives credit it recovers as an interest charge the interest which it is itself paying. This is unlike many manufacturers who include in their selling price a period of credit; or who if they do charge interest charge it at a rate probably lower than that charged by the export house.

   Export houses refinance most of their sales in London, i.e. the interest they pay is a U.K. domestic payment in sterling, whereas the interest they receive is a foreign exchange earning. In some traditional markets of the sterling area, such as Australia and South Africa, many bills are "negotiated," i.e. the negotiating bank transfers the debt immediately to its opposite number in the buyer's country, and thus the debt is carried in the buyer's currency; in such cases there is of course no foreign exchange earning on account of interest.

4. *Recovery of Expenses.* Export houses, particularly those serving the buyer, in many cases supplement their very narrow margins of commission by recovering from their clients some of the expenses actually incurred in U.K. on their behalf, such as cable and postage expenses, bills of lading and shipping charges (in addition to freight), bank charges for opening letters of credit, etc.; sometimes E.C.G.D. premia are recovered over and above commission. It is difficult to arrive at any precise figures for these items, but in the calculations made by the British Export Houses Association (outlined below) an allowance for the recovery of expenses is made within the average commission of $2\frac{1}{2}$ per cent used.

92.   In order to arrive at *net* earnings of foreign exchange, these four sources of gross foreign income have to be reduced by subtracting expenses incurred abroad (including commissions paid abroad); losses from bad debts; and interest paid abroad.

93.   In attempting to assess the foreign earnings of the export houses on this basis, the Committee was helped by the British Export Houses Association, which had already initiated an independent inquiry into the foreign earnings of its members. Though the terms and definitions used in this inquiry were not completely in line with the requirements of the Committee, it was decided to use the results as a basis for its work.

94.   The B.E.H.A. inquiry was conducted by the Export Research Group in conjunction with B.E.H.A., under the direction of Professor G. M. Sharman. The results are set out in an interim report in Appendix A. As the report shows, a turnover of £700 million is estimated for members of the British Export Houses Association, of which about 75 per cent concerns exports from the United Kingdom, i.e. about £525 million a year.

95.   On this basis the B.E.H.A. submitted the following estimates to the Committee:

"To arrive at a total invisible earnings figure for the Export houses needs a great deal more research, but the following calculation based on Professor Sharman's researches, could be a starting point.

Total Turnover	Turnover	Earnings
of BEHA members	£700 million p.a.	
add for non-members 50%	£350 million p.a.	
Total Export House Turnover	£1,050 million p.a.	
of which U.K. goods, say 75%	£787$\frac{1}{2}$ million p.a.	
foreign goods, say 25%	£262$\frac{1}{2}$ million p.a.	
Commission		
on total turnover at average $2\frac{1}{2}$%		
Total Commission Earnings		£26$\frac{1}{4}$ million p.a.
		£26$\frac{1}{4}$ million p.a.

£26¼ million p.a.

INTEREST

> For cash—say one-third of turn-
> over; for credit—say two-
> thirds of turnover, i.e. at aver-
> age 120 days at 7½% p.a. £700 million p.a.

Total Interest Earnings £17½ million p.a.

Total Export House Earnings £43¾ million p.a.

This turnover of U.K. goods represents approximately 15 per cent of Britain's annual exports. According to the Census of Distribution for 1950, it has been estimated that the Export house share was approximately 35 per cent; undoubtedly the pattern of U.K. exports, i.e. the trend for consumer goods to capital goods, has the effect of reducing the Export house share, but opinions are strongly held that the reduction is not so great as indicated by the above researches and estimate. They should therefore be regarded as very provisional and interim, and the figure of £43½ million p.a. as a minimum figure."

96. The Committee has two comments to make on these estimates:
1. The B.E.H.A. sample, which forms the basis of the calculations, may be biased towards the larger firms. A comparison with the Board of Trade enquiry of 1959 suggests that this may be so (see the *Board of Trade Journal* for April 7, 1961). On the other hand, the estimated turnover based on the B.E.H.A. figures shows export houses handling only about 15 per cent of British exports (compared with 35 per cent in the Board of Trade enquiry of 1951). It seems unlikely that the proportion has fallen as sharply as this.
2. It must be stressed that, while the average amount of commission, the average period of credit, and the average rate of interest assumed have been based on actual information and experience available to B.E.H.A., such information has not been comprehensive and there has had to be an element of estimating. The Committee, therefore, is prepared to accept the estimates, with these reservations in mind. This leads to two further questions:
   (i) How far are the amounts concerned included in the present official statistics?
   (ii) How far can they fairly be credited to the export houses in any estimate of the earnings of "the City" in its broadest sense?
   (a) The £26¼ million commission is implicitly assumed to be three-quarters on exports of British goods and one quarter on third country trade. The commission on U.K. exports *should* already be included in the f.o.b. values of visible exports for customs purposes. The B.E.H.A. believes this to be generally so for houses serving the manufacturer, but believes that houses serving the buyer (mainly confirming houses) perform services "paid for by the buyer over and above the price for the goods." Although this may be so, the sums concerned may not be large.
   Commission on third country trade is covered by the esti-

mate of merchanting earnings referred to in Chapter VI though this is not entirely satisfactory; one reason being that the classification of export houses does not include those merchants who trade solely in commodities or who are members of the various commodity exchanges and markets, export houses trading basically in manufactured goods. Interest on credit extended for less than 180 days is at present assumed to be included in the price returned to Customs & Excise, and no separate estimate is made. Credit of over 180 days is estimated and included in the "interest, profit and dividend" category of the balance of payments.

In so far as export houses' earnings on U.K. goods fail to get included in the official figures, therefore, it is likely to be because the declared value of exports may not include all receipts by British residents in respect of services and short-term credits. Such omissions can affect other sectors too, and there is a clear need for further study.[1]

(b) The commission earnings in respect of both U.K. and third country exports can fairly be credited to the export houses in a calculation of the earnings of the City. Interest earned by export houses is, however, in a different category. The Association states that, "Export houses refinance most of their sales in London." Most, if not all of this will be done with banks and a great deal of it will have been included by the banks in their return to the Committee. It would be quite impossible to estimate from our information the amount of overlap between the interest item shown by the banks and the export houses. In any estimate of the earnings of the City, therefore, the Committee believes that in the present state of knowledge only the banks' figures for interest earned should be used though it recognizes that this will result in some under-estimation. Thus in Chapter XIII where the Committee attempts to bring together the earnings of "the City," the contribution of the export houses is put at £26 million (i.e. £43¾ million less the interest item of £17½ million).

97.   In considering ways in which the export houses might expand their invisible earnings the Committee was mindful of the two quite different sources of such earnings, i.e. deriving from the services they provide directly to visible exporters, and deriving from the services they render in international trade to both overseas buyers and sellers. In both respects they are at a disadvantage, i.e. compared with the U.K. manufacturers they are helping, and with their international competitors: the U.K. exporters of manufactured goods receive a repayment of the Selective Employment Tax plus a premium, as well as an export rebate, where appropriate; the export houses receive neither. The issues involved in both cases are raised in more general

1. See recommendations at end of chapter and Appendix B.

terms in Chapter XVIII. Beyond these two tax questions, the export houses put forward several proposals to provide incentives designed to raise their foreign earnings. They included assistance for overseas travel (either individually or in sponsored missions), special allowances for domestic travel and entertainment and for specialized export training and a scheme to bring E.C.G.D. facilities (not rates) on External Trade Policies into line with those on Comprehensive Policies (i.e. U.K. goods policies). Suggestions were also made about adjusting the tax structure in order to permit a company to retain a larger share of its profits when earned in foreign exchange. Most of the proposals were intended, directly or indirectly, to reduce costs, to reduce risks or reduce taxation, i.e. generally to raise retained profits, in relation to earnings of invisible income.

RECOMMENDATIONS

98.   The broader questions of how far Britain can provide tax incentives to earners of invisible income, without running counter to international agreements under G.A.T.T., O.E.C.D., etc. are examined later in Chapter XVII. But the Committee believes that the following proposals are worthy of further study.

1. It recommends that the British National Export Council should study the question of how far the present system of visible export missions can be extended in their present form, where appropriate, to invisible exporters. Under this scheme help is available through the British National Export Council for export missions which meet certain requirements, such as a minimum number within the mission, market and product approved in advance by Board of Trade officials, sponsored by a non-profit-making body, report to be made public etc.

2. The Committee recommends that the Export Credit Guarantees Department should consider how far it could extend the facilities it provides on External Trade Policies as a direct stimulus to the earning of invisible income. Such a move would not, it is clear, help British visible exports; but in the light of the importance of invisible income to Britain's payments balance, the Committee believes that a general re-consideration of E.C.G.D. policies to reflect an invisible export drive as well as the accepted visible export drive is now necessary.

3. The Committee believes that the contribution of the export houses needs to be evaluated more closely in statistical terms than has been done so far. Since, as is shown in the Committee's examination of the commissions on exports and imports in Appendix B, there is a strong case for an official survey of these commissions and of the values shown in customs documents, the Committee recommends that such an official examination might be combined and co-ordinated with a more detailed survey by the British Export Houses Association of the earnings of their members.

APPENDIX A(1): CHAPTER V

EXPORT RESEARCH GROUP IN CONJUNCTION WITH THE BRITISH EXPORT HOUSES ASSOCIATION

Interim report of investigation into turnover and activity of British Export Houses

By Professor G. M. Sharman

THREE-HUNDRED AND EIGHTY-SIX questionnaire forms were issued by the Director of the British Export Houses Association to their members and of these 172 were returned, i.e. just over 45 per cent. A further 160 were issued to known export houses who were not members and of these 15, i.e. just under 10 per cent were returned. Some of these forms were negative, or so incomplete as to be unusable. One form gave information which, if correct, was so out of line with all other replies and for such a large figure that it would have distorted the results. Finally one form was received after the analysis had been completed.

One hundred and seventy-eight forms were analysed and because of the variation in size of operation it was necessary to sub-divide them into more or less comparable groups for this purpose. It will be seen from TABLE 22 that 10 firms accounted for 40 per cent of the total turnover, 20 firms accounted for 60 per cent of the turnover and that 90 firms (or about 50 per cent) accounted for 95 per cent.

We, therefore, did the analysis twice; once making groups in turnover ranges and once making groups according to the number of employees reported. It was thought that these two divisions would enable firms to compare their own situation with that of the average of the two groups into which they fitted. In deciding on these ranges we attempted to group not less than 20 and not more than 30 firms together in fairly logical divisions.

The analysis is set forth in TABLES 23-27 inclusive, which are attached. The code to both the activities and the groups precedes these tables in the Appendix.

Because we are only dealing with less than half the membership of the Association (probably about a quarter of the known number of firms engaged in this trade) it is impossible to postulate exact findings. However, the Director of B.E.H.A. (who has been supplied with a list of the numbers of the forms returned) gives as his opinion that we have a fair cross-section of replies. If this opinion is correct, the figures shown could very well be double, suggesting a total turnover, so far as the Association is concerned, of about £700 million a year, of which about 75 per cent concerns exports from the United Kingdom, i.e. about £525 million a year. This would mean that about 10 per cent of our export trade is handled through or financed by export houses who are members of the Association.

Looking at the individual activities, nearly two-thirds of the firms act in more than one capacity. It would appear that in the analysis by activity there must be a margin of error, since there is evidence that some export houses interpret their activities differently from the generally understood definition. Bearing in mind the activities of export houses which are not members of the Association, the actual figure of exports for which export houses are responsible must be considerably higher. Moreover, no account has been taken in this investigation of the activities of overseas establishments and associated companies, which make a significant contribution to foreign exhange earnings. The investigation is being continued with the co-operation of B.E.H.A., as a result of which it is hoped that additional detailed turnover figures will be obtained to enable a further and more conclusive report to be made.

We had hoped that the enquiry would produce some indication of rates of growth or decline in this trade and in the various activities. Unfortunately no clear pattern has emerged. As the widest possible generalization, it seems that the larger firms (especially those dealing with confirmation of orders and financing of export business) have had recent growth and expect future growth; whereas some of the small firms (especially those acting as merchants and as suppliers' selling agents) appear to have had and to expect some decline. However, the writer does not believe that any firm reliance can be made of this subjective assessment and would recommend that a selective sample survey might be held, going into much more detail on this point and also into the commodity composition and the market distribution of such trade. He believes it would be especially useful to know whether in the terms of these last two matters the pattern of trade through export houses was or was not changing at the same rate as the national trend.

We believe that the figures we have been able to produce enable an "identity kit likeness" of these export houses to be built up. In total about one-quarter of the activity lies in merchanting and most of this is done by the smaller companies. The buying agents and confirming houses ought to be considered together and they amount to 55 per cent of the activities. Here it is the medium to larger firms that are strongest in this field. Finance houses, although few in number and restricted to the medium to large firms, appear to be developing rapidly and this could very well indicate a change in activity that should be developed. The writer believes that there is a very good case for specialist firms with knowledge of the money market who would bring together the products of manufacturers and loan capital to enable credit to be given more effectively and efficiently than if this is left to be done by the manufacturers from their own working capital.

The percentage of trade from suppliers outside the United Kingdom increases as the size of the company grows. In TABLE 24 the figure against A1 is distorted by virtue of the fact that there was one company in this group all of whose trade was external to the United Kingdom.

Looking at the firms who are engaged in one activity only, apart from those engaged in finance activities, most of them appear to fall into the small to medium groupings.

This is the first known attempt to measure and identify the activity of this type of firm. They employ around 4,000 (say up to 10,000 if we attempt to postulate regarding those whose forms were not returned).

96

APPENDIX A(2): CHAPTER V

SURVEY OF BRITISH EXPORT HOUSES

The following code applies to the tables setting out the
results of the survey

ACTIVITIES

(*a*) Merchants buying *and* selling as principals.
(*b*) Purchasing agents and Indent Houses.
(*c*) Confirming Houses other than on (*b*) above.
(*d*) Suppliers' U.K. export agents or Export Managers.
(*e*) Factors (in the financial sense).
(*f*) Export Finance Houses.
(*x*) Exports from non-U.K. supplies.

GROUPS

A—By Turnover

1.	up to £	99,000
2.	£ 100,000 up to £	149,000
3.	£ 150,000 up to £	299,000
4.	£ 300,000 up to £	599,000
5.	£ 600,000 up to £	999,000
6.	£1,000,000 up to £1,999,000	
7.	£2,000,000 up to £2,999,000	
8.	£3,000,000 and up.	

B—By number of Employees in the U.K.

11. 1-3
12. 4-5
13. 6-7
14. 8-10
15. 11-19
16. 20-49
17. 50 and up.

97

TABLE 22

CUMULATIVE NUMBER OF FIRMS (RANKED IN ORDER
OF DESCENDING TURNOVER) CONTRIBUTING TO 5%
STEPS OF TOTAL TURNOVER

Percentage of Turnover	Cumulative number of Firms	Percentage of total number of Firms
10	1	0·5
15	2	1·1
20	3	1·7
25	4	2·2
30	6	3·4
35	8	4·5
40	10	5·6
45	12	6·7
50	14	7·9
55	17	9·6
60	20	11·2
65	23	12·9
70	26	14·6
75	33	18·5
80	40	22·5
85	50	28·1
90	65	36·5
95	90	50·6
100	178	100·0

TABLE 23

NUMBER OF FIRMS ENGAGED IN EACH ACTIVITY

A=Divided by TURNOVER GROUPS 1–8   B=Divided by EMPLOYEE GROUPS 11–17

Activity	Total	a	b	c	d	e	f	x
A – 1	27	18	10	8	9	1	0	16
2	20	20	11	4	8	0	2	14
3	26	21	8	8	8	0	1	11
4	26	16	10	13	9	1	4	19
5	20	11	12	14	8	0	1	15
6	24	13	17	12	3	1	1	22
7	17	13	14	9	6	0	2	14
8	18	8	4	9	3	0	8	14
B – 11	25	20	7	8	4	0	0	15
12	27	20	14	9	11	1	1	18
13	27	20	13	7	12	–	4	16
14	29	16	14	15	9	2	2	22
15	24	18	12	14	6	0	3	19
16	30	16	20	13	7	0	5	22
17	16	10	6	11	5	0	4	13
Total	178	120	86	77	54	3	19	125
Percentage of Total		67	48	43	30	2	11	70

98

Table 24

TURNOVER AND PERCENTAGES OF EACH ACTIVITY OF ALL FIRMS

A=Divided by Turnover Groups 1–8   B= Divided by Employee Groups 11–17

	Turnover £'000s	*a*	*b*	*c*	*Activity d*	*e*	*f*	*x*
A 1	1,300	38·5	23·5	15·2	21·4	1·4	–	21·9
2	2,422	69·5	12·5	3·6	13·2	–	1·2	8·4
3	5,195	64·8	10·7	12·3	12·0	–	0·2	6·2
4	11,307	41·7	12·5	27·4	16·5	0·2	1·7	23·1
5	14,462	25·5	36·3	28·9	8·5	–	0·8	17·6
6	34,714	27·0	35·4	29·2	7·5	0·1	0·8	27·7
7	55,433	28·1	30·3	32·3	1·2	–	8·1	27·7
8	171,435	19·1	8·3	46·5	0·8	–	25·3	29·6
B 11	2,759	75·2	8·4	14·1	2·3	–	–	14·9
12	5,951	45·9	14·5	12·2	26·9	0·3	0·2	17·5
13	7,961	37·1	38·7	15·0	6·6	–	2·6	21·3
14	19,639	22·7	35·4	26·6	14·3	0·3	0·7	14·9
15	28,060	36·6	20·5	21·9	4·2	–	16·8	24·3
16	91,611	18·2	24·1	20·9	0·9	–	35·9	23·5
17	140,287	23·9	7·9	61·3	1·2	–	5·7	33·6
Total	296,268	24·6	17·5	38·7	3·2	–	16·0	27·5
Unanalysed	52,292							
Total	348,560							

Table 25

NUMBER OF FIRMS ENGAGED SOLELY (OR ALMOST SO) IN ONE ACTIVITY *a–f*

A=Divided by Turnover Groups 1–8   B=Divided by Employee Groups 11–17

Activity	*Total*	*a*	*b*	*c*	*d*	*e*	*f*
A 1	10	5	2	2	1	0	0
2	8	8	0	0	0	0	0
3	15	12	1	1	1	0	0
4	10	5	2	3	0	0	0
5	5	2	2	1	0	0	0
6	8	1	4	2	1	0	0
7	1	1	0	0	0	0	0
8	10	1	1	5	0	0	3
B 11	13	9	2	2	0	0	0
12	10	7	1	1	1	0	0
13	9	6	2	1	0	0	0
14	14	7	2	3	2	0	0
15	6	3	2	1	0	0	0
16	10	2	3	2	0	0	3
17	5	1	–	4	0	0	0
Total	67	35	12	14	3	0	3
Percentage of all	39	29	14	18	6	0	16

N.B. Some of these firms were also engaged in non-U.K. exports. Additionally one firm (falling in groups 1 and 14) was solely engaged in such trade.

TABLE 26

TURNOVER AND PERCENTAGES OF EACH ACTIVITY OF FIRMS ENGAGED SOLELY (OR ALMOST SO) IN ONE ACTIVITY

A=Divided by TURNOVER GROUPS 1–8   B=Divided by EMPLOYEE GROUPS 11–17

		Turnover £'000s	a	b	c	d	e	f
					Activity			
A	1	344	42·7	25·9	18·3	13·1	–	–
	2	906	100·0	–	–	–	–	–
	3	2,790	83·1	5·0	6·3	5·6	–	–
	4	3,230	60·2	10·5	29·3	–	–	–
	5	3,349	39·0	52·4	8·6	–	–	–
	6	10,135	15·6	42·6	24·5	17·3	–	–
	7	2,235	100·0	–	–	–	–	–
	8	67,313	7·8	7·0	52·7	–	–	32·5
B	11	1,444	85·7	10·0	4·3	–	–	–
	12	1,451	78·8	5·9	12·2	3·1	–	–
	13	2,342	41·6	47·5	10·9	–	–	–
	14	7,857	28·9	14·6	32·7	24·3	–	–
	15	4,935	37·8	49·9	12·3	–	–	–
	16	33,140	8·9	19·4	5·6	–	–	66·1
	17	39,133	13·3	–	86·6	–	–	–
Total		90,302	17	13	44	2	–	24

TABLE 27

NUMBER AND TURNOVER (IN TOTAL AND UNDER EACH ACTIVITY) OF FIRMS ENGAGED SOLELY (OR ALMOST SO) AS A PERCENTAGE OF THE WHOLE

A=Divided by TURNOVER GROUPS 1–8   B=Divided by EMPLOYEE GROUPS 11–17

		Number of Firms %	Total %	a %	b %	c %	d %	e %	f %
A	1	37	26	38	37	40	21	0	–
	2	40	40	62	0	0	0	0	0
	3	58	56	73	27	30	26	–	0
	4	38	29	54	31	40	0	0	0
	5	25	23	43	40	8	0	–	0
	6	33	29	23	48	13	94	0	0
	7	6	4	20	0	0	0	–	0
	8	56	39	22	47	62	0	–	42
B	11	52	52	70	73	19	0	–	–
	12	37	24	51	12	30	3	0	0
	13	33	30	42	46	27	0	–	0
	14	48	40	60	20	55	80	–	–
	15	25	17	24	57	13	0	–	0
	16	33	36	25	38	13	0	–	87
	17	31	28	23	0	60	0	–	0
Total		38	30·5	29·5	30·2	47·4	28·8	0	26·8

100

APPENDIX B: CHAPTER V

COMMISSIONS ON IMPORTS AND EXPORTS

Commissions on imports and exports appear as "other services" in Table 11 of the official balance of payments "pink book." The figures for 1964 and 1965 were:

	£ million	
	1964	1965
Commissions, etc. on exports (debit)	60	66
Commisions, etc. on imports (credit)	77	82

These entries in the accounts arise essentially from the need to adjust the figures of visible trade so as to give a true picture of the balance of payments. The valuation of imports is at "open-market values," including "all other costs, charges and expenses incidental to the sale and delivery of the goods . . . at the place of importation." Some of these costs are commissions paid to British firms. It would, of course, be possible to deduct these from the value of imports (as freights earned by British ships are deducted), but the established practice is to regard them, instead, as an offsetting export of a service to the overseas supplier, and so to include them in invisible earnings. A similar treatment must, therefore, be accorded to exports; where the f.o.b. value includes commissions paid to non-residents, these must be entered as an invisible import. Though the concepts are symmetrical the operations involved in deriving estimates are not, so the two are considered separately in the following paragraphs.

IMPORTS

It is necessary first to mention certain adjustments made by the Department of Customs and Excise in preparing the Trade Returns, which are collectively know as "uplift." For the great majority of transactions, the invoice price is accepted. The main exceptions are:

1. Consigned goods, where values are based on the actual selling price.
2. Imports brought in at privilege prices by associate firms.
3. Preferential prices allowed to sole concessionaires to cover U.K.
4. Other cases where the U.K. selling price is used (e.g. second-hand cars.

The total amount of "uplift" is about £10 million. This sum appears in the trade accounts but, since it is earned by residents, it is deducted from the trade figures when these are converted to a balance of payments basis.

To estimate total commissions earned by British firms in respect of imports, and included in the trade returns, the C.S.O. and Customs and Excise have examined trade in various commodities to discover the proportion which took place in various ways (i.e. through agents, associated houses, sole concessionaires or direct purchase), and the rates of commission (including "uplift") contained in the recorded values. This detailed study covered 80 per cent of imports, and the average rate of commission found to apply to this 80 per cent is applied to the remaining 20 per cent. However, the gross figure thus obtained includes "uplift," which is already deducted in calculating the balance of payments value of imports. A corresponding sum is, therefore, deducted from the gross estimate of commissions to produce the figure which appears in the official balance of payments "pink book."

The detailed study referred to above was last made in 1961. In subsequent calculations it has been assumed that there has been no change in the way trade in each commodity is conducted, or the rates of commission, though allowance is made for changes in the commodity pattern of trade. The official view is that detailed surveys will be needed from time to time to provide "benchmark" data but, in view of the complexity of the work involved and the fact that trading practices change only slowly, the interval can be fairly long—say seven to ten years.

EXPORTS

The value of exports in the Trade Accounts is defined as, "the cost of the goods to the purchaser abroad, including packing, inland and coastal transport in the U.K., dock dues, loading charges, and all other costs, profits, charges and expenses (e.g. insurance and commission) accruing up to the point where the goods are deposited on board the exporting vessel or aircraft." The recorded values should, therefore, include commission earned by overseas agents for services performed up to the time when goods are loaded, but Customs and Excise believe that this is not always so.

The only information available about the amount of these commissions is derived from Exchange Control transactions and covers only remittances to non-sterling area countries. In compiling the estimates in the official balance of payments it is assumed that exports to the sterling area involve payment of the same average rate of commission as exports to the non-sterling area.

The Exchange Control estimates are available only for the years 1954-56 and 1964-65. The average rates were as follows:

Year	1954	1955	1956	1964	1965
Percentage	1·66	1·53	1·48	1·35	1·38

The difference between the highest and lowest of these figures is equivalent to about £15 million a year but, in the present state of knowledge, there is no adequate explanation of the variations.

CONCLUSIONS

The figures of commissions on exports, as at present estimated, may therefore be inaccurate for one or more of the following reasons:

1. Only commissions resulting in cash flows to non-sterling area are identified by Exchange Control. A corresponding estimate is made for payments to the overseas sterling area.
2. There may be differences in the average rate of commission between exports to the sterling area and non-sterling area. This might work either way.
3. There may be a failure to include commissions in the export values returned to Customs. This would produce an under-valuation of exports, and so an understatement of the credit position on visible

and invisible items together. One of the ways in which this could arise would be when a manufacturer prepares the customs documents on the basis of his own invoice, but an agent invoices the goods to an overseas buyer at a figure including commission.

Errors arising from 1. and 3. must work in opposite directions, while those arising under 2. may work in either direction. It is thus impossible to say whether the net result is an over- or -under-statement of net current account earnings from exports.

Information about exports is much less full than that about imports both in respect of the precise basis of valuation and the way in which the trade is conducted. There is a strong case for a survey that would cover both commissions and the more general problem of how far Customs documents do in fact represent the full value of exports according to the official definition. Such a survey would be expensive but, once done, it could be used as a "benchmark" and need not be repeated for a number of years.

CHAPTER VI

COMMODITIES

99. In Britain's commercial history three main types of commodity markets have developed: auctions; sale rooms; and commodity exchanges and futures markets. These have reflected the variety of commodities being sold, for some can be sold by description only, some by sample and description and some on individual merit. In many cases it has been sufficient to establish an agreed description of a commodity. In others samples have needed examination and assessment. And in others again experts have been essential to evaluate and judge quality. Differing facilities have thus been required and different markets have grown up to provide them. Each type of market has tended to develop in its own way, though all face similar problems:

1. THE AUCTION ROOMS

100. These handle commodities, such as tea, furs etc., in which the size of consignments is relatively small or where the quality is most important, or in some cases where the quality is not assessable except by inspection. The foreign exchange earnings derived from these auctions are twofold:

    i. From the physical consignment of goods to this country, their insurance, their valuation by the auction and their despatch abroad or retention here, according to the buyer's instructions.

    ii. From the opportunity for U.K. buyers to see the available supply as favoured clients and to be involved with the creation of ancillary activities—tea blending, dressing and making up of furs, etc.

101. The object of the Auction Rooms is plainly to establish the value of the goods by competitive bidding. If London has secured and can maintain the most respected Auction Room in any particular commodity, it is likely the best will be sent here. The qualities and prices available here will react on the producers whether they be foreign or British owned companies abroad.

2. COMMODITY EXCHANGES

102. In the Commodity Exchanges, with their allied Futures Markets, the commodity itself never appears. Examples are grain, oils and fats on the Baltic Exchange, sugar, cocoa, rubber, coffee, shellac, copra and palm oil on the London Commodity Exchange, copper, tin, lead and zinc on the London Metal Exchange. Not so long ago a Wool Futures Market was established, linked closely with Bradford.

103. The role of the market is similar in each case; the commodity is defined by weight and quality according to the individual international

standard. The rules for conducting transactions in the commodity are established by a Trade Association and the members of the market have to accept the definitions, the rules and the arrangements for settling disputes.
104. The objective is to provide a service for both producers and consumers on as wide an international basis as possible. The service consists of:

(a) Establishing a value for the commodity not only for prompt delivery but for periods of time ahead.

(b) Laying down the conditions for delivery by producers to consumers and ensuring that these are fulfilled.

(c) Providing quick and expert arbitration for quality or breaches in the conditions of sale.

(d) Providing the opportunity for producers and consumers to sell or buy their supplies simply and in large amounts, if necessary spread over several months ahead, to and from anywhere in the world.

The market consists of three categories of people: producers or their agents; consumers or their agents; and intermediaries (brokers or merchants). The difference between the broker and the merchant is simple—the title of goods passes from the producer or his agent to the consumer or his agent via the broker, but never becomes the property of the broker. The merchant accepts title to the goods and resells them.
105. The foreign exchange earnings of these markets comes from both the trade in the physical goods ("actuals") involving agency or brokerage commissions (not only for the sale or purchase of the goods but usually for providing financial insurance and shipping services as well) and the merchants' margins. In addition earnings flow from the futures markets where a "price" insurance arrangement is established for which producers and consumers pay a premium type fee, but where merchants can also deal.

3. THE SALE ROOMS
106. These cover such commodities as spices, herbs, gums, nuts, citrus juices, fibres, etc., which are usually not sufficiently uniform in quality to permit a basic standard suitable for trading on description only. Although the range in qualities is not vital enough for a special auction room to be required, the variations between shipments and origins are important enough for buyers to want to know in some detail the type, standard and availability.
107. As a result a series of bilateral deals has become the main activity with the producer's agent or the consumer's agent seeking each other to establish a bargain. The trades suffer from three current trends:

(a) Replacement by synthetics, which may not be so good but are consistent in quality and regularly available.

(b) Interchangeability such as in edible oils where lard, palm oil, fishmeat oil, etc., are all useable.

(c) Elimination by vertical integration—the producer deciding he would be better off establishing the next process of manufacture either in his own country or in the main market, or the buyer. buying direct from the producer or going into partnership with him.

Earnings of Commodity Markets

108. The foreign earnings of commodity markets appear as part of two items in the balance of payments pink book. Earnings in respect of imports to the U.K. are included along with similar earnings by other import merchants in "Commissions, etc. on imports" in Table 11 of the Pink Book. Earnings in respect of trade, outside the U.K., are recorded under the heading of "Financial and allied services" in the same table. This item is defined in a footnote as, "Including brokerage, merchanting, arbitrage, banking charges and commissions, underwriting and other insurance."

109. No breakdown is available of the Central Statistical Office's estimate of commissions. (For the method of estimation, see Appendix B to Chapter V on "Commissions on Imports and Exports.") The other element (earnings from third country trade) is in three categories:

1. Trade covered by exchange control forms EC (G) 60 and EC (G) 68.
2. Trade in the following, "scheme" commodities: cotton, coffee, copra, cocoa, grain, rubber, sugar, copper, tin, lead, zinc.
3. Other outer sterling area trade not included in 2.

It is estimated that in 1965 these three items came to over £20 million. (But this figure includes earnings under 1 and 3 on certain goods other than primary commodities.)

110. The following points about these official estimates of third country trade should be noted:

(a) For all categories, the estimate of earnings is made by applying assumed rates of profit or commissions to a turnover figure. The rates are, of course, chosen in consultation with representatives of the trades concerned, but some members of the markets are not entirely happy about them.

(b) Turnover figures are derived from exchange control records and information received from certain members of "scheme" commodity markets. Trade in category 3 is assumed to be 30 per cent of that covered by EC (G) 68.

(c) No account is taken of the earnings of terminal markets, the official view being that insufficient evidence is available as to their invisible earnings.

(d) The commodities treated as "scheme" commodities are those in which international trade through the U.K. market is conducted under special Exchange Control arrangements. Typical amongst those not so far included are wool, oil and oilseeds (except copra), tea and animal feeding stuffs. These are included in categories 1 and 3.

111. Privately the sugar trade commissioned a survey by the Economist Intelligence Unit covering the years 1956/57/58, and in conjunction with the Bank of England a follow-up survey for 1963. For other commodities the

Committee felt the need for further information and obtained figures from the following markets for 1964 and 1965: coffee, cocoa, rubber, the London Metal Exchange (a combined figure for copper, tin, lead and zinc), the grain trade of the Baltic Exchange, and feeding stuffs covered by the Cattle Food Trade Association (average of 1963 and 1964).

112. Members of the associations concerned were asked to estimate (where relevant):

Their gross profit earned in trade from non-residents.

Gross commissions paid to them by non-residents.

Total differences received from or paid to non-residents in respect of terminal market contracts.

The results are shown in TABLE 28.

TABLE 28

EARNINGS OF SOME COMMODITY MARKETS

Returns made to the Committee

£ million

	1964	1965
Coffee	0·3	0·5
Cocoa	0·9	1·6
Grain		0·3[1]
Rubber	1·2	1·3
Sugar	3·7[2]	—
Copper ⎫ Tin ⎬ Lead ⎪ Zinc ⎭	3·2	4·3
Cattle foods	1·8[3]	

113. The figures given to the Committee were higher than some of the earlier official estimates, in spite of the fact that the returns to the Committee were voluntary and therefore somewhat incomplete. For the markets where figures are available for 1965 (coffee, cocoa, rubber and metals) the reported earnings are £7·7 million, much greater than the equivalent official estimates. However, the market returns include earnings in respect of U.K. imports, and there is no way of separating these. There are considerable difficulties in collecting statistics from the markets, but the official estimates can hardly be regarded as satisfactory, and there now seems to be a strong case for occasional comprehensive surveys to provide "benchmarks" for future estimates.

114. From the point of view of an estimate of the earnings of the City, which is discussed in more detail in Chapter XIII, the returns given to the Committee are more relevant than the official estimates. The part of the market's earnings that is related to U.K. imports is—as already noted—estimated in the official figures, but is inextricably mixed up with a number of other items. The big difficulty about using the returns to the Committee

1. Returns from Baltic Exchange, 1966.
2. Figures refer to 1963 but it is estimated that the results of 1964 were very similar. The private surveys for 1956/57/58 and 1963 all indicate a yearly net earning of £0.6 million excluding Terminal market transactions and commissions on U.K. imports and exports.
3. Average of 1963-64.

for this purpose is the limited area covered purely by the "scheme" commodities. There is no indication of the size of non-scheme commodity trade, so that a straight "grossing up" of the sample might be subject to large errors of unknown dimensions.

115. As already noted, the official view is that the settlement of differences in terminal market contracts may produce a debit item or a credit, so that, on balance, there is no stable pattern in their contribution to the balance of payments. The sugar market estimates—on the basis of the returns to the Bank of England for the years 1962/65 inclusive—show that the terminal market produced net overseas earnings averaging £1,465,000, but this included a debit of around £50,000 in 1962 and a credit of about £3 million in 1963. The other terminal markets for which information is available report much smaller figures, as follows:

			£'000		
			1963	1964	1965
Coffee ..	..	..	—9	—38	104
Cocoa ..	..	..	nil	40	—186
Rubber	..	..	—1	—	7

The figures for these three markets are clearly not inconsistent with the official view, but it must be remembered that the trading on the terminal markets is usually only one aspect of a normal transaction.

116. The contribution of terminal markets to the balance of payments is largely an indirect one—through their attraction of other business to London and through the service which they provide for producers and users of commodities. However, it is quite possible that they may, on average, also make a direct contribution. Unfortunately, however, there is a serious difficulty. The figures already quoted suggest that there are very large year-to-year fluctuations in the balance from terminal market settlements. Thus, the occasional surveys which would be adequate for other purposes, would not give an accurate picture of the earnings of terminal markets, whose results should be examined over a period of several years.

117. To sum up the Committee's statistical findings: foreign earnings from commodity traders are at present included in different sections of the official balance of payments; some of these estimates are more accurate than others; in the case of the individual markets where the Committee made a spot check on recent figures, the earnings were found to be higher than the official estimates. The Committee thus felt the need for occasional inquiries in depth for individual commodities to provide "benchmarks" for the official statisticians. Nevertheless the pattern of trade can plainly change quite rapidly, so that there is also a need for checks between such detailed studies.

RECOMMENDATION

118. The Committee recommends, therefore, that in order to provide more frequent statistical "benchmarks" the British Federation of Commodity Associations should consider, after discussions with the Bank of England,

what regularity would be acceptable to members and at the same time most fruitful to the official statisticians.

STIMULATING COMMODITY EARNINGS

119. The Committee, in considering how invisible earnings from commodity merchants might be expanded, was conscious of the complexities of the individual markets and of their variety. It was plainly impossible to assess prospects of each market. Yet it was equally clear that two problems were common to most: the rapidly changing world climate in which they were operating; and the efforts of maintaining internal efficiency.

120. It is an axiom that an efficient market will bring foreign exchange into this country, not only directly but indirectly by stimulating the use of the City's services, and that the size of the inflow is determined as much by the activity of the commodity in world trade as by the productivity of the commodity firms involved. This wider world background needs consideration first.

121. The international movement of basic commodities (i.e. raw materials and foods) cannot claim to have achieved a generally acceptable pattern of distribution. The United Nations Conference on Trade and Development in emphasising the low level of commodity prices; the attempts to bridge the gap between rich and poor countries; and the political pressure to create international commodity agreements or arrangements, all indicate that "the authorities" whoever they may be, are unhappy with the existing pattern of the commodity trades. Secondly, the activities of the communist block countries, with centrally planned economies, have also to be considered. They attempt to balance supply and demand by barter in volume terms making the cost in money equivalent subordinate, whereas the countries with relatively free economies use the price level as the method of adjusting supply and demand. Thirdly, even within the free world, governments (as well as private commodity producers) have been playing larger roles in commodity trading, often either restricting or by-passing commodity markets. These trends have already led to some diminution in the turnovers of individual commodity markets in the United Kingdom. Yet within the international movement of goods, there is still complete freedom of choice to nations and companies on where to establish their market centres. History, individual personalities, social conditions, political and economic background, etc., all influence the choice. Probably of major importance is security; that is the reliability of the spoken or written word, the convertibility of the money used, the integrity of arbitration machinery, the secrecy if required of the principal to the contract, its private terms, etc., etc. Second to security comes the general advantage to the predominant side (i.e. producer or consumer). For example, in a commodity which is generally in short supply the centre will tend towards the country of major size as a producer (e.g. wool). In a commodity generally in surplus the centre tends towards the country/countries of major size as an importer (sugar, coffee, cocoa).

122. Within the private sector of trade, however, the U.K. has a significant advantage in that history has centred a large number of the markets here by free choice, and as long as the security of the business is maintained, sterling remains freely convertible and the reputation of the markets for justice is unsullied, it should be possible to maintain them. The successful re-establishment of the U.K. commodity markets after the last war illustrates that once freedom and security are assured the U.K. will tend to attract world traders back.

123. The Committee believes that the commodity markets are not designed to make large profit margins. In fact, with the United Kingdom a heavy importer of raw materials and food, the competitive power of British industry as a whole could well be damaged by trying to promote larger profit margins in the markets. The aim, therefore, should be to encourage the growth of invisible earnings by the efficiency and increased volume of the markets and by their growing importance in world trade as a whole. This kind of expansion will clearly depend on success in three main areas:

1. An increase in world trade in free monetary terms in contrast with barter or closed bilateral accounts.
2. The retention of the United Kingdom's cost advantage in providing freight, shipping, insurance and financial services against other world centres.
3. The cost and efficiency of the markets' international communications network.

124. The first and second are outside the scope of the markets themselves, but Government policy can and should continue to provide indirect support for the use of Britain's commodity markets. In entering into commodity agreements, internationally or regionally, the Government can stress the need for an internationally free price. In concerning itself with future world food production and distribution, the Government can emphasize that the actual job of handling the trade will require the evaluation of a world price and a market mechanism for the speediest and cheapest distribution. On the third point of communications, although certain advantages remain, competition from other centres has increased. London still has the most favourable geographic situation in that London commodity firms can work with their clients from 6 a.m. to midnight during their clients' eight hours office day, because at 6 a.m. Hong Kong, Singapore, etc., are still in their offices and at midnight Chicago, San Francisco and Vancouver are in theirs. For efficiency and low cost the tele-communication network from London, particularly in Commonwealth under-water cables, was in the lead for a period after the last war, but it has now lost its pre-eminence to New York and perhaps even to Moscow, and the standard of service has become very mixed since competition was eliminated. "Early Bird" or satellite communications, the markets hope, will be important and may put London back amongst the leaders both for coverage and price. This area may well be worth a major study between the G.P.O., the Government and the markets as a whole.

110

CHAPTER VII

STOCK EXCHANGE AND CAPITAL MARKET

125. The London Stock Exchange is a market with two main functions:
1. A primary market, raising money for governments and companies (both domestic and foreign).
2. A secondary market, whereby securities can be bought or sold by investors throughout the world.

Over the centuries it has risen in importance, and today it is believed to be the largest Exchange in both its functions, second only to New York.

126. The membership of the London Stock Exchange, which numbers approximately 3,300 at present, is divided into two categories who elect to act either as jobbers or as brokers. There is a clear and fundamental difference between these two groups. Jobbers act as principals and attempt to make a profit on dealing in securities in which they specialize. They deal with brokers and are prohibited from dealing direct with the public. Brokers act as agents for the public in buying and selling securities and charge a commission for their services. They deal with the jobbers.

127. In July, 1965, the Federation of the Stock Exchanges in Great Britain and Ireland[1] was formed to promote and co-ordinate the interests of the various existing stock exchanges. Its principal aims are (a) to promote the co-ordination of the activities of all affiliated Stock Exchanges and (b) to provide good service to, and safeguards for, the investing public—including the regularizing of requirements for companies having or seeking a quotation.

128. The London Stock Exchange trades in over 9,500 securities of all descriptions of which the present market value is over £82,000 million. The bulk of new issues are for domestic borrowers, as the following figures regularly compiled by the Midland Bank show. They exclude Government borrowings:

£m

		Home	Commonwealth	Foreign	TOTAL
1961	..	553·5	48·9	6·3	608·7
1962	..	565·2	29·1	10·7	605·0
1963	..	534·6	53·8	4·6	592·9
1964	..	464·4	22·6	20·9	507·9
1965	..	764·1	5·3	1·1	770·5
1966	..	836·2	13·5	6·9	856·6

129. The question faced by the Committee has been how much of the activities of both the new issue market and the secondary market is devoted to foreign business and thus earns invisible income. An estimate is at present

1. For details of the Federation see Appendix A.

compiled by the Bank of England which is not published separately, but is included under the heading, "financial and allied services" in the official balance of payments pink book. The Committee felt that this was not entirely satisfactory and decided to undertake a direct inquiry with the help of the Council of the London Stock Exchange.

130. At the outset four types of overseas earnings appeared relevant:

1. Broker's commission on dealings on behalf of overseas clients (excluding new issues).
2. Profits from arbitrage.
3. Earnings of jobbers from overseas business.
4. Commissions on new issues of overseas securities.

1. BROKER'S COMMISSION

131. The Committee was informed by the Stock Exchange that of about 200 broker firms, "no more than 30 to 40 would be continuously interested in foreign business, and of these about a dozen would be responsible for the majority of it." Although different firms have different accounting methods it was assumed that it would be quite feasible for them to give information about their overseas commissions.

2. ARBITRAGE

132. Arbitrage may be carried on both by brokers and jobbers, but the amount undertaken by jobbers was believed to be small. "Joint account" business (i.e. where a London firm has a joint account with a firm or firms abroad) requires the sanction of the Council. The number of firms operating joint accounts is small, and it was felt that those accounting for the greater part of arbitrage business would be able to give figures of their profits from this source without undue difficulty.

133. In so far as overseas firms receive payments from London firms on joint account, it was plainly desirable to have a separate record of these.

3. JOBBERS' EARNINGS

134. There are at present about 40 firms of jobbers and only a few deal in foreign securities. There are two difficulties in the way of collecting estimates of overseas earnings from jobbers:

(a) Jobbers deal with brokers, not with the public, so that they do not ordinarily know whether a purchase or sale originates from an overseas order or not.

(b) The jobber's profit is the balance of receipts and payments over a series of transactions, and cannot be allocated to any particular deal.

These two difficulties present insuperable obstacles to the collection of the relevant information by direct inquiry.

4. NEW ISSUE BUSINESS

135. New issues of overseas securities are usually handled by brokers in conjunction with merchant banks. In so far as this is so certain foreign earnings are likely to be covered by the questionnaire to the banks described

112

in Chapter IV. But since some firms receive commissions for this type of business from other sources, it was decided to ask firms for receipts *other than from banks* in respect of new issue business.

136. In the light of all this the London Stock Exchange expressed its willingness to ask broker members for overseas earnings in respect of commissions, arbitrage and new issues. Accordingly a questionnaire[1] was agreed and distributed to members by the Council.

137. Because of the difficulties involved in collecting figures for past periods, the Council asked the co-operation of members in providing those for the calendar year, 1966. The results were as follows:

Overseas Earnings by Stock Exchange Firms

(£.).

			(*Total estimates included*).
1. Brokers commission on dealings on behalf of overseas clients.		1,430,004	(405,557)
2. Arbitrage and share of joint account profits and losses—net profits.		914,348	(431,708)
3. Fees in respect of new issues of overseas securities:			
(*a*) received from a U.K. banker	114,820		(3,000)
(*b*) other fees	82,769		(2,000)
		197,589	(5,000)
4. Any other revenue by way of remuneration from services rendered to overseas sources		37,673*	(375)
		£2,579,614	(£842,640)

* Fees for foreign dividend collections, interest on currency deposits etc.

This total figure of £2,579,614 for 1966 does not, of course, include the overseas income of jobbers. It is possible, therefore, according to assessments made by the Committee, that the total overseas income of the Stock Exchange (including the jobbers) may be between £3 million and £4 million. This is referred to again in Chapter XIII.

138. In considering what might be done to expand the London capital market and to develop London's international role, without putting inordinate pressure on the pound, the Committee examined the recent development of the international market in foreign currency issues—the so-called

1. See Appendix B.

Euro-bond market. This evolved from the late 1950s onwards, partly as a result of the gradual removal in most European countries of restrictions on outward portfolio investment by residents. In essence, this is a new issue market for foreign borrowers where bonds are sold mainly to non-residents of the countries in which the main issuing houses are situated.

139. Statistical difficulties arise in determining the size of the market because, for example, a part of some issues is sometimes taken up by residents of the countries of the issuing houses. Moreover it is only in the past year or so that figures have been assembled by responsible bodies, e.g., O.E.C.D. Issues are usually arranged by a small group of up to four or five banks and issuing houses from two or more countries, and these in turn organize a wider syndicate of banks and other houses (sometimes as many as 50) and the bonds are usually placed with investors, who hold them as a long-term investment. The issues are normally quoted on at least two stock exchanges (often London or New York and Luxembourg or one other), but the secondary market for post-issue transactions is still fairly small. London banks were amongst the first to pioneer Euro-issues, even though they could not sell Euro-bonds to U.K. residents, except for subscription with so-called investment currency (i.e. the proceeds of disinvestment abroad by residents), and London expertise has played a prominent part in the development of the market.[1]

140. Considerable stimulus to the market came from the introduction by the U.S. Government as from mid-1963 of the Interest Equalisation Tax, which increased the interest cost of borrowing on the New York market for developed and certain other countries by about 1 per cent. This effectively diverted many would-be borrowers to Europe. As the figures in TABLE 29, Appendix D, show, the market expanded rapidly in 1964 and 1965, and was particularly affected in 1965 by the introduction of U.S. policies designed to restrict the outflow of capital for direct U.S. investment abroad. From the second quarter of 1965 a large number of U.S. corporations have issued bonds in Europe, often with an option for conversion into shares at a later date; and while European borrowers accounted for over two-thirds of total Euro-bond issues in 1963 and 1964, with Japan taking part of the remainder, U.S. corporations issued over one-third of total issues in 1965 and over one-half in 1966. In line with increased U.S. borrowing, the proportion of issues denominated in dollars has grown significantly, although issues continue to be denominated e.g. in units of account[2], Deutschemarks, sterling with a Deutschemark option etc. No statistics are available to show the source of subscription to these issues. A sizeable proportion comes from European residents but funds emanate also from a variety of sources in other parts of the world.

141. The development of the market was affected during 1966 by extremely tight monetary conditions and the high cost of borrowing in most European countries but, with easier conditions and a decline in rates, particularly

1. See Appendix C.
2. A term derived from the accounting unit of the European Payments Union and its successor the European Monetary Agreement. A unit is the equivalent of one U.S. dollar defined in terms of the gold parity.

during the first quarter of 1967, there has been a sharp increase in the amount of capital raised in the market. It should be noted that the Euro-bond market is different from the Euro-dollar market, described in Chapter IV, which is a market for short and, to a lesser extent, medium-term, bank deposits in dollars, which has also developed in Europe during the past decade.

142. Thus, so far as the London market is concerned, there are now two potential sources of overseas earnings: earnings by brokers and jobbers from transactions on behalf of non-residents in the secondary market; and those by brokers and banks in connection with overseas issues in sterling in London as well as with so-called Euro-bond issues. The first will depend on widening the market; the second on encouraging the raising of new money through London whether from British investors or from non-residents. Like New York, London has the current advantage of a wide secondary market[1]. The Committee, therefore considered what might be done to widen it further, so that, for example, a Frenchman selling an Italian share to a German through London might become commonplace.

143. The Committee has been told both by brokers and merchant banks that this should involve further quotation of British firms abroad as well as more quotations of foreign firms in London. The Committee believes that there is ample scope for both. On the London Stock Exchange about 4,000 public companies have a quotation for their ordinary shares. In contrast the following table shows the number of quotations of United Kingdom companies in the Common Market countries and the United States of America:

	Official	Unofficial
Belgium (Brussels)	11	12
France (Paris)	14	9
Germany (Dusseldorf) ..	1	
Holland (Amsterdam) ..	12	
Italy	Nil	
Switzerland (Zurich) ..	4	
U.S.A.	32	

There are also a few fixed interest stocks quoted abroad. Even among these figures there is some overlapping because the same firm is quoted in different places i.e. Imperial Chemical Industries (5), Bowater (4), Shell (4) and Courtaulds (3) to take a few examples.

144. Apart from enhancing the status of London as a financial centre, the introduction of foreign shares on the Stock Exchange results in a variety of professional, printing and other fees. In addition, to the extent that deals

1. As the *O.E.C.D. Observer* (April, 1967) put it, in commenting on the report of the O.E.C.D. Invisible Transactions Committee on members' capital markets:
"Contractual savings institutions have assumed primary importance in the provision of resources to the capital markets in the Netherlands, Sweden and the United Kingdom, where they account for 30-40 per cent of all such funds, and in the U.S. where they provide some 20 per cent of the resources.
"O.E.C.D.'s Invisible Transactions Committee considers it no coincidence that these are the same countries where the financial markets are generally acknowledged to be the most efficient. Individual investors lacking a broad knowledge of the market and of alternative investment opportunities, entrust their savings to experts who can keep the cost of transactions down and invest the money well."

are made in London rather than in foreign centres it ensures that at least part of the commissions, currency transactions etc. are earned in the U.K. There are also grounds for supposing that the satisfactory introduction of a foreign company's shares to the London market might encourage them to prefer using London for Euro-bond or other capital raising operations.

145. Apart from the possibility of getting more United Kingdom companies quoted abroad it is also desirable to have more information on United Kingdom companies available on the Continent. At present material of this kind is provided by a few London stockbrokers with Continental connections but it seems desirable to enlarge the concept of investment in United Kingdom securities by foreigners. The main investment advisers on the Continent are the domestic banks along with brokers in a few countries, and it is for them to educate their clients. They need help. Whilst in the United Kingdom there are the usual statistical services for foreign companies, it would be a benefit if our companies' statistics were published abroad in a similar manner. Many of the large Continental companies publish their annual reports not only in their native tongue but also in English. The Committee believes that large British companies might be encouraged to publish their reports in at least German and French for overseas investors.

146. The Committee also feels that the use of Deposit Receipt Certificates might well be extended on the Continent. As such Continental Deposit Receipts would be in bearer form, they would help to overcome the overseas investor's dislike of waiting for some form of ownership on buying United Kingdom shares. If C.D.R.'s were introduced abroad, it might, of course, lead to a local market in them, and commission and profits might not come to London. But if the control and issue of C.D.R.'s was in the hands of Continental branches of London banks, their profit on handling would add to the City's invisible earnings.

147. While it is clear that any hopes of increasing sterling issues for foreign borrowers in London must await a significant improvement in the United Kingdom's balance of payments, the expansion of international issues, denominated in foreign currencies and subscribed to by non-residents, needs further encouragement. The Committee believes that every help should be given to enable London to maintain its position as the main entrepot centre for international operations of this kind. Although the market continues to grow rapidly, competition is increasing and London appears to be hampered by a number of what appear to be unnecessary restrictions.

148. It was represented to the Committee that the Stock Exchange's Certificate of Exemption from the requirements of the Companies Act in practice limits the exemption only to those sections of the Act which are unduly burdensome for the borrower. Sections which are virtually meaningless in the context of a foreign loan, it was complained, are nevertheless enforced. The borrower is compelled to go through unnecessary and irritating technicalities. The Stock Exchange Council by a simple directive, it was suggested, could assist invisible earnings.

149. At present, although U.K. residents are unable to subscribe to foreign

currency issues in London, the authorities allow the banks concerned to use official dollars for underwriting purposes. In addition to this valuable concession, it is suggested, it would be useful for such banks to know the limit, in terms of time, of such facilities provided to trade in the issues and to ensure an adequate after-market.

150. In broader terms, it has been represented to the Committee, both the present form of the Companies Act and the current Stock Exchange regulations are not drawn up with Euro-bond issues in mind. Various clauses in the Act and in the regulations are either inappropriate or difficult to interpret. The result is that unnecessary impediments are apparently placed in the way of such international issues organized through London.

RECOMMENDATION

151. While the Committee did not feel competent to make specific recommendations on any of these detailed points, it was convinced that London's role in this new international capital market, already active and rewarding, needed further positive encouragement. The Committee recommends that the Bank of England, the Accepting Houses Committee, the Issuing Houses Committee and the Council of the London Stock Exchange undertake a specific inquiry to examine the technical obstacles standing in the way of further earnings from the arranging of such international issues through London.

EFFICIENCY OF THE MARKET

152. There remains the question of the efficiency of the London stock market and of London as an international capital centre. It is rather a problem of how to measure it. As in so many other areas of invisible earnings, the Committee has not found a satisfactory measuring rod. If measured by results, London's merchant banks, brokers etc. have already shown their initiative in developing many parts of the new international bond market. London claims for itself the first international loan following the American introduction of the Interest Equalization Tax as well as the first borrowing by an American group utilizing a Luxembourg holding company. The Committee was also impressed by the role of London brokers in providing a secondary market for these new foreign currency bonds, though estimates of turnover in the Euro-bond market remain sketchy[1]. In considering the efficiency of the domestic stock market and that of the issuing mechanism in London, the Committee made an attempt to measure relative costs in London and other centres. The results were encouraging without being conclusive.

153. In comparing issue costs in London and elsewhere, the Committee relied on a recent survey of Europe's capital markets undertaken by the Invisible Transactions Committee of O.E.C.D. The survey provided the following evidence:

"The marketing costs for share issues proper will depend on whether

1. One unofficial estimate has calculated that turnover in the secondary Euro-bond market is bigger than that of domestic bonds in certain Continental stock exchanges.

it is a rights issue or a new issue; rights issues are generally considerably less expensive. Issue costs are difficult to compare since sometimes they exclude underwriting commissions. A few examples follow: in the United Kingdom, new issue costs vary between 2 and 5 per cent (including an underwriting commission) whilst rights issues costs are under 2 per cent (if not underwritten). In France costs vary between 2·5 per cent for a rights issue in the case of a small unquoted enterprise where all the shareholders are known (1 per cent capital duty, 1·5 per cent legal fees) and 8·5 per cent for a rights issue for a small quoted enterprise involving underwriting commissions, advertising, and the use of banks as paying agents—the average cost of a large rights issue being about 6·50 per cent; in the Netherlands a new issue costs between 5·12 and 5·65 per cent inclusive of registration tax (2·5 per cent) and underwriting charges; in Japan rights issues are estimated to cost about 1·6 per cent whilst in the United States the rate for a large issue is about 2·75 per cent for a rights issue and 5 per cent for a new issue inclusive of underwriting commissions, with costs climbing steeply for smaller issues.''

154. In a similar comparison of *issue* costs for private industrial bonds, the United Kingdom also emerges with one of the lowest non-recurring costs. The typical cost of such things as bank and broker's commissions, Stock Exchange quotation fee, printing and advertising charges etc. on a private industrial bond issue in 1966 was put at 4·198 per cent for the U.K. Only Japan, Sweden, Norway and the U.S. had lower charges: every Common Market country was higher.

155. When *dealing* costs in different countries were compared the answer was quite different. The Committee worked out the cost to an individual resident in each of the following centres to switch £10,000 out of one equity into another. The results were as follows:

London[1] £288; Frankfurt £224; Paris £162; Luxembourg £160; Brussels £126; Amsterdam £124; Milan £110; Zurich £104. The difficulty is that other costs,[2] often more important, are not so simple to compare. For example, one of the advantages of the breadth of the London market and of the unique system of jobbing employed in it is the relatively narrow gap between selling prices and buying prices. London's advantage in this respect often completely offsets the apparent high cost of dealing shown above. The Committee formed the view that when all factors had been taken into account, total dealing costs in London remained highly competitive. But it was harder to be convinced that foreign investors necessarily thought so. The Committee believes that, unless the Stock Exchange deliberately goes out of its way to stress the virtues of dealing in London, an impression of high commission and tax costs may continue to curb the growth of potential business.

1. In London the percentage cost rises sharply as the total involved falls, being £35 for £1,000's worth. Correspondingly, it falls relatively with larger amounts, being £2,250 for £100,000. In the other centres the relation of cost to value will vary little within this range.
2. It has to be borne in mind that under U.K. legislation change of ownership of shares takes place by transfer at a company's registered office, compared with "bearer" delivery on the Continent. This raises British costs.

APPENDIX A: CHAPTER VII

The Federation of Stock Exchanges in Great Britain and Ireland consists of the following exchanges with centres or local associations:

Stock Exchange	Centre or Local Association
The Stock Exchange, London	London
Belfast Stock Exchange	Belfast
Cork Stock Exchange	Cork
Dublin Stock Exchange	Dublin
Midlands & Western Stock Exchange	Birmingham
	Bristol
	Cardiff
	Nottingham
	Swansea
Northern Stock Exchange	Bradford
	Halifax
	Huddersfield
	Leeds
	Liverpool
	Manchester
	Newcastle-upon-Tyne
	Oldham
	Sheffield
	Northern Country Brokers' Association
Scottish Stock Exchange	Aberdeen
	Dundee
	Edinburgh
	Glasgow
	Scottish Country Brokers' Association
The Provincial Brokers' Stock Exchange	(An association of stockbrokers in smaller provincial towns, without a trading floor)

Dealings take place on trading floors in each region and also between country firms and London broker firms. The largest proportion of country business—i.e. orders to buy or sell received by country brokers from their clients—is done by passing the order to a London broker who will do the transaction on behalf of the country firm in the London market.

APPENDIX B: CHAPTER VII

The following details were requested by the Council of the London Stock Exchange from member firms for 1966:

OVERSEAS EARNINGS 1966

In respect of bargains struck, or new issues made, during the year ended December 31, 1966.

1. Broker's commission on dealings on behalf of Overseas clients   £
   N.B. The address of the client with whom the Broker deals must be outside the United Kingdom, whether in the sterling area or not, i.e. business transacted through an agent in the United Kingdom or by a United Kingdom office of the client is excluded.
   The gross commission is to be included, but any amounts paid to an overseas agent under a sharing arrangement must be deducted. Amounts received by allocation from other Brokers must not be included.
2. Arbitrage and share of joint account profits/losses   £
3. Fees in respect of new issue of Overseas securities:
   (a) Received from a U.K. banker   £
   (b) Other fees   £
   —————————£
4. Any other revenue by way of remuneration from services rendered to Overseas sources..............................   £
   N.B. Where this figure is greater than one-tenth of the totals of the three preceding groups, please give a brief description of the nature of the service given.
* Indicates that amount has been estimated.
NIL RETURNS ARE REQUESTED

APPENDIX C: CHAPTER VII

FOREIGN CURRENCY ISSUES IN LONDON: MARCH 1963-APRIL 1967

MARCH 25, 1963-MARCH 24, 1964

Date	Company	Amount	Security
12.7.63	Autostrade-Concessionie	15,000,000	$5\frac{1}{2}$% Guaranteed Bonds 1972-78
15.1.64	Norges Kommunalbank	10,000,000	$5\frac{3}{4}$% 20-year External Loan of 1964
29.1.64	Austria (Republic of)	18,000,000	6% Bonds 1979-84
5.2.64	Wolfson Clore Mayer Corp. Ltd.	5,000,000	$6\frac{1}{2}$% Debenture Stock 1983-88
12.2.64	Oslo (City of)	15,000,000	$5\frac{3}{4}$% Bonds 1964
12.2.64	Copenhagen Telephone Co. Ltd.	12,000,000	$5\frac{3}{4}$% External Loan 1970-84
28.2.64	Takeda Chemical Industries Ltd.	15,000,000	6% Convertible Debentures (due March 31, 1984)
6.3.64	Teijin Ltd.	10,000,000	$6\frac{1}{4}$% Convertible Unsecured Debentures 1974-84
18.3.64	Mortgage Bank of the Kingdom of Denmark	12,000,000	$5\frac{5}{8}$% Bonds of 1964 Ser. XIX

$U.S.112,000,000

MARCH 25, 1964-MARCH 24, 1965

Date	Company	Amount	Security
25.3.64	Tyssefaldene Hydro-Electric Power Co.	10,000,000	6% 1st Mortgage Loan 1974-84
25.3.64	Itoh (C) & Co. Ltd.	12,500,000	$6\frac{1}{4}$% Convertible Unsecured Debentures 1984
3.4.64	Denmark (Kingdom of)	25,000,000	$5\frac{1}{2}$% 20-year External Loan of 1964
4.5.64	Jutland Telephone Co. Ltd.	10,000,000	$5\frac{3}{4}$% Bonds of 1964
11.5.64	Norway (Kingdom of)	25,000,000	$5\frac{1}{2}$% 20-year External Loan of 1964
5.6.64	Toyo Rayon Co. Ltd.	15,000,000	$6\frac{1}{4}$% Convertible Bonds of 1964
19.6.64	Rautaruukki Oy (Ironworks Co. Ltd.)	8,000,000	$6\frac{1}{4}$% 15-year External Loan of 1964
26.6.64	I.R.I. (Institute per la Ricostruzione)	25,000,000	$5\frac{3}{4}$% Bonds of 1964 due 1975-79

Date	Company	Amount	Security
26.6.64	Denmark (Associated Municipalities of)	15,000,000	$5\frac{3}{4}$% 20-year External Loan of 1964
3.7.64	Portugal (Republic of)	20,000,000	$5\frac{3}{4}$% Bonds 1979-84
7.7.64	Midtkraft Electricity	8,000,000	$5\frac{3}{4}$% Bonds 1979
10.7.64	Hitachi Ltd.	10,000,000	$6\frac{1}{4}$% Convertible Unsecured Loan Stock 1979
5.10.64	Komatsu Manufacturing Co. Ltd.	10,000,000	$6\frac{1}{2}$% Convertible Unsecured Debentures 1984
5.10.64	Rauma-Repola Oy	10,000,000	$6\frac{1}{2}$% 15-year External Loan of 1964
9.10.64	Bergen (City of)	10,000,000	$5\frac{1}{2}$% 20-year External Loan of 1964
9.11.64	Roldal-Suldal Kraft	15,000,000	$5\frac{3}{4}$% 20-year Secured Debenture Loan 1964
13.11.64	European Coal & Steel Community	30,000,000	$5\frac{1}{4}$% 20-year Bonds of 1964
18.1.65	Norwegian State & Municipal Power Consort	25,000,000	$5\frac{3}{4}$% 20-year External Loan of 1965
25.1.65	Ericsson (L.M.) Telefonaktiebolaget	20,000,000	$6\frac{1}{2}$% Loan 1986
22.2.65	Cassa Per Ll Mezzogiorno Southern Italy Development Fund	20,000,000	6% Guaranteed Bonds 1985

$U.S.323,500,000

MARCH 25, 1965-MARCH 24, 1966

Date	Company	Amount	Security
25.3.65	Norway (Kingdom of)	30,000,000	$5\frac{1}{2}$% 20-year External Loan 1965
5.5.65	Australia (Commonwealth of)	25,000,000	20-year $5\frac{1}{2}$% Bonds due 1.5.85
11.6.65	Asea (Allmanna Svenska)	1,500,000	6% 15-year External Unsecured Loan of 1965
8.7.65	New Zealand	20,000,000	20-year $5\frac{3}{4}$% Bonds due 1.7.85
25.10.65	Roldal-Suldal Kraft A/S	15,000,000	$6\frac{1}{4}$% 20-year Secured Debenture Loan of 1965
9.11.65	Australia (Commonwealth of)	25,000,000	20-year $5\frac{3}{4}$% Bonds due 1.11.85
15.11.65	Copenhagen (City of)	15,000,000	6% 20-year External Loan of 1965
24.1.66	Mortgage Bank of the Kingdom of Denmark	12,000,000	$6\frac{1}{4}$% 20-year External Loan of 1966 Serv. XX
31.1.66	S.G.I. International Holdings S.A.	15,000,000	$6\frac{1}{2}$% Guaranteed Bonds 1980
21.2.66	S.G.I. International Holdings S.A.	5,000,000	$6\frac{1}{2}$% Guaranteed Bonds 1980 Second series
28.2.66	Transalpine Finance Holdings S.A.	27,500,000	$6\frac{1}{2}$% Loan 1985
14.3.66	Ericsson (L.M.) Telefonaktiebolaget	20,000,000	$6\frac{1}{2}$% Loan 1986
18.3.66	New Zealand	15,000,000	20 year $6\frac{1}{2}$% Bonds due 15.3.86

$U.S.226,000,000

MARCH 25, 1966-MARCH 24, 1967

Date	Company	Amount	Security
16.5.66	International Utilities Overseas Capital Corpn.	12,000,000	$5\frac{1}{4}$% Guaranteed Convertible Bonds 1986
26.5.66	Jutland Telephone Co. Ltd.	5,000,000	$5\frac{3}{4}$% Bonds of 1964 Second Series
13.6.66	European Coal & Steel Community	15,000,000	$6\frac{1}{2}$% 20-year Bonds of 1966
11.7.66	Austrian Electricity Guaranteed Loan 1986	15,000,000	$6\frac{5}{8}$% Bonds 1986
18.7.66	Transalpine Finance Holdings S.A.	20,000,000	$6\frac{3}{4}$% Loan of 1985
19.7.66	Beecham International Holdings S.A.	15,000,000	$5\frac{1}{2}$% Guaranteed Convertible Debentures 1981
16.9.66	New Zealand	10,000,000	10-year 7% Bonds due 15.9.76
19.9.66	Philips International Finance S.A.	25,000,000	$6\frac{3}{4}$% Loan 1976

Date	Company	Amount	Security
17.10.66	Kockums Mekaniska Verkstads	5,000,000	6¾% 10-year Guaranteed External Loan of 1966
28.11.66	European Coal & Steel Community	20,000,000	6½% Bonds of 1966 due 1.12.86
19.12.66	British Petroleum Co. Ltd.	25,000,000	6¾% Loan 1978
6.2.67	Norwegian State & Municipal Power Consortium	15,000,000	6¾% 10-year External Loan of 1967
20.2.67	Transalpine Finance Holdings S.A.	30,000,000	6¾% Loan 1982
21.2.67	Nacional Financiera S.A.	20,000,000	7¼% External Loan due 1972
24.2.67	European Coal & Steel Community	25,000,000	6½% Bonds of 1967 due 1.3.87
27.2.67	Mortgate Bank of the Kingdom of Denmark	12,000,000	6¾% 15-year External Loan of 1967 Ser. XXII
15.3.67	Imperial Chemical Industries Ltd.	30,000,000	6½% Bonds 1982
20.3.67	Austria (Republic of)	22,500,000	6¾% Bonds 1982

$U.S.321,500,000

AFTER MARCH 25, 1967

18.4.67	Copenhagen (City of)	25,000,000	6¼% 20-year Eighth Century Loan of 1967

APPENDIX D: CHAPTER VII

TABLE 29

BORROWING ON THE EURO-BOND MARKET

(U.S. $m.)

	1963	(%)	1964	(%)	1965	(%)	1966	(%)	1967 1st Quarter	(%)
By borrower:										
U.S.	—	(—)	—	(—)	331	(32)	540	(56)	279	(39)
E.E.C. institutions	5	(4)	187	(29)	51	(5)	101	(10)	70	(10)
Italy	—	(—)	46	(7)	80	(8)	40	(4)	25	(3)
Scandinavia	33	(25)	149	(23)	187	(18)	90	(9)	89	(12)
U.K.	73	(54)	—	(—)	46	(4)	25	(3)	30	(4)
Other	23	(17)	271	(41)	352	(33)	172	(18)	230	(32)
TOTAL	134	(100)	653	(100)	1,047	(100)	968	(100)	723	(100)
By currency:										
U.S.$	72	(54)	468	(72)	504	(48)	832	(86)	590	(81)
DM	—	(—)	149	(23)	321	(31)	42	(4)	79	(11)
Units of Account	48	(36)	10	(1)	—	(—)	74	(8)	—	(—)
Swiss fcs.	14	(10)	—	(—)	—	(—)	—	(—)	34	(5)
£/DM	—	(—)	—	(—)	11	(1)	20	(2)	20	(3)
Other	—	(—)	26	(4)	211	(20)	—	(—)	—	(—)
TOTAL	134	(100)	653	(100)	1,047	(100)	968	(100)	723	(100)

Figures have been extracted from a variety of published sources.

CHAPTER VIII

A. TRANSPORT (SHIPPING)

156. Foreign earnings from transport services in the case of the United Kingdom are naturally derived from shipping and aviation. Until the early 1950's the first was a significant earner of foreign exchange; and aviation has become one. Shipping is treated in the first part of this chapter; aviation in the second part.

157. The merchant fleet owned and registered in the United Kingdom amounted to 17·4 million gross registered tons in June 1966 and was just over three million tons less than the United Kingdom registered fleet, which includes Commonwealth owned ships and ships owned by Commonwealth associates of United Kingdom companies. It has been thought convenient to analyse the fleet itself since 1958 and TABLE 30 contains a breakdown into categories, both foreign-going and coasting and home trade.

158. Over this period, the foreign-going liner fleet has fallen by almost 1½ million gross tons and, although a split between passenger-cargo and cargo liners is not available for 1958-60, it is clear that the greater part of the decrease has been in passenger tonnage. The deep-sea tramp and tanker sections have both increased, particularly the latter, so that the total foreign-going fleet has grown over the period by about 400,000 tons. Among the coasting and home-trade ships the three categories (liners, tramps and tankers) have all decreased, so that the total is now under one million tons. The result is that the grand total for the whole fleet has remained at a fairly constant level of just over 17 million tons for the past nine years.

159. Over these years the active world fleet has grown from about 100 million gross tons to 155 million tons. Among the major increases of fleets by flag are Japan (an increase of approximately 8 million tons), Liberia (10·5 million tons), Norway (7 million tons) and the U.S.S.R. (5·5 million tons). The steady growth of world sea-borne trade has therefore been accompanied by an immense amount of building of more efficient tonnage. Competition has intensified and freight earnings have been under pressure, while costs generally have continued to rise. Other factors affecting profitability have been the continuing practices in large parts of the world of flag discrimination in its varied forms.

160. The contribution made by the British shipowning industry—that is, shipowning companies which are resident in this country, but not those which are resident in other parts of the Commonwealth—to the invisible side of the balance of payments relates to United Kingdom shipping companies. It includes figures relating to the companies' own ships (the United Kingdom owned and registered fleet as shown in TABLE 30), together

TABLE 30

MERCHANT SHIPS OWNED AND REGISTERED IN THE UNITED KINGDOM

	June 30, 1958	June 30, 1959	June 30, 1960	June 30, 1961	June 30, 1962	June 30, 1963	June 30, 1964	June 30, 1965	June 30, 1966
FOREIGN GOING									
Passenger-Cargo Liners									
No.	—	—	—	157	136	127	116	116	89
g.t. (000)	—	—	—	2,372	2,176	2,072	1,948	1,917	1,598
Average age (years)	—	—	—	14·7	14·2	14·5	15·1	15·9	15·6
Cargo Liners									
No.	—	—	—	904	883	843	800	787	784
g.t. (000)	—	—	—	5,987	5,886	5,688	5,468	5,459	5,602
Average age (years)	—	—	—	11·5	11·4	11·4	11·3	11·5	12·2
Total Liners									
No.	1,131	1,120	1,077	1,061	1,019	970	916	903	873
g.t. (000)	8,658	8,647	8,376	8,359	8,062	7,760	7,416	7,376	7,200
Average age (years)	12·5	12·6	12·8	12·4	12·2	12·2	12·3	12·7	12·9
Tramps									
No.	468	471	440	452	450	419	398	393	375
g.t. (000)	2,765	2,845	2,790	2,911	3,041	2,989	2,923	3,081	3,201
Average age (years)	9·5	8·7	7·4	7·2	7·2	6·6	6·8	6·7	6·6
Tankers									
No.	452	459	464	416	391	366	348	327	325
g.t. (000)	4,641	4,951	5,346	5,188	5,304	5,493	5,690	5,782	6,079
Average age (years)	8·4	8·0	7·4	6·9	6·6	6·4	6·4	6·4	6·7
Total Foreign-going									
No.	2,051	2,050	1,981	1,929	1,860	1,755	1,662	1,623	1,573
g.t. (000)	16,064	16,443	16,512	16,458	16,407	16,242	16,029	16,239	16,481
Average age (years)	10·8	10·6	10·1	9·7	9·4	9·2	9·2	9·3	9·4

	June 30, 1958	June 30, 1959	June 30, 1960	June 30, 1961	June 30, 1962	June 30, 1963	June 30, 1964	June 30, 1965	June 30, 1966
COASTING AND HOME TRADE									
Liners									
No.	315	302	292	282	276	258	243	251	236
g.t. (000)	437	396	388	378	378	358	342	356	350
Average age (years)	16·1	15·5	15·6	15·5	15·1	15·3	14·7	14·8	14·4
Tramps									
No.	599	542	506	472	455	440	407	409	391
g.t. (000)	639	571	514	472	477	468	442	452	443
Average age (years)	13·3	12·4	12·1	12·8	12·9	13·4	13·6	13·2	12·8
Tankers									
No.	133	138	140	142	140	141	137	120	115
g.t. (000)	102	107	111	113	112	116	114	104	93
Average age (years)	15·2	14·8	15·4	14·4	14·7	14·7	15·4	15·0	13·6
Total Coasting and Home Trade									
No.	1,047	982	938	896	871	839	788	780	742
g.t. (000)	1,178	1,074	1,013	963	967	942	898	913	886
Average age (years)	14·5	13·8	13·8	14·0	14·0	14·2	14·3	14·0	13·5
GRAND TOTAL									
o.	3,098	3,032	2,919	2,825	2,731	2,594	2,450	2,403	2,315
g.t. (000)	17,242	17,517	17,525	17,421	17,374	17,184	16,927	17,152	17,367
Average age (years)	11·0	10·8	10·3	10·0	9·7	9·5	9·5	9·6	9·6

The average ages are based on tonnage.

with those relating to the foreign tonnage time-chartered to those companies.
161. For balance of payments purposes, imports and exports are both valued f.o.b. and the recipient of the goods is deemed ultimately to bear the freight. The effect of this is that payments for freight on U.K. imports carried in foreign ships and receipts for freight on U.K. exports carried in U.K. ships are included in the balance of payments. But freight on imports carried in U.K. ships and on exports carried in foreign ships is excluded, because the former involves transactions between U.K. residents and the latter between non-residents.

TABLE 31

GROSS EARNINGS OF UNITED KINGDOM SHIPPING ENGAGED IN OVERSEAS TRADE

	1958 (a) £m.	1959 (b) £m.	1960 (b) £m.	1961 (b) £m.	1962 (a) £m.	1963 (b) £m.	1964 (b) £m.	1965 (b) £m.
Receipts:								
Freight on U.K. imports	235	244	256	250	243	241	236	240
Freight on U.K. exports	150	148	148	148	135	141	146	161
Freight on cross voyages	338	328	337	341	348	355	374	391
Total freights	723	720	741	739	726	737	756	793
Passage money collected in U.K.	28	27	25	27	33	33	34	36
Passage money collected abroad	51	49	50	46	47	49	49	52
Time-Charter hire from abroad	23	24	24	28	32	27	35	40
Time-Charter hire from U.K. non-shipowners	8	N/A	N/A	N/A	15	N/A	N/A	N/A
Total receipts	834	820	840	840	853	846	874	921
Disbursements abroad:								
Bunkers (c)	99	92	89	89	88	88	81	81
Canal dues	18	18	23	23	23	22	23	25
Port and other expenditure	174	181	186	195	199	197	206	218
Time-Charter hire	137	149	172	180	180	182	187	185
Total disbursements abroad	428	440	470	487	490	489	497	509

(a) Results of complete inquiry.
(b) Estimates based on sample inquiries.
(c) The cost of bunkers taken abroad, whether or not paid for in the United Kingdom.

162. TABLES 31 and 32 give the gross earnings of United Kingdom shipping engaged in overseas trade and the contribution of United Kingdom shipping to invisible exports[1] together with the net expenditure by the United Kingdom on overseas shipping and the resultant balance on total shipping account. The gross earnings of the British shipping industry increased by about £105 million between 1958 and 1965 (allowing for an estimated growth in time charter hire receipts from U.K. non-shipowners) but this increase has been accompanied by an approximately equivalent rise in expenditure abroad, particularly "port and other expenditure" and "time-charter hire." The net contribution to invisible exports has followed a U-shaped curve, the fall from £128 million to £72 million having been followed by a rise to £137 million. The major increase in earnings from abroad has been in freights on cross-voyages.

1. This contribution in Table 32 is based on Chamber of Shipping definitions.

126

Table 32

I CONTRIBUTION OF THE UNITED KINGDOM SHIPPING INDUSTRY TO INVISIBLE EXPORTS

II NET EXPENDITURE BY THE UNITED KINGDOM ON OVERSEAS SHIPPING

I	1958	1959	1960	1961 (b) £m.	1962 (a) £m.	1963 (b) £m.	1964 (b) £m.	1965 (b) £m.
Receipts from abroad:								
Freight on U.K. exports	150	148	148	148	135	141	146	161
Freight on cross voyages	338	328	337	341	348	355	374	391
Passage money from non-U.K. nationals	54	52	53	48	50	51	52	55
Time-Charter hire	23	24	24	28	32	27	35	40
Total	565	552	562	565	565	574	607	647
Disbursements abroad:								
Bunkers (c)								
Canal dues	300	299	304	313	313	309	313	325
Port and other expenditure								
Time-Charter hire	137	149	172	180	180	182	187	185
Total	437	448	476	493	493	491	500	510
Net contribution to invisible exports (d) (e)	128	104	86	72	72	83	107	137

II EXPENDITURE BY THE UNITED KINGDOM ON OVERSEAS SHIPPING (f)

				1961 £m.	1962 £m.	1963 £m.	1964 £m.	1965 £m.
Freight on U.K. imports	143	151	189	175	169	188	228	228
Passage money from U.K. nationals	6	7	6	7	6	8	10	10
	149	158	195	182	175	196	238	238
Disbursements in the U.K. by overseas shipping	64	66	72	74	82	89	97	105
Net expenditure	85	92	123	108	93	107	141	133
Balance on shipping account (g)	+43	+12	—37	—36	—21	—24	—34	+4

(a) Results of complete inquiry.
(b) Estimates based on sample inquiries.
(c) The cost of bunkers taken abroad, whether or not paid for in the United Kingdom.
(d) The "net contribution to invisible exports" is the total of the amounts of freight, passage money and charter hire which the United Kingdom shipping industry earned abroad less the total amount of disbursements (including time charter hire paid to foreign tonnage) which it incurred abroad.
(e) Freights earned by the industry in carrying imports to this country, which represent a saving of foreign exchange rather than a direct contribution to invisible exports, are not credited in these calculations, even though related foreign disbursements are debited.
(f) Estimates made by the Government and published in the Shipping table in "United Kingdom Balance of Payments."
(g) The difference between the net contribution to invisible exports by the United Kingdom shipping industry and the net expenditure by this country for the use of overseas shipping. The small discrepancies between these figures and the net balances in "United Kingdom Balance of Payments" are due in the main to small differences of definition.

163. The net contribution to invisibles by British shipping is however only one part of the "shipping" section in the country's balance of payments account. The other part is the net expenditure by this country on the employment of foreign shipping to bring that part of our imports not carried by the British shipping industry. This net expenditure has moved up from £85 million to £133 million so that the balance on total shipping account dropped into deficit in 1960 and continued in deficit until 1965 when a small surplus reappeared. The provisional figures for 1966 suggest that this improved trend is continuing.

164. The trades in which the British shipping industry is engaged affect in a complementary fashion these two parts in the shipping account in the

balance of payments. The net expenditure by this country on the use of foreign shipping to bring our imports would be reduced if more of our own shipping were employed in these trades. In that event, however, those ships would be earning less in the export or cross-trades so that the net contribution of British shipping to the balance of payments might remain unchanged.

165. The Committee concerned itself with two main issues in examining the earnings of the shipping industry. One was the basis and reliability of the balance of payments statistics. The other was the reason for the drop in net earnings. First the statistics. Earnings of British shipping in carrying imports to Britain are regarded as transactions between residents and are therefore excluded from the final figures, though they play an important part in the process of estimation. On the credit side of the payments balance are recorded freights earned by British shipping in the export trade and in cross trades, passenger revenue, receipts from time charters, and the expenditure of foreign ships in British ports. The corresponding debit items are earnings of foreign-owned ships carrying British imports, passenger fares paid by British residents to overseas shipping companies, payments for time charter hire, and disbursements by British ships in overseas ports.

166. The main sources of information are studies by the Chamber of Shipping, and by the Board of Trade, and this is supplemented by information derived from Exchange Control records.

THE CHAMBER OF SHIPPING RETURNS

167. The chamber has conducted full scale enquiries, with a more than 99 per cent response rate in 1947, 1952, 1958 and 1962 and another is being undertaken for 1966. For intervening years since 1959 a sample has been taken. The following information is provided:

(i) Freight earnings from imports, exports and cross trades.
(ii) Passage money.
(iii) Time charter receipts and payments.
(iv) Disbursements abroad, subdivided into:
    (a) Bunkers,
    (b) Canal dues, and
    (c) Other expenditure.

168. Figures for freights are compiled for each country (or pair of countries in the case of cross trades) and passenger receipts and disbursements abroad are also analysed by country, though none of these figures are published.

BOARD OF TRADE ESTIMATES

169. The Board of Trade studies are concerned mainly with estimating the earnings by foreign ships carrying British imports, and the expenditure of foreign shipping in British ports. For the disbursements of foreign ships in British ports, the Board of Trade estimates payments for stevedoring; port and pilotage dues; repairs; agency fees; stores; and crews' spending. These are based mainly on occasional enquiries with adjustments for known

changes in prices, wages, etc., between enquiries. Information on payment for bunkers is provided by the Ministry of Power.

170. An estimate of passenger fares paid to overseas shipowners is compiled by the Bank of England from Exchange Control records.

171. Improvements in the collection of shipping statistics are still continuing. The Chamber of Shipping inquiry relating to 1966 is again introducing a number of new refinements (on passenger expenditure, disbursements abroad, fares, etc.). The Chamber of Shipping also informed the Committee that it was not entirely satisfied with the figures showing the shipping industry's contribution to the balance of payments. It was, therefore, in the process of undertaking an examination of the basis of the shipping account, with particular reference to the following:

(a) The proper allocation of foreign tonnage time-chartered by British owners (i.e. should it belong to the section of United Kingdom expenditure on overseas shipping).

(b) The question of any foreign tonnage time-chartered in from abroad by United Kingdom non-shipowners, which, if employed in export or cross-trades, is outside the present scope of the shipping account.

(c) The question of foreign tonnage voyage chartered for export and cross trades by both United Kingdom shipowners and non-shipowners which also does not come within the ambit of the shipping account.

(d) The basis of calculating freights on cargoes carried by tanker companies (either in their own or time-chartered tonnage) for their oil company parents.

172. In the light of this statistical investigation, which was still proceeding as the Committee prepared its report, the Committee did not feel able to comment in detail on the shipping statistics. But it came to two general conclusions about possible improvements.

RECOMMENDATIONS

173. 1. The Committee recommends that more of the information already collected should now be published. In particular this might be done for the earnings of liners, tramps and tankers separately. It is suggested that talks might take place between the Central Statistical Office and the Chamber of Shipping about the kind of breakdown that might be provided without disclosing confidential information about individual firms.

2. The Committee recommends that efforts be made to get shipping statistics available earlier, although the Committee recognizes that there are practical difficulties involved and earlier figures might produce inaccuracies. The results of the Chamber of Shipping surveys (both the annual samples and the periodical full-scale inquiries) are not available until some time after the end of the year to which they refer. This is a clear handicap in the preparation of quarterly figures. Any progress that can be made without

throwing an unreasonable amount of extra work on the shipping companies would be welcome.

174. The second major issue considered by the Committee was the drop in the net earnings of the U.K. shipping industry since the beginning of the 1960s. As shown in TABLE 32 the net shipping account was in surplus throughout the 1950s and, after moving into deficit between 1960 and 1964, managed to produce a small surplus in 1965 and a further one in 1966. The large surpluses of the early 1950's, however, have clearly gone. Part of the explanation seems to lie in certain structural changes. In the first place, as mentioned earlier, world tonnage has been rising faster than British tonnage. This has been true in recent years; it has been equally true over the past fifty years. World tonnage has increased five times since 1914, while British tonnage has roughly doubled.

175. Secondly there has been a significant change in the pattern of our external trade. TABLES 33 and 34 bring this out. By and large, freights are rather more closely related to the weight of the cargo than to its value. In 1966 British exports (including coal) amounted to only 34 million tons whereas imports weighed 163·5 million tons, a ratio of almost 1 to 5. During the period 1958-66 the weight of exports increased by 14 per cent. Imports rose by 57 per cent so that the basic imbalance in the volume of U.K. trade seems to be increasing. This has also been a long-term trend. Since 1914 import tonnages have doubled, while export tonnages have actually declined. This remarkable change can only be explained by the technological strides made by industry in recent years and the increasing sophistication of the country's output and exports. The heavy bulky low-value items of earlier years have given way to highly processed, lighter and more valuable products. Coal, iron and steel, and textiles together comprised 44 per cent of exports in 1913, and no more than 13 per cent in 1964. In the case of imports, particularly of food and raw materials their volume seems likely to grow, with the rise in population and living standards. The recent increase in oil imports is also likely to continue.

TABLE 33

UNITED KINGDOM EXPORTS

(000 tons)

	1958	1959	1960	1961	1962	1963	1964	1965	1966
Exports	23,496	24,277	25,140	23,406	26,232	27,999	26,098	28,291	30,037
Re-Exports	751	796	518	479	533	498	305	318	334
Total (exc. coal)	24,247	25,073	25,658	23,885	26,765	28,497	26,403	28,609	30,371
Coal Exports	5,763	4,986	6,789	7,139	6,539	10,024	7,387	4,822	3,752

Source: Liverpool Steam Ship Owners' Association.

CLEARANCES WITH CARGO

(000 tons net)

	1958	1959	1960	1961	1962	1963	1964	1965	1966
British Ships	32,140	33,124	32,698	32,594	32,590	32,375	31,524	31,222	28,308
Foreign Ships	19,252	20,828	22,108	21,083	23,727	26,034	26,303	26,545	30,060
Total	51,392	53,952	54,806	53,677	56,317	58,409	57,827	57,767	28,368
% British	63	61	60	61	58	55	55	54	48

Source: Board of Trade.

Table 34

UNITED KINGDOM IMPORTS

(000 tons)

	1958	1959	1960	1961	1962	1963	1964	1965	1966
Food, Beverages and Tobacco	21,300	21,500	20,300	20,300	22,200	20,200	20,200	20,400	19,700
Basic Materials	29,300	30,200	38,300	33,600	30,800	33,200	39,800	40,100	35,400
Mineral Fuels and Lubricants	47,300	53,700	60,200	62,400	70,300	75,500	80,000	87,400	97,400
Manufactured Goods	6,300	6,500	9,400	8,400	8,700	9,800	11,700	11,500	11,000
Total	104,200	111,900	128,200	124,800	132,000	138,700	151,700	159,400	163,500

Source: Liverpool Steam Ship Owners' Association.

ENTRANCES WITH CARGO

(000 tons net)

	1958	1959	1960	1961	1962	1963	1964	1965	1966
British Ships	41,668	43,309	44,886	45,849	46,788	48,059	49,675	49,381	43,404
Foreign Ships	38,197	41,470	46,739	45,857	48,645	50,029	54,183	58,852	65,024
Total	79,865	84,779	91,625	91,706	95,433	98,088	103,858	108,233	108,428
% British	52	51	49	50	49	49	48	46	40

Source: Board of Trade.

176. The effect of all this on the foreign exchange earnings of the British shipping industry is clear. Since incomes relate to the volume rather than the value of consignments, the total of freights charged on imports is now about 50 per cent more than that on exports. And as British ships handle just under half of all incoming and outgoing cargoes, the balance of foreign payments and receipts has moved against Britain.

177. Thirdly, as TABLES 33 and 34 also show, the British proportion of clearances and entrances with British cargo is clearly declining. Between 1955 and 1966 the share of British clearances dropped from 63 per cent to 48 per cent and that of British entrances from 52 per cent to 40 per cent. Although, in this context, British includes United Kingdom, Commonwealth and Eire tonnage, United Kingdom tonnage is the main constituent. However, these entrances and clearances are in net tonnages and some qualification is necessary as the contribution, in balance of payments terms, of different types of ship may vary considerably. A more accurate measure of the proportion of the carryings by United Kingdom ships in our export and import trades was recently made available by the Board of Trade for the year 1965 (see TABLE 35). It will be noticed that United Kingdom ships carry a greater proportion of our import and export trades by value than by weight (for example, by value 55 per cent of British imports and 61 per cent of British exports are carried in British ships).

178. Finally, over the long period another important structural factor has been the change in re-exports. This was once a purely entrepot trade, mainly linking the American and European ports, reaching its peak at the end of the last century. It was a traffic that, historically, was bound to decline. As other nations acquired their own fleets and ocean passages became quicker and more reliable, it was inevitable that transiting through the U.K. should

TABLE 35

UNITED KINGDOM SEABORNE TRADE—1965

WEIGHT AND VALUE, AND PROPORTIONS IN UNITED KINGDOM REGISTERED SHIPS

Imports	Weight		Value	
	Total Weight of Imports by Sea (mn. tons)	Propn. in U.K. Ships	Total Value of Imports by Sea (£mn.)	Propn. in U.K. Ships
Bulk cargoes	42·8	46%	778	39%
Other dry cargoes	26·9	49%	3,698	60%
Total dry cargoes	69·7	47%	4,476	57%
Tanker cargoes	87·1	38%	615	40%
All cargoes	156·8	42%	5,090	55%

Exports	Weight		Value	
	Total Weight of Exports by Sea (mn. tons)	Propn. in U.K. Ships	Total Value of Exports by Sea (£mn.)	Propn. in U.K. Ships
Bulk cargoes	6·9	29%	42	28%
Other dry cargoes	16·6	51%	3,856	62%
Total dry cargoes	23·5	44%	3,898	61%
Tanker cargoes	10·8	66%	99	69%
All cargoes	34·3	51%	3,997	61%

be abandoned. Re-exports, which accounted for over 20 per cent of total British exports in the 1870s, fell away in the inter-war period to around 15 per cent and, after 1945, dwindled further, amounting to just over 5 per cent of total exports in 1964. The disappearance of this trade did not affect the visible balance, since it was for all intents and purposes an entry on both sides of the ledger. However, being largely in the hands of British merchants, consignments in the re-export trade, moved generally in British bottoms; and, being bulky cargoes, they earned more in total. The closure of this traffic therefore directly affected British shipping income. Of itself it may have accounted for 7 per cent of the fall in the British share of entrances and clearances from British ports, with a consequent adverse change in the balance of shipping payments.

179. These four factors help to explain some of the decline in foreign earnings from shipping. They do not, in the view of the Committee, necessarily explain the whole of the decline. The Committee was conscious, however, that in any attempt to pursue these questions and to provide appropriate recommendations, it would be in danger of duplicating the work of the special Committee of Inquiry into shipping set up, under the chairmanship of Lord Rochdale, by the President of the Board of Trade earlier this year. Its terms of reference were as follows: "To review, in the light of current commercial and technological developments, the organization and structure of the U.K. shipping industry, its methods of operation and any other factors which affect its efficiency and competitiveness; and to recommend what action should be taken by shipowners, seafarers and Government to bring about changes which would improve the position of the industry in these respects. The Committee is to be concerned primarily with the shipping activities of persons resident in the United Kingdom, though it may take into account, to the extent that it finds them relevant,

similar activities of other persons in respect of any ship registered in the United Kingdom. The Committee is to have regard to the international character of the industry, including the effects of the actions and regulations of foreign and other Commonwealth governments and to the nature of the relations between governments on shipping matters. The Committee should also take account of the first and subsequent Reports of Lord Pearson's Court of Inquiry into certain matters concerning the shipping industry."

180. The Committee on Invisible Exports, in deciding not to duplicate the work to be undertaken by the new Committee of Inquiry, nevertheless felt it necessary to suggest the examination of certain points emphasized to it both by the shipping industry and others:

1. Some examination is clearly needed of the expenditure of British traders, etc., on foreign vessels. That there is scope for saving in foreign currency through shipping is made clear from the invisible export returns for the industry, showing that about £200 million was spent on time charter hire paid abroad in 1964, most for foreign tankers. In addition, more than £200 million was spent on import freights in foreign ships, mainly liners and tramps. Insufficient is known at present to be certain why there are not sufficient British ships to enable these two main items of expenditure to be substantially reduced.

2. There is a general feeling that most exporting firms prefer to sell goods on f.o.b. terms as presenting the least difficulties and as meeting the preference of overseas buyers. The United Kingdom, however, imports more commodities and goods, both by value and by volume, than it exports and this gives the United Kingdom traders generally a very extensive influence to determine the form of quotation under which the goods are shipping. It is said that it would be of great help and encouragement to British shipowners if United Kingdom exporters and importers of goods tried to sell c.i.f. and buy f.o.b. whenever possible. Their success would give them control over the shipment of cargoes with a consequent ability to use British ships if and when available. This question needs considering.

3. There was strong criticism in the shipping industry of the cheap credit made available to foreign buyers in U.K. shipyards because of E.C.G.D. facilities. The shipping industry argued that, where the trading opportunities existed, the operation of a British owned ship contributed more foreign currency to the United Kingdom balance of payments than did the sale of a similar ship on E.C.G.D. terms to a foreign owner. British shipowners believed that, in the national interest, they ought to have had access to shipbuilding finance on the same terms as foreign owners who build in United Kingdom yards. This position has now been rectified by the home credits made available under the Shipbuilding Industry Act.

4. A major factor in determining the amount of investment in British

shipping is the application of government fiscal policy and its effect on the industry. The combination of corporation tax, accounting to the Revenue for tax deducted from dividends, and capital grants is said to bear more heavily on shipping than the system of income and profit taxes and investment allowances which prevailed before the 1965 Finance Act.

5. One result of the replacement of the investment allowances by capital grants is to increase the amount of taxes payable by United Kingdom shipping companies in some countries with which the United Kingdom has no double taxation agreement (and the shipping industry is anxious that such agreements should be reached wherever possible). It should be a fundamental aim of the Government to see that the application of capital grants produces no anomalies in its effect on British shipping. This is particularly important in the rapidly developing field of container traffic.

6. Besides measures which can be regarded as coming within the domestic environment of British shipping, it is important that, in the international field, the Government continues to resist the encouragement of flag discrimination and the incursion into international seaborne commerce of fleets subsidized and assisted by the state, and to be alive to the dangers in the actions of certain governments in regulating shipping services in the sole interest of their own foreign commerce.

BALTIC EXCHANGE

181. So far attention has been concentrated on foreign earnings from vessels based on freight, outward, homeward and cross voyages. In addition there is the invisible income arising from the employment of members of the Baltic Exchange, domiciled in the U.K., earning commissions, brokerage, fittages, port agencies, professional fees and payment for services by reason of a contractual relationship with foreign shipowners.

182. The Baltic Mercantile and Shipping Exchange Ltd., commonly known as the Baltic Exchange, was opened in its present form in 1903 and now performs the following functions:

1. As a property company owning and administering[1] the Exchange and offices.
2. As an Exchange for:
   (i) The chartering of both ships and aircraft.
   (ii) The sale and purchase of ships.
   (iii) The sale and purchase of grain and a "futures" market.
   (iv) The sale and purchase of oil and oil seeds.
   (v) Miscellaneous activities connected with the above.

1. The Baltic Exchange as an administrative unit is small. It is organized as a private limited company in which members of the Exchange (700 limited companies comprise the bulk of the members, there being few individual members now) *must* hold shares and representative principals, i.e. the senior staff of member companies, principally directors, and clerks of five years standing *may* hold shares. Some 2,400 individuals, representing member companies, are entitled to use the Exchange.

183. Shippers and merchants in all parts of the world are represented on the Exchange by chartering agents: similarly, practically every deep sea shipowner of every nationality is also represented, either directly or through a broker. The method of doing business is simple. A shipowner's broker, with knowledge that a ship will be empty in a certain port at a certain time, approaches a chartering agent who, he knows, represents shippers of commodities or merchants with interests in that part of the world, and tries to negotiate the chartering or "fixing" of the vessel for a cargo. Similarly chartering agents, with knowledge of the movement of tramp ships, approach shipowners' brokers with the same object. The market is completely free, the charterer taking the vessel most suited to his requirements at the best rate and conditions obtainable. Thus ore from Australia to Japan can be carried in a Norwegian vessel, or grain from the River Plate to the Mediterranean in a Greek-owned vessel registered in Panama, Honduras or Liberia. The nationality of the vessel, places of origin and destination of the cargo have little or no bearing on the contract of carriage.

184. Changes, of course, are taking place. Bulk carriers are now being built which will carry in one bottom with hardly any increase in crew, four, five and six times the amount hitherto carried in one post-war conventional tramp.

185. The development of such ports as Rotterdam, Tilbury and others elsewhere is encouraging shipowners to build and fix bulk carriers: until the National Ports Council can authorize and build suitable ports in the right parts of the U.K. imports of bulk cargo may continue to be transhipped to, say, 5,000-ton vessels, possibly specially built for the individual trade. As a result of all this it is possible that, with increasing long-term contracts, there may be less *ad hoc* chartering and the role of the Baltic broker may change.

186. As for the market for the sale and purchase of ships, this is fully international in character. Members operating on this market as sale and purchase brokers also maintain information services to their clients and keep in touch with shipbuilding developments. In addition members in this market act as valuers of ships on a wide scale.

187. The market operates through the activities of about half a dozen specialist companies and a score or so of other broking companies which maintain a department for the sale and purchase of ships.

188. The commissions earned by U.K. sale and purchase brokers on the sale of ships to, from and between foreign shipowners is obviously an invisible export: in addition, such brokers have large sums of purchase money emanating from foreign shipowners lying to their credit in London banks pending completion of the sale which are utilized on the money market.

189. Since the founding of an international air market on the Baltic in 1947, a great deal of varied business has taken place, on a similar basis to the Baltic Exchange shipping market. Employment is found for British and foreign aircraft and aircraft sought for freight or passengers on a full or part load single user basis from specified points to specified points. Airbrokers

representing over a hundred operators, both I.A.T.A. airlines and independents, by making contact with users or their agents on the market, arrange loads (either cargo or passengers as required by the operators) on the basis of a Charter Party at rates and on terms which fluctuate freely. Primarily *ad hoc* business is the speciality of the market, such as, for example, the rapid movement of urgently required cargo, ships' spares, ships' crews, football teams, parties of men needed quickly for emergencies, etc., but much forward work for series of flights or contract work is included as well as many charters to cover inclusive tour holidays. Obviously freight or hire and brokerage accrue to sterling credit where foreign charterers come to the market to fix British aircraft and where British and foreign aircraft are fixed in cross trades.

190. There are three principal developments at present. First the evolution of larger aircraft both for passengers and cargo; second the rapidly increasing use of specialized all-freight aircraft with a pallet and/or container capability; third the continuing expansion of the air tourist market. There seems to be no reason to believe that the services of Baltic brokers should diminish as a result of these changes.

191. The Committee found that no official estimate had been published of the foreign earnings of the members of the Baltic Exchange separately from other foreign earnings of financial and allied institutions. Nor had any recent attempt been made to compare turnover on the Baltic with other shipping centres abroad. The Baltic itself claims to be the only truly international freight market in the world. Other centres deal with specific trading areas, and communist countries, whenever possible, fix their own ships for their own cargoes. Of the reported fixtures, the Committee was informed, almost the whole of those concluded from South Africa, Australia and the River Plate were fixed in the London market. Of the balance, i.e. those from American Atlantic and Pacific coasts, some are concluded by American cable brokers through London, and some by London offices or associated companies of American charterers. This is particularly true of the grain trade. Most Chinese chartering is said to be done through London and fixtures for account of the Indian Government are for the most part fixed in London if they do not concern American flag tonnage. Fixtures outwards from this country and homewards to this country from the Mediterranean are also likely to have been fixed in London if they are reported here at all.

192. The Baltic Exchange, accordingly, is convinced that it accounts for close on two-thirds of the free world's fixtures (i.e. excluding the Soviet block, U.S. tied cargoes and coastal shipping). But in order to assess this for the first time the Baltic Exchange has agreed to undertake a special inquiry. Preliminary inquiries have already begun.

193. In addition the Baltic agreed to initiate a pilot inquiry into the invisible earnings of its members, on behalf of the Committee. This has already been completed.

194. The questionnaire, an analysis of the returns, and the results of the pilot inquiry are set out in detail in Appendix A. They are referred to in Chapter XIII.

195. 1. The Committee recommends that the Baltic Exchange, in collaboration with the Bank of England and the Central Statistical Office, should consider undertaking an inquiry into members' invisible earnings on a regular basis in future.

Lloyd's Register of Shipping
196. Invisible earnings also accrue to the Society known as Lloyd's Register of Shipping. The Society's main activity is the surveying of ships whilst under construction and at intervals throughout their lives to ensure that they are kept up to the right standards. The phrase "A.1 at Lloyd's" is a direct reflection of the classification work done by Lloyd's Register of Shipping which is an independent, non-commercial society whose aim is the establishment of standards of construction and maintenance and the provision of a technical service to enable owners to maintain such standards. Over 1,400 surveyors are employed exclusively by Lloyd's Register of Shipping and the world tonnage classed with the Society exceeded 62 million tons gross in June 1966. Lloyd's Register Book is published annually in four volumes and contains particulars of all known ocean-going merchant ships in the world of 100 tons gross and over, whether classed with Lloyd's Register of Shipping or not, and extensive information about shipowners' fleets, shipbuilders, dry and wet docks, off-shore drilling rigs, refrigerated stores and cargo containers. The Society also publishes Rules and Regulations covering the classification of ships. One side of the Society's activities that is perhaps not so well known concerns the Non-marine work. It provides an extensive international inspection service covering the fabrication and the erection on site of a wide variety of manufactures, notably large pressure vessels and other components for nuclear reactors, oil refineries, power stations, pipelines, water and steam turbines, penstocks, bridging material, etc. Although this work at the moment represents only about 15 per cent of Lloyd's Register's total activities, it is growing as these services become better known.
197. In the financial year ended June 30, 1967, the net foreign currency earnings of Lloyd's Register of Shipping amounted to the equivalent of £3,000,000 compared with £2,750,000 the year before.

B. TRANSPORT (CIVIL AVIATION)
198. The foreign earnings of civil aviation include those of the two nationalized corporations (British European Airways and British Overseas Airways Corporation), which according to the National Plan[1] account for around 80 per cent of the industry's turnover, and those of about 30 privately-owned airlines. From the end of the 1950s onwards the civil aviation account (i.e. not including overseas airlines) produced a significant and growing surplus in the balance of payments. Since 1963 it has levelled off, though remaining above the £20 million mark (see Table 36).
199. The Committee first turned its attention to the statistics. The foreign

1. Cmnd. No. 2764.

earnings of civil aviation comprise (i) receipts by the U.K. airlines from overseas residents for passenger fares, freight, mail and charter lines, and (ii) disbursements in the U.K. by foreign airlines. We deal with each category in turn.

TABLE 36

CIVIL AVIATION

(Balance of Payments Contribution)

£m

	Debit	Credit	Net
1955	40	37	—3
1956	45	44	—1
1957	52	49	—3
1958	60	68	+8
1959	64	82	+18
1960	78	96	+18
1961	85	108	+23
1962	97	118	+21
1963	105	129	+24
1964	117	141	+24
1965	135	158	+23
1966	152	175	+23

RECEIPTS OF FOREIGN CURRENCY BY U.K. AIRLINES

200. In 1965, the foreign receipts of U.K. airlines were estimated at £123 million. This figure was derived from two sources: (a) quarterly returns completed by the two public corporations B.O.A.C. and B.E.A. and (b) the quarterly estimates of the overseas transactions of independent airlines compiled by the Central Statistical Office, in conjunction with the Board of Trade. Since the earnings of B.O.A.C. and B.E.A. totalled £116 million in 1965, the independents accounted for only 6 per cent of the total foreign earnings in that year.

201. Passenger revenue relates to *all* tickets sold *outside* the U.K. and used on British aircraft. No distinction is made between fares paid abroad by U.K. and overseas residents, but it is thought that the small amount of ticket sales to U.K. residents abroad is counterbalanced by sales in the U.K. to overseas residents.

202. Each month a summary of the activities of the aerodromes of the U.K. is published, including details of passengers handled, freight traffic, and aircraft movements by destination and origin. For U.K. operators, separate particulars are given for the public corporations and other airlines. Data is also available on average passenger fares and cargo costs. It is on the basis of this kind of information, on detailed annual figures supplied regularly by a major independent airline and on data supplied on one occasion to the Central Statistical Office by several other independents, that the foreign earnings of all British independents are calculated.

EXPENDITURE BY FOREIGN AIRLINES IN THE U.K.

203. Information on expenditure in the U.K. by overseas airlines (which in 1965 totalled £35 million) is obtained from various sources. It covers such

138

items as (i) all airport charges, (ii) purchases of fuel and stores, (iii) crews' expenses, (iv) office rentals and expenses, (v) salaries and wages of staff at U.K. offices.

204. Initially, a dozen of the more important airlines were approached to provide details of their U.K. expenditures, but while some gave this for one year, few have continued to provide regular information. The C.S.O. currently base their estimates more widely using the following sources:

(a) returns provided by the British Airports Authority and Board of Trade on "non-export" expenditure by overseas airlines at United Kingdom airports (about £6 million in 1965). This includes the cost of landing fees, use of airport buildings by passengers, rent of offices at the airports and other similar airport services, but it excludes fuel and stores;

(b) estimates of oil bunkers lifted by overseas airlines, derived from total deliveries of aviation fuels for civilian use at United Kingdom airports (a figure supplied to the C.S.O. by the Minister of Power) *less* amounts lifted by United Kingdom airlines;

(c) information provided by a few overseas airlines of their *total* expenditure in the United Kingdom adjusted for overlap with returns received under (a) and (b); and,

(d) a notional addition for non-reporting airlines based on (c).

205. The main gap from this list would appear to be items (iii) and (v) above and the "stores" and "other than airport office expenses" components of (ii) and (iv). Clearly, comprehensive data on these items can only be supplied by the airlines themselves. At the moment a few airlines provide the C.S.O. with estimates of their *total* expenditure, but none give any breakdown. Moreover, the information is contained in an informal exchange of correspondence between C.S.O. and the airline. There appears to be no pro-forma used at present. The C.S.O. estimate that the total expenditure in categories (iii) and (v) (and part of (ii)) is quite small.

206. It is clear that the expansion in civil aviation earnings has been going hand in hand with the expansion of tourist spending. In the early 1950s tourist-class fares were introduced by the international airlines leading to a progressive growth in economy class travel. Later, charter flights provided a similar stimulus. Freight traffic too has been increasing. The important point is whether Britain's earnings compare favourably with those of other countries. This is difficult to establish since the I.M.F. statistics enable civil aviation transactions to be separated from the transport item for only three countries; the U.S., the U.K. and Italy. Even for these three countries the statistical presentation is not uniform. Scant though it is the available information is shown in TABLE 37.

207. On the basis of these five years civil aviation has shown a marked tendency to grow relative to the total transport item. Freight credits and debits and port disbursements (except for the U.S.) have been fairly constant so that most of the growth has been in passenger fares which are, for all the countries, the largest item.

TABLE 37

COMPARISON OF CIVIL AVIATION EARNINGS

$ U.S. millions	1960 Credit	Debit	1961 Credit	Debit	1962 Credit	Debit	1963 Credit	Debit	1964 Credit	Debit
United States										
1. Air Freight	55	52	46	22	51	26	53	26	64	26
2. Passenger Fares	126	301	174	291	180	341	195	390	223	420
3. Port Disbursements[1]	147	181	163	168	175	169	187	178	190	195
Total	328	504	383	481	406	536	435	594	477	641
% of Total Transport	18·7	26·3	21·2	24·8	20·7	25·2	20·6	25·6	20·6	26·0
United Kingdom										
1. Air Freight					20	17	23	17	25	22
2. Passenger Fares					199	78	218	87	238	98
3. Port Disbursements					64	162	64	171	73	176
4. Other[2]	268	218	299	238	39	6	44	6	42	6
Total	268	218	299	238	322	263	349	281	378	302
% of Total Transport	13·1	10·5	14·3	11·3	15·1	12·5	15·8	12·9	16·1	12·9
Italy										
1. Air Freights	6	8	10	10	12	12	14	14	17	15
2. Passenger Fares	50	19	62	23	80	25	96	30	106	31
3. Port Disbursements	23	15	26	23	27	27	30	29	32	34
4. Coastal		3		3		3		4		3
Total	79	45	98	59	119	67	140	77	155	83
% of Total Transport	15·8	7·4	17·5	8·6	19·6	9·5	20·3	8·9	20·9	9·2

Notes: 1. The I.M.F. figures do not distinguish air and sea port disbursements. This figure was taken from the "U.S. Abstract of Statistics: 1966."

2. The figures for 1960 and 1961 are civil aviation totals. The itemized account is not available.

208. It is interesting to notice that the U.S. has higher debits and credits than the U.K. largely, in the case of debits, because of its relatively high port disbursements. The U.K.'s foreign receipts from passenger fares are actually higher than the U.S.'s. Further the U.S. has a consistent deficit on civil aviation. Both the U.K. and Italy show a useful surplus.

209. Will these encouraging trends continue for the U.K.? The Committee considered the prospects outlined in the National Plan. The forecasts contained there were mainly based on the forecasts of the two nationalized corporations, B.E.A. and B.O.A.C., plus estimates for the independent airlines. According to the National Plan physical output of the civil aviation industry, in terms of capacity ton-miles flown was expected to increase up to 1970 at a rate of about 10 per cent per annum. This was a slightly slower rate of growth than in the past, largely reflecting the diminishing scope for the diversion of traffic to air from other forms of transport. In terms of foreign exchange earnings the contribution of air transport was "expected to grow in the future." The Plan concluded: "The exact rate of increase is difficult to predict but by 1970 the total will probably have grown by between 40 and 50 per cent at 1964 prices." Since the domestic economic basis of the Plan has now been changed, reflecting the lower prospects for economic growth at home, it would be unwise to attach too much credence to the actual figures but the Committee believes that the *trend* of earnings may still be near the mark. The outstanding problem is whether the prospective rise in turnover can continue to offset the probably continued lowering of fares and freight charges at a time when airline costs are likely to go on rising.

210. In considering prospects it has to be borne in mind that, in spite of

the potential growth of air travel, British airlines, both nationalized corporations and independents, operate under conditions partially imposed by governments at home and abroad. Overseas routes and the frequency of their operations are dependent on negotiations undertaken by the U.K. Government with foreign governments. This involves a certain amount of "give and take," but it is clear that several former Commonwealth territories no longer offer the same rights as in the past. Moreover, because governments have become heavily involved in air transport in most countries, airlines have tended to become instruments of government policy. Thus political influences have become stronger, with preferences and privileges often being given to small airlines that otherwise might not be competitive.

211. Britain's privately owned, independent airlines also complain that they have been kept out of most of the busiest international routes, and are convinced that two or more British operators on some international routes would attract a larger share of the traffic to Britain. The Committee did not feel equipped to judge either the strength of these arguments or the feasibility of such a sharing of overseas routes. But it was convinced of the need for an assessment of the potential growth of individual overseas routes and, in the light of such findings, of the need for a reappraisal of Government policy relating to the licensing of such routes as between private and public carriers.

212. Other factors beyond the control of individual airlines are the political unrest in various territories (e.g. as in Nigeria, Greece and the Middle East during parts of 1967, which can quickly reduce potential traffic) and currency regulations which can restrict the carrying of a particular country's nationals to its own airline, or, by reducing overseas travel allowances, can cut down potential tourist markets.

213. One final important element must be mentioned: the possible cost of buying and operating foreign, particularly U.S., aircraft. This applies especially to the future purchase of Boeing aircraft, for example, by B.O.A.C. which is already committed to the purchase of six Boeing 747s and two Boeing 707-336C freighters. All of these will be financed by U.S. loans which will be repaid during the years up to 1977—the main exchange impact coming in the last seven years when the repayments on the Boeing 747s will be made. The purchase of more of these aircraft may be necessary and the future foreign exchange cost must be taken into account in assessing Britain's possible invisible earnings from civil aviation. But B.O.A.C. feel confident that future earnings will more than offset the cost. The independent lines, however, made it clear to the Committee that they were often inhibited from buying all the foreign aircraft they needed because of the import duty imposed by the British Government, even in cases where a comparable British aircraft was not available.

214. In view of the Committee of Inquiry set up to examine the future of the air transport industry, announced in July, 1967, the Committee on Invisible Exports did not feel it appropriate to make any specific recommendations but draws the attention of the new Committee to the problems outlined above, particularly to the potential invisible earnings of the industry.

APPENDIX A (1): CHAPTER VIII

BALTIC EXCHANGE: EARNINGS INQUIRY

THE QUESTIONNAIRE

(a) Gross commissions, brokerages, agency fees or fittages earned in the U.K. from Non-Residents in respect of:

    1. *Shipping*

        (a) Freight on British exports (liner and/or tramp).

        (b) Freight on British imports (liner and/or tramp).

        (c) Freight on cross voyages or third country trade (line and/or tramp).

        (d) Time Charter.

        (e) Sale and Purchase of Ships.

        (f) Building and repair contracts.

        (g) Bunker contracts.

        (h) Port Agency.

    2. *Grain*

    3. *Oil and Oilseeds*

    4. *Air*

        (a) Freights on British exports (I.A.T.A. and/or Chartered flights).

        (b) Freight on British imports (I.A.T.A. and/or Chartered flights).

        (c) Freight on cross flights or third country trade (I.A.T.A. and/or Chartered flights).

        (d) Time Charter.

        (e) Sale and Purchase of aircraft.

(b) Any other gross earnings in the U.K. from Non-Residents (please specify nature, e.g., general retainers, professional fees and merchanting profits, etc.).

(c) Payments in the U.K. to Non-Residents in respect of the above transactions.

APPENDIX A (2)

NUMBER OF RETURNS
1. Blank returns despatched by the Baltic Exchange to members   696
2. Completed returns received   237
   Note: Six of the above returns cover 19 members thus the returns were in respect of 250 members.
3. Analysis of completed returns received:

	Number	Percentage of Returns Received		Percentage of Returns Despatched	
		%	%	%	%
(a) Giving details sufficient to enable information to be analysed:					
(i) Reported to other City organizations	2		0·8		0·3
(ii) Not reported to other City organizations	163		65·2		23·4
	165		66·0		23·7
(b) Not giving details sufficient to enable information to be analysed	23		9·2		3·3
	188		75·2		27·0
(c) "Nil" returns:					
(i) Unable to supply information	7	2·8		1·0	
(ii) No information given as this has already been reported to other organizations	4	1·6		0·6	
(iii) New member who does not consider information should be included for period prior to membership	1	0·4		0·1	
(iv) No reason stated	50	20·0		7·2	
	62		24·8		8·9
	250		100%		35·9

APPENDIX A. (3): THE RESULTS

SUMMARY OF INVISIBLE EXPORT EARNINGS BY MEMBERS OF THE BALTIC EXCHANGE

	Reported to Other City Organizations £	Not Reported to Other City Organizations £	Total £	£
A. Gross commissions, brokerage, agency fees or fittages earned in the U.K. from non-residents in respect of:				
1. Shipping				
(a) Freight on British exports (liner and/or tramp)	549	890,503	891,052	
(b) Freight on British imports (liner and/or tramp)	—	584,083	584,083	
(c) Freight on cross voyages or third country trade (liner and/or tramp)	—	2,298,495	2,298,495	
(d) Time charter	—	2,005,327	2,005,327	
(e) Sale and purchase of ships	270	418,938	419,208	
(f) Building and repair contracts	—	90,908	90,908	
(g) Bunker contracts	—	179,369	179,369	
(h) Port agency	—	335,349	335,349	
		6,802,972		6,803,791
2. Grain	819	269,076		269,076
3. Oil and Oilseeds	—	297,728		297,728
4. Air				
(a) Freight on British exports (I.A.T.A. and/or chartered flights)	—	147,087	147,087	
(b) Freight on British imports (I.A.T.A. and/or chartered flights)	—	16,479	16,479	
(c) Freight on cross flights or third country trade (I.A.T.A. and/or chartered flights)	64	8,384	8,448	
(d) Time charter	—	3,600	3,600	
(e) Sale and purchase of aircraft	—	—	—	
	64	175,550		175,614
	883	7,545,326		7,546,209
	21,732,698	1,798,059		23,530,757
B. Any other gross earnings in the U.K. from non-residents (principally freight)	21,733,581	9,343,385		31,076,966
Deduct:				
C. Payments to non-residents in respect of the above transactions	10,843,388	667,939		11,511,327
Add:				
D. Total net earnings in the U.K. from non-residents in respect of members whose returns do not give sufficient information to analyse their earnings under the above headings	10,890,193	8,675,446		19,565,639
	—	2,050,772		2,050,772
	£10,890,193	£10,726,218		£21,616,411

144

CHAPTER IX

INSURANCE

215. The United Kingdom insurance market is made up of over 500 insurance companies, British, Commonwealth and foreign, of insurance brokers and of Lloyd's underwriters and brokers. The foreign business undertaken by this market represents a high proportion of its total turnover. But this share is higher for some types of business than for others; and the structure of the insurance companies differs from that of Lloyd's. They are better described separately.

1. THE INSURANCE COMPANIES

216. There are at present roughly 500 insurance companies operating in the United Kingdom, of which about 400 are incorporated in Great Britain, 50 in other Commonwealth countries[1], and the remainder elsewhere abroad. The first main subdivision of insurance business is into life and non-life (or general) business, and life assurance again falls into two principal divisions: ordinary life and industrial life. General insurance is traditionally divided into three main branches: fire, accident and marine. Within these branches there are, however, a large number of separate classes of insurance (for example, motor insurance is nowadays the largest component of accident, and aviation insurance is usually classed under marine) though some companies do not undertake all classes of business. Finally, there is the re-insurance market. All general insurance companies reinsure at least a proportion of their risks, and the practice also extends to life assurance, although (except for small or very new companies) normally only in respect of unusually large risks.

217. This is the structure of the insurance company market. Its foreign business varies widely. While the business of U.K. life assurance companies is predominantly domestic in origin, a number of companies transact ordinary life business overseas, principally within the Commonwealth and the Republic of South Africa. In the past few years this source of business has in fact been expanding at a slightly faster rate than that originating in the U.K., and in 1965 constituted some 10 per cent of worldwide premium income of British life companies.[2] Overseas business is much more highly concentrated than is home business, the four leading companies overseas— the Prudential, Standard Life, Norwich Union Life and Legal & General— together accounting in 1963 (the latest year for which figures are available)

1. Of these, some 275 U.K. and Commonwealth-registered companies, accounting for over 95 per cent of the premium income of the whole company market, are members of the British Insurance Association.
2. According to figures provided by the Life Offices' Association, the Associated Scottish Life Offices and the Industrial Life Offices Association, whose members transact virtually all the life assurance and annuity business in the U.K.

for more than three-quarters of total overseas premium income of U.K. life companies. In all there are about 25 U.K. companies transacting ordinary life business overseas on any significant scale[1]; no U.K. companies transact industrial life business overseas.

218. Much the larger proportion of U.K. companies' overseas insurance business is in general insurance. In 1959 the Radcliffe Committee estimated that general business arising overseas was double that at home (although since then there has probably been a slight decline in the overseas proportion). The U.S.A. is the largest single overseas market; in 1965 branches and local subsidiaries of British companies wrote premiums in that country valued at some $1,000 million, equivalent to well over 40 per cent of total overseas premium income of U.K. companies in respect of general insurance. In 1965 four composite groups (the Royal, Northern & Employers, General Accident and Commercial Union) accounted, with their American subsidiaries, for over two-thirds of the premiums earned by British companies in that country. Canada, where U.K. companies and their Canadian subsidiaries wrote premiums worth over $C.330 million in 1965, is probably the second most important overseas market. The four British groups with the largest interests in Canada (the Royal, Commercial Union, Northern & Employers and the Guardian) accounted in 1965 for well over half the net premiums written by U.K. companies and their Canadian subsidiaries. Details of British insurers' business in other overseas countries is not easily available but they are known to have substantial interests in Australia, the rest of the Commonwealth and South Africa. A certain amount of business is also transacted in other parts of the world, the most important being continental Europe and South America.

219. Details of income derived from the operations of overseas branches, subsidiaries and agencies of non-life U.K. companies are collected by the British Insurance Association (some of the information being obtained quarterly and some annually). At present, the B.I.A. provides the Board of Trade annually with a world wide return of the *earnings* of its members divided into three major geographical divisions (sterling area excluding U.K., U.S.A. and Canada, and the rest of the non-sterling area). The Board of Trade draw upon data from other sources to make an estimate of a further geographical breakdown of this income. Since 1963, these earnings have been incorporated in the figures published on *direct* investment income. (See Table 12/14 Balance of Payments pink book 1966).

2. Lloyd's

220. Lloyd's[2] is established in London and members must conduct their underwriting in the Underwriting Room. In the same way as the Stock Exchange deals in stocks and shares, Lloyd's is an insurance exchange where the underwriters and insurance brokers in the Room correspond to the

1. Taking as "significant" in this context overseas premium income exceeding £100,000 in 1963.
2. The constitution of Lloyd's and the basis on which business is transacted by its Members are governed by Lloyd's Acts, 1871-1951, and by bye-laws made under them. Lloyd's is a Society, incorporated by Act of Parliament in 1871, whose Members, known as Underwriting Members (or, sometimes, Underwriters or Names), transact insurance for their own account and risk with unlimited liability.

jobbers and stockbrokers of the Stock Exchange. Underwriters are not permitted to accept insurance business other than through the intermediary of Lloyd's brokers, who alone have the right of entry to the Underwriting Room to place insurance for their clients.

221. The total number of Underwriting Members has steadily increased over the years and is now in the region of 6,000. About two-thirds of this number comprise members who, although personally liable (as is every member) to the full extent of their means for risks accepted on their behalf, are not otherwise connected with Lloyd's and whose day-to-day occupations are concerned with the professions, industry and commerce, etc. The remaining members (approximately 2,000) are engaged in the operations of the Lloyd's Market—some as underwriting agents, active underwriters or their employees, and others as principals or staff of firms of Lloyd's brokers.

222. The income of Lloyd's underwriters and brokers derived from business undertaken for foreign clients can be subdivided into:

(i) Business underwritten at Lloyd's.

223. Under the existing system of accounting and recording employed at Lloyd's, it is not possible to produce actual premium income figures relating to all overseas business. However, figures are available to show that U.S. and Canadian dollar business has for a considerable period of time represented approximately 50 per cent of Lloyd's total premium income, and it is reasonable to estimate that other foreign business accounts for a further 25 per cent. Accordingly, Lloyd's net premium income from all overseas business (on the basis that it is equal to 75 per cent of the total premium income) has progressively increased from approximately £130 million in 1955 to approximately £216 million in 1965. Since April, 1964, Lloyd's have supplied quarterly figures to the Board of Trade on foreign income earned by its underwriters. This represents the difference between the premiums earned in a given year and the claims *paid out* in that year. The data are collected direct from the underwriters. Prior to April, 1964, information was only available on Lloyd's U.S. dollar business via U.K. exchange control. Income earned on non-dollar business was included indistinguishably in the estimates of all other insurance earnings. Information is at present given to the Board of Trade for marine and non-marine business separately and also broken down by broad geographical areas.

(ii) broker's commission.

224. All business transacted at Lloyd's has to be negotiated between the underwriters and a U.K. broker. Although Lloyd's brokers form an integral part of the Lloyd's market, Lloyd's is essentially a society of underwriters. Sometimes foreign business is commissioned directly from a U.K. broker, but more often than not through an overseas agent or subsidiary of the broker. In the former case, the U.K. broker would expect a commission of about 20 per cent of premium income; in the latter about 5 per cent. Lloyd's estimate that foreign earnings of brokers in respect of insurance business transacted at Lloyd's is currently well in excess of £10 million. In addition, brokers earn commission from non-Lloyd's business and some-

times from business transacted between overseas clients and overseas insurance companies (including reinsurance business).

225. The Board of Trade receives quarterly details of brokerage on foreign transactions. This information is voluntarily obtained direct from brokers, and the estimated coverage is 60/80 per cent.

3. EARNINGS ON PORTFOLIO INVESTMENTS

226. Income earned on foreign securities held by insurance companies in head office portfolios makes a significant contribution to the market's foreign earnings. No separate statistical return is made for this item. The Board of Inland Revenue provides global estimates to the Central Statistical Office of the interest and dividends received on foreign government and municipal stocks, and/or paid through U.K. paying agents and coupon dealers, but there is no way of separately identifying in these estimates the portfolio income received by insurance companies. Such income is included indistinguishably in the total figure for portfolio investment receipts published in Table 12 of the Balance of Payments Pink Book, 1966. The B.I.A. has made an estimate that the net income earned on the foreign portfolio investments (excluding investments in land, property and ground rent) of its members in 1965 was around £25 million. This calculation is based on the knowledge that the book value of these investments at the end of that year was £454 million. (This figure is derived from the holdings returns of member companies.) The notional rate of return assumed for this calculation is $5\frac{1}{2}$ per cent.[1]

COVERAGE AND RELIABILITY

227. All these items of insurance earnings are incorporated in the balance of payments. The income from portfolio investment is included in Table 12 and most of the income from foreign insurance business is classed as earnings on direct investment. Yet it remains impossible to separate the insurance market's contribution from the rest. The Committee, therefore, considered not only what improvements might be made in the figures but also whether some attempt might be made to provide a separate item for insurance earnings.

228. During the last two years or so, the coverage of the foreign earnings of insurance companies included in the published statistics has improved considerably. The B.I.A. (which covers the bulk of the insurance company market), Lloyd's and the Corporation of Insurance Brokers each feel satisfied that there is comparatively little of their overseas business which is not incorporated in one or other of the sections of the balance of payments accounts. But certain improvements could be made in attempting to provide regular information about the insurance industry. There could be considerable improvement in the way in which the data on the *portfolio* investment income of insurance companies is collected and it is believed in the industry that it might be possible to record this type of information in the quarterly and annual reports submitted to the Board of Trade.

1. 7 per cent on equities and 4 per cent on bonds.

148

229. There are two other and comparatively minor deficiencies in the coverage of insurance statistics. The first concerns the earnings of the subsidiaries and branches of *life* insurance companies overseas. Although the B.I.A. claim that very little of the earnings of these companies are remitted back to the U.K. they might, nevertheless, be included in the balance of payments statistics. The B.I.A. say that this is unlikely to be a significant omission. The other deficiency relates to the companies' foreign underwriting business transacted in the U.K. (known as home/foreign). The B.I.A. says that apart from marine underwriting (including aviation and transit), earnings from which are already included in the returns to the Board of Trade, income from this business would be very difficult to estimate and it is doubtful whether a reliable figure could be obtained at all. In any case, the amount is almost certain to be very small as, where a significant volume of business is obtained from any overseas territory, it is normally transacted locally through a branch office, subsidiary company or agency.

230. Finally, a certain amount of insurance is undertaken by other than insurance companies, e.g. by mutual indemnity companies. It is thought that such companies are largely confined to the shipping industry, e.g. Liverpool Shipowners Mutual Indemnity Society, and that their total premium income (at home and overseas) is not more than a few million pounds.

231. The Committee requested the different parts of the insurance industry to provide it with statistical information from which an estimate of the industry's foreign income could be made for the first time. All sectors of the industry agreed to do so and the following figures were assembled for the year 1965:

	£ *million*
Companies:	
overseas branches, subsidiaries and agencies	19
marine and other "home-foreign" business	2
head office overseas portfolio investment income	25
	——
	46
Lloyd's (underwriting and interest)	13[1]
Brokers[2]	22
	——
	81

RECOMMENDATIONS

232. 1. The Committee recommends that, following talks between the Board of Trade, the British Insurance Association, Lloyd's and the Corporation of Insurance Brokers, efforts should be made to fill the statistical

1. Annual average 1964-1966.
2. Actual average of £21·6 million a year from mid-1964 to end of 1966.

deficiencies relating to the insurance industry's portfolio investment, the foreign earnings of life insurance companies overseas and "home-foreign" underwriting business (other than marine) transacted in the U.K.

233. 2. The Committee also recommends that an estimate of the insurance industry's foreign earnings should be published annually in future.

STIMULATING INSURANCE EARNINGS

234. In considering what might be done to encourage further foreign earnings from insurance, the Committee was conscious of the drop in underwriting profits and the losses faced by both Lloyd's underwriters and insurance companies in certain overseas markets in recent years. The two classes of business worst affected have been motor and industrial fire, with the adverse trends widespread throughout most industrialised countries. The U.S.A. and Continental Western Europe have been particularly bad examples; Far Eastern and Middle Eastern markets have generally continued to provide satisfactory profits. In the past three or four years marine insurance has also begun to deteriorate in profitability, as, more recently still, has aviation insurance.

235. According to the insurance industry foreign earnings from underwriting overseas have declined for very much the same reasons that underwriting profits in the home market have been declining; that is to say, the effects of inflation on claim costs have outstripped increases in premiums. There are other factors as well, including the world-wide trend towards greater fire damage, increased claim consciousness on the part of the insuring public and higher third party awards. In addition, premium rate levels have been influenced considerably by competition in most of the major territories, including, for instance, the United States, Canada and Australia. The incidence of Hurricane "Betsy" in the U.S. in September, 1965, leading to heavy claims payments to overseas clients, also considerably affected the results for 1965 and, to a lesser extent, for 1966.

236. The Committee was informed that in the United Kingdom rates are being raised to a more realistic level and other corrective underwriting measures are being applied. To a varying extent the same is true of the overseas territories but in some areas, and notably in the United States, insurers are not completely the masters of their own destinies. There has also been a permanent loss of earnings from some of the less developed countries where the business of British and other foreign insurers has either been expropriated (e.g. Burma, Ceylon, Tanzania) or is in the process of being diverted to national companies. In other countries, e.g. Rhodesia, there are of course restrictions on remittances of earnings to this country. In the view of the insurance industry, the overall trend should be one of slowly improving underwriting results over the next few years.

237. The existing pattern, particularly in the United States, of a loss on underwriting being off-set by a profit on investment is not one which the insurance industry regards as satisfactory and the Committee share this view. In a buoyant investment market like the United States the profit on

investments has generally exceeded underwriting losses by appreciable amounts and national companies there have, therefore, continued to increase their unprofitable insurance business merely to obtain further funds for investment. British companies have felt that, provided they are not making an overall loss on their operations, they should remain and continue to compete with the national companies against the time when an improvement in underwriting occurs. It is difficult to foresee a rapid and radical change in the present position in the United States. However, there is undoubtedly a growing awareness there on the part of all the major companies, both domestic and foreign, of the unsatisfactory underwriting situation. There are also signs of more sympathetic treatment by the State Supervisory Authorities of applications for rate increases.

238. Other factors have also been influencing insurance results abroad. One disturbing trend has been the growing tendency of overseas Governments to place various legislative controls on domestic insurance operations which have, directly or indirectly, operated to the disadvantage of the U.K. insurance market. While outright discrimination against foreign companies is unusual, any regulations requiring a minimum proportion of premiums to be retained in a country, or for funds to be invested locally in certain specified ways, tend to reduce the flexibility and thus the competitiveness of British insurers. This is because their overseas operations have been built up to their present position largely on the basis of the ability to transfer funds freely from one place to another as needed. Since the principle of insurance consists of the accumulation of funds from many sources available to cover any of a wide variety of risks, regulations that split up reserves into a number of small amounts not available for use except in one particular country inevitably reduce efficiency. Although it is understandable that a developing country may wish to mobilize its own savings for domestic use, or may wish to conserve foreign exchange, there is little doubt that they have contributed to, and are likely to go on contributing to, a slower rate of expansion overseas by British insurance companies.

239. One way in which British insurance companies might improve their earnings would be by further investment in insurance companies overseas. Such investment would bring with it by way of return not only dividends receivable from the overseas companies but also probably a more substantial and immediate return in the form of re-insurance business. This is at present largely prevented by the current restrictions on overseas investment in the non-sterling area and the so-called developed countries of the Commonwealth. The longer these restrictions persist in hindering the free flow of capital to finance expansion, it was represented to the Committee, the more difficult will it be for British insurance companies to retain even their present share of overseas markets. Furthermore, the restrictive attitude currently adopted by the U.K. authorities towards overseas investment is said to aggravate foreign opinion and further encourage the imposition of controls on the remittance to parent companies of cash balances, profits and dividends arising from British insurance operations abroad. In this context a special case

with particularly unhappy consequences, according to both Lloyd's and the insurance companies, has been the publicly announced ban on the remittance of insurance funds to Rhodesia; this has already provoked the threat of legislation adverse to the interests of British insurers in South Africa, and has certainly already resulted in the loss of a certain amount of business, both there and elsewhere.

EFFICIENCY

240. When considering the insurance industry it was clear to the Committee that conditions had become more competitive, both at home and abroad, and that in these circumstances efforts had been made to maintain the profitability of operations by increasing efficiency; these efforts can be grouped under three main headings: action taken by individual companies; action taken collectively by the company market as a whole; and action taken by Lloyd's.

241. Individual insurance companies have sought to improve efficiency of operations by the rationalisation of administrative procedures such as organisation and methods study, by the introduction of computers and by mergers with other companies, aimed at reducing overheads. A survey of 30 member companies (including all the largest groups and a sample of the smaller companies) undertaken by the British Insurance Association early in 1964 showed that nine had formal Organisation and Methods departments and 19 had other arrangements for reviewing O. & M. periodically. In addition, six companies had engaged outside management consultants to advise them on particular aspects of reorganisation.

242. The same survey showed that at that time 14 companies had installed one or more computers, and some of them had already accumulated several years' experience in their use. Six other companies were in the process of installing computers or had them on order, and most of the rest (apart from the very smallest concerns, some of which intended to buy computer time as needed) had begun seriously to consider placing orders. It is too early to try to assess the overall economic benefits derived from computerisation in insurance, since many companies are still only at the running-in stage, but it is possible that it has been a contributory factor in halting the previous tendency for insurance employment to rise inexorably year by year as the volume of business expanded.

243. While insurance mergers are by no means a new phenomenon, the number of mergers, many of them between major companies, has been markedly higher during the past decade than at any time since the period immediately succeeding the First World War. The merger movement reached a peak during the years 1959-61, when among the more important amalgamations were those concerning the following companies:

1959   Royal Exchange/Atlas
        Eagle Star/Midland Employers' Mutual
        Commercial Union/North British & Mercantile
        Norwich Union/Scottish Union & National

1960	Guardian/Union of Canton
	Northern/Employers' Liability
	Sun/Alliance
	London/Sea
1961	Royal/London & Lancashire

244. Since 1961 mergers have been fewer (although 1965 was notable for the absorption of the London Assurance into the Sun Alliance group), partly because many of the major groups have been concentrating on the integration of earlier acquisitions.

245. Beyond the work of individual companies the B.I.A. has also initiated collective efficiency efforts. In 1963 it set up a Productivity Sub-Committee to start projects designed to assist member companies to improve their operating efficiency. The first major result was the commissioning of McKinsey & Co., the management consultants, to carry out a full-scale study of the problems prevailing in U.K. motor insurance and to recommend means of dealing with them. The McKinsey report on motor insurance appeared in 1965, and has been followed by detailed work to implement many of its proposals, carried out by a number of B.I.A. project groups.

246. Other productivity projects carried out under the auspices of the B.I.A. have included a second study by McKinsey's, on ways of achieving the greatest financial benefit from the application of computers to insurance operations, and an investigation into the advantage of substituting premium acknowledgements for premium receipts, resulting in the recommendation of the former system to members. The Committee was informed that several further projects are now either in progress or under consideration.

247. In the case of Lloyd's, the Committee was informed, efforts to improve efficiency have already included the introduction of modern computer systems, not only in Lloyd's Policy Signing Office, but also in the offices of many underwriting agents and/or the firms of accountants who keep their books, and the introduction of a central accounting system which has removed the necessity for individual accounting as between the many Lloyd's syndicates and Lloyd's brokers.

248. The total staff of Lloyd's includes underwriting agents, active underwriters and their staffs, and the staff of the Corporation of Lloyd's. No running totals are maintained, but a recent survey shows that there are approximately 3,000 persons (male and female) who are either principals or employees of Underwriting Agents, in addition to which there are approximately 2,000 persons (male and female, clerical and non-clerical) employed by the Corporation. Active underwriters sit in the underwriting room so that the whole market, comprising nearly 300 Syndicates, is accommodated under one roof and this enables overheads to be kept to a minimum. The expenses of underwriters over the last 10 years have amounted to an average of approximately 2·5 per cent of net premium income, and this ratio has fluctuated only marginally during this period.

249. 1. The Committee recommends that the Insurance Companies and Lloyd's should continue to study ways and means of improving their underwriting results in North America.

2. The Committee recommends that the insurance companies and Lloyd's should be given government support abroad:

(*a*) in cases where insurance control regulations require the immobilisation of funds in any country beyond those required to establish normal technical reserves and where companies are required to maintain funds and no suitable avenues of investment exist.

(*b*) in cases where discriminatory legislation imposes greater restrictions upon British companies and Lloyd's than upon national companies.

CHAPTER X

TRAVEL

250. As was shown in Chapter III, travel has become one of the fastest growing elements in the world's invisible transactions. Of the four broad categories analysed by the International Monetary Fund it was the fastest growing between 1952 and 1964, quadrupling in that period. The share of travel in the world's invisible transactions correspondingly grew from 14 per cent to 21 per cent. Britain has naturally shared in this growth, though in terms of the balance of payments, expenditure by British visitors abroad has persistently exceeded that spent here by foreign visitors. Throughout the

TABLE 38

BRITAIN'S TRAVEL PAYMENTS AND RECEIPTS (1958–1966)[1]

(£m.)	1958	1959	1960	1961	1962	1963	1964	1965	1966
Debits:									
Irish Republic	24	26	30	37	39	41	50	57	55
Other overseas sterling area countries	16	13	14	12	14	14	14	18	20
Western Europe	101	112	127	135	139	166	174	188	192
North America	8	9	10	11	12	13	14	14	16
Other non-sterling countries	3	4	5	5	6	7	9	13	14
Total Debits	152	164	186	200	210	241	261	290	297
Credits:									
Irish Republic	10	10	13	14	16	19	21	23	27
Other overseas sterling area countries	40	39	46	49	48	42	38	40	38
Western Europe	27	32	37	41	46	53	53	55	63
North America	49	52	58	54	54	55	60	61	71
Other non-sterling countries	8	10	15	18	19	19	18	14	20
Total Credits	134	143	169	176	183	188	190	193	219
Travel (net):									
Irish Republic	−14	−16	−17	−23	−23	−22	−29	−34	−28
Other overseas sterling area countries	+24	+26	+32	+39	+34	+28	+24	+22	+18
Western Europe	−74	−80	−90	−94	−93	−113	−121	−133	−129
North America	+41	+43	+48	+43	+42	+42	+46	+47	+55
Other non-sterling countries	+5	+6	+10	+13	+13	+12	+9	+1	+6
Total Travel (net)	−18	−21	−17	−24	−27	−53	−71	−97	−78

1. Source: *United Kingdom Balance of Payments*, 1967.

post-war period Britain has had a payments deficit on travel. Up to the early 1950's the strictness of exchange controls and the deliberate control of personal travel allowances kept spending outside the sterling area damped down, but from the later 1950's onwards overseas spending rose rapidly. So did foreign spending in Britain, but the resulting payments gap began to widen from 1962 onwards. As TABLE 38 brings out, spending abroad almost doubled between 1958 and 1965, rising from £152 million to £290 million. The rise accelerated from 1962 to 1965, though not rising quite so sharply in 1966. By 1965 close on two thirds of the total spending was taking place in western Europe, the result of rising living standards in Britain, its limited sunshine and the availability of cheap "package" tours using chartered and scheduled airlines.

251. Spending by foreigners in the United Kingdom has also expanded over the past two decades, though not so rapidly as British spending overseas. Europeans doubled their spending here between 1958 and 1965 and so did visitors from Ireland. Total foreign spending seemed to lose its momentum after 1961, giving another spurt in 1966. In the three years 1958-61 total foreign expenditure rose by 31 per cent; in the following four year period, 1961-65, it rose by only 9 per cent. One immediate result was that the United Kingdom's travel deficit began to widen significantly, from £27 million in 1962 to £97 million in 1965, though narrowing to £78 million in 1966. While the expected net surplus with North America remained fairly stable, the net deficit with Ireland more than doubled and that with Western Europe rose by four-fifths.

252. In the light of the widening deficit in the 1960's, the Committee felt obliged to concentrate on Britain's gross earnings from travel and to examine how far Britain's experience was shared by other industrialized countries and what was being done and might be done to encourage foreign spending in Britain.

BALANCE OF PAYMENTS STATISTICS

253. Views about Britain's travel earnings are based on the balance of payments statistics. The Committee had to consider at the outset, therefore, how reliable they were and how they compared with those of other countries. The item described as "travel credits" (Table 10 in the *United Kingdom Balance of Payments*, 1966) covers the estimated personal expenditure of overseas residents visiting the U.K. In conformity with international recommendations, the cost of sea or air travel from and to the U.K. is not included; nor is the expenditure by visitors on (*a*) goods already accounted for in visible exports or (*b*) real estate bought while in the U.K.

254. Broadly speaking two main methods of estimating tourist receipts are used by member countries of the Organization for Economic Co-operation and Development (O.E.C.D.): (*a*) the bank reporting or ticket system method (used by 16[1] O.E.C.D. countries), (*b*) the estimation method (used by 5[2] countries):

1. viz. Austria, Belgium, Denmark, France, Germany, Greece, Iceland, Italy, Japan, Luxembourg, Netherlands, Norway, Portugal, Spain, Sweden and Turkey.
2. viz. Canada, Ireland, Switzerland, U.K. and U.S.A.

(a) The *bank reporting* method obtains data on foreign "means of payments" for purposes of tourism through the banks. The term "means of payments" covers notes and coins as well as cheques, letters of credit and other means of payments denominated in a foreign currency; the term "banks" extends to all types of institutions authorized to deal in foreign currency. Such transactions may be reported to the collecting agency either on a case by case basis or at intervals of time. Though accurate and suitable for implementation in countries which operate pretty stringent exchange control mechanisms, the system is incomplete as it does not cover use of domestic means of payments outside the banking channels. Neither does it allow that part of the movements in domestic currency used for the purposes of tourism to be statistically identified.[1] In countries which have liberalized their control mechanism in recent years and value freedom of action in monetary affairs, the system is regarded as either impracticable or an improper interference into the operation of local banks by the central bank.

(b) The *estimation method*. Here tourists' receipts and expenditures are estimated either by (i) obtaining the information direct from a random sample of tourists entering or leaving the country in question and/or (ii) from data supplied by hotel associations, travel agencies, transport companies and so on.

255. The U.K. uses the second of these methods. Since 1962, estimates of travel earnings have been based on sample surveys of air and sea passengers leaving the U.K., conducted by the Social Survey for the Board of Trade.[2] The results of these international passenger surveys are published in the *Board of Trade Journal*[3] and now cover the routes used in about four-fifths of the number of visits to this country by overseas residents[4]. Data in respect of both numbers of visits and expenditure are classified according to (a) purpose of visit, e.g. holidays, business etc., (b) length of visit, (c) form of travel and (d) residence of visitors. Various improvements have been made to the survey since it was first undertaken in 1962, and its coverage has been gradually extended.

256. Details of the sampling method used in connection with passengers travelling from the U.K. by sea and air are given in Appendix A. In all, about 7 per cent of the outgoing passengers and 4 per cent of the incoming

1. As the *O.E.C.D. Observer* put it (October, 1966):
   "Nearly all European countries have established an allowance permitting the individual traveller to export and to import a certain amount in domestic notes and coins when leaving or entering a country. There is no possibility of finding out, however, how much the individual traveller takes with him when leaving his home country, as measures to do so would seriously hamper the flow of travel. Thus, the balance of payments statistician does not know, under this method, how much is taken out through these channels and there seems no way of estimating this amount. A large part of the domestic currency taken out of the country in this manner may find its way to banks in the countries visited and will be exchanged into foreign currency; what happens to the rest cannot be ascertained." (P.13-14.)
2. Previously, estimates of travel were derived as a product of numbers of passengers and rough estimates of average expenditure per head supported by information made available from partner countries.
3. See particularly issues dated August 23, 1963, August 28, 1964, September 10, 1965 and September 16, 1966.
4. The principal omission from the figures is traffic between the U.K. and the Irish Republic. The Central Statistical Office for the Irish Republic provides estimates, based on sample inquiries of travel credits and debits for this traffic.

passengers on long air and sea routes are sampled; the proportion is considerably smaller for the short haul routes.

257. An estimate of the total traffic is obtained from information supplied by the main air and seaports. Not all air and sea routes are surveyed at all times, however, and there is a "grossing up" problem involved. The Board of Trade feel, however, that the margin of error is fairly small, as 90 per cent of the air and sea routes are regularly surveyed.

258. In effect the estimation system adopted by Britain should, and probably does, produce a more comprehensive picture of the tourist trade than the bank reporting method but it suffers from two defects. In the case of the direct samples only small numbers of passengers can be interviewed and there is a danger of obtaining biased information; in the case of the direct information from hotel associations, travel agencies etc. the difficulty is to obtain reliable and comprehensive data.

259. The Committee, in examining British travel statistics, has been concerned with two issues: the reliability of the balance of payments figures as such and the question of whether they are useful enough for the purpose of formulating policy. On the first of these points the Committee, while satisfied that Britain's statistics are as good as, and usually more accurate and representative than, those of other countries, also feels that further improvements are possible:

1. Two questions arise from the methods used, one general, one specific. Has there been enough experience of the sampling techniques for the Board of Trade to be satisfied that new and important shifts in spending by foreign visitors are immediately reflected? Secondly, since passengers on inclusive tours are unable to distinguish the cost of their fares from the cost of accommodation and other expenditure abroad, does this lend a bias to the estimates of expenditure?

2. Apart from goods carried in the luggage of tourists, all goods bought in the U.K. by foreign tourists are excluded from U.K. "travel" earnings. Although such goods naturally appear in the visible export figures, it would be useful, in analysing and comparing the tourist industry, to know their value. This is particularly so in comparing the U.K.'s travel earnings with those of other countries; some O.E.C.D. countries *include* the purchase of goods by foreign visitors in their trade credits.

3. International fare payments (i.e. the earnings of British carriers from foreign visitors) are also excluded from the U.K.'s travel earnings. They are, of course, included in the U.K.'s invisible accounts under "transport" but are not recorded separately. There are grounds for arguing, as the British Travel Association does, that Britain's earnings from international fare payments should be added to the travel account of the balance of payments. In Britain's case this would reduce the overall travel deficit since Britain still has a surplus though perhaps a narrowing one in air and shipping fare

TABLE 39

BRITAIN'S TOURIST TRADE 1964 AND 1965

Nationals of	Holiday Visitors 1964	Holiday Visitors 1965	Business Visitors 1964	Business Visitors 1965	Total by Sea 1964	Total by Sea 1965	Total by Air 1964	Total by Air 1965	Total by Sea and Air 1964	Total by Sea and Air 1965	Expenditure 1964 £m	Expenditure 1965 £m
Belgium-Luxembourg	70,000	75,200	20,000	20,800	60,300	64,100	30,200	32,200	90,500	96,300	2·5	2·5
Denmark	26,200	31,800	11,000	11,600	21,500	24,500	16,100	19,300	37,600	43,800	1·9	2·1
France	269,000	302,600	53,600	59,000	176,200	194,400	149,300	169,100	325,500	363,500	10·1	10·2
Germany	173,800	199,100	51,800	57,700	143,700	155,000	84,100	104,000	227,800	259,000	8·5	8·8
Italy	57,200	63,800	17,900	19,600	34,700	36,900	41,400	47,600	76,100	84,500	5·3	5·0
Netherlands	92,000	108,400	54,100	59,700	70,800	79,100	76,000	89,600	146,800	168,700	4·1	4·0
Norway	17,100	19,100	8,500	9,300	12,300	12,500	13,700	16,200	26,000	28,700	1·3	1·2
Spain	16,800	19,000	6,800	7,800	9,100	9,300	15,200	18,300	24,300	27,600	1·6	1·7
Sweden	46,600	57,200	16,300	18,800	29,000	34,800	34,500	41,800	63,500	76,600	3·3	4·0
Switzerland	35,400	39,800	14,900	16,100	15,900	16,700	36,400	41,300	52,300	58,000	4·0	4·1
W. EUROPE	805,000	916,000	255,100	280,400	573,500	627,300	496,900	579,400	1,070,400	1,206,700	42·6	43·6
U.S.A.	474,300	532,900	82,100	93,000	145,300	150,600	443,900	523,600	589,200	674,200	45·5	46·2
Japan	13,500	14,300	9,100	8,400	1,600	1,800	21,200	21,100	22,800	22,900	n.a.	n.a.
South Africa	30,300	30,900	6,100	6,200	14,100	12,200	23,900	26,300	38,000	38,500	4·9	5·0
Other foreign countries	156,700	174,700	40,800	43,800	69,700	72,900	132,000	150,000	201,700	222,900	20*	19*
TOTAL FOREIGN VISITORS	1,479,800	1,678,800	393,200	431,800	804,200	864,800	1,117,900	1,300,400	1,922,100	2,165,200	113*	114*
Australia									34,000	40,000		
Canada									160,000	175,000		
New Zealand									14,000	16,000		
Commonwealth residents in U.S.A.									40,000	47,000		
**Other Commonwealth residents in other countries									286,000	333,000		
TOTAL COMMONWEALTH									534,000	611,000	56*	56*
GRAND TOTAL									2,456,000	2,776,000	190*†	193*†

The estimates of expenditure in Britain by overseas visitors in 1965 are provisional figures based on the International Passenger Survey, a large scale sample survey carried out at airports and seaports for the Board of Trade by the Government Social Survey.
To the total revenue figure of £193 million may be added an estimate made by the British Travel Association of international fare payments by visitors to Britain to British carriers giving estimated total tourist earnings of £321 million in 1965. This total excludes visitor spending on special purchases such as cars and antiques which are included under "physical" exports in the balance of payments.

NOTE 1 Figures in the table are for the calendar years 1965 and 1964.
NOTE 2 Expenditure figures are estimated expenditure in Britain and exclude international fare payments by visitors to Britain to British carriers.
NOTE 3 The analysis into holiday and business visitors excludes long stay visitors (staying more than three months) and those arriving via the Republic of Ireland; these two categories of visitor are included in the means of transport breakdown.

**NOTE 4 Figure rounded to nearest £1 million.
***NOTE 5 Including Commonwealth residents of South Africa.
*†NOTE 6 Including the estimated expenditure of residents of the Republic of Ireland—£23 million in 1965; £21 million in 1964.

159

payments. The reason for this surplus seems to be that most British travel abroad is "short-haul" to Europe and largely carried by British companies whereas large number of Commonwealth and American visitors to Britain travel on British carriers and naturally pay a much higher fare per head for their longer journeys. The reasons given for adding this surplus to the net travel account are twofold: (a) to obtain an overall picture of the importance of travel as a whole, (b) to compare Britain's figures with those of countries that include fare payments in "travel." (e.g. Austria and, partially, Sweden and U.S.). The B.T.A. has estimated Britain's international fare payments to British carriers as £118 million in 1964 and £128 million in 1965. This, if accurate, would give a total earnings figure for 1965 of £321 million (i.e. £193 million plus £128 million), as shown at the foot of TABLE 39.

4. The British Travel Association has some doubts about some of the expenditure figures derived from the passenger survey. For example, the rise in the spending of overseas visitors here has not apparently kept pace with the rise in the number of such visitors:

	Number of Visitors	% Rise	Expenditure £m.	% Rise
1961	1,823,000	–	176	–
1962	1,955,000	7·2	183	4·0
1963	2,159,000	10·4	188	2·7
1964	2,456,000	13·8	190	1·0
1965	2,776,000	13·0	193	1·6
1966	3,176,000	14·3	219	13·4

To some extent this smaller rise in spending may be a reflection of the drop in their average length of stay, perhaps due to rising air travel, to package tours and special limited duration excursion tickets. But the Committee believes that it may bear statistical investigation.

5. One of the main problems in handling travel statistics is the difficulty of comparing those of one country with those of another. Some countries include international fare payments; others do not. Some include *all* purchases of foreign visitors; others do not. Some figures are complicated by the problem of border traffic (e.g. on the Continent) where workers commuting from one country to another can be mixed up with genuine visitors; others (e.g. the U.K., apart from border between Eire and Northern Ireland) are not. Some include capital transactions such as the sale of villas etc.; others do not. Above all, some use one method of estimating, others another.[1]

1. The O.E.C.D., which has studied these problems of comparability, while realizing the costs of changing statistical methods in industrial countries, has strongly urged the following:
    (a) A reciprocal use of both groups of methods to improve the data available.
    (b) A standardisation of definitions, e.g. in respect of treatment of (i) transport (ii) expenditure of frontier and foreign workers (iii) purchase of goods by tourists.
    (c) An exchange of information on the purchase of domestic banknotes (particularly important for countries using the bank reporting method).
    (d) The collection of gross (rather than net) data on an international tourist payments and receipts to indicate the full impact on the economies of individual member countries.

RECOMMENDATIONS

260   1. The Committee recommends that separate figures for international fare payments, at present included under transport, should be prepared and published by the Board of Trade. This would allow the British Travel Association and others involved with the potential of travel to the British economy to know their significance. The Committee, however, is *not* persuaded that the form of the balance of payments should be altered in order to add the fare payments to the "travel" account.[1]

       2. The Committee recommends that the Board of Trade should consider estimating the spending of foreign travellers on goods etc., not at present included in the "travel" account in the balance of payments. Such figures would be of prime significance in assessing Britain's travel potential and in comparing Britain's experience with that of other countries. Again no change in the present form of the balance of payments accounts need be contemplated.

STIMULATING TRAVEL EARNINGS

261. In considering ways of raising Britain's earnings from travel and of reducing the net deficit in the balance of payments, the Committee has been conscious of the number of bodies already engaged in similar pursuits. The British Travel Association is the Government's chosen instrument for the promotion of overseas visitor traffic to this country and three quarters of its £2,500,000 income comes from the Board of Trade in the form of a grant-in-aid, the remainder being from membership contributions and sales of advertising space and publications. Beyond this association are bodies and associations concerned with different trades and industries involved in travel: the Economic Development Committee for Hotels and Catering, the British Hotels and Restaurants Association, the Hotel Sales Managers Association, the Association of British Travel Agents etc., etc.

262. The survey of accommodation and catering requirements of overseas visitors to Britain, undertaken by the Economic Development Committee for Hotels and Catering earlier this year (*Visitors to Britain*, H.M.S.O., 3s. 6d.), naturally focused its attention on hotels and restaurants. These are also the focus of most overseas spending. Apart from fares, spending on accommodation and food are the largest items in a tourist's expenditure. Of the £215 million spent in Britain in 1966, £110 million went on hotels and restaurants. The British Travel Association is convinced that the proportion will be higher by 1970. On average the 1966 figure amounted to 10 per cent of the turnover of British hotels and restaurants; and in some areas (particularly London) the proportion is far higher. As the British Hotels and Restaurants Association has pointed out, for example, the percentage of foreign exchange earnings for room charges alone at four leading groups of hotels is well above the average:

1. For one thing the balance of payments accounts need to conform to the international usage of the I.M.F. For another, it would involve other complications such as the problem of how to treat the corresponding foreign costs attributable to fares, such as fuel, port charges etc.

Associated Hotels	40 per cent
Grand Metropolitan Hotels	55 per cent
Lyons Group	48 per cent
Savoy Group	73 per cent

263. The question is whether the accommodation and food offered to overseas visitors is adequate both in quantity and quality. The conclusions of the survey undertaken by the Economic Development Committee for Hotels and Catering (mentioned above) were as follows:

"There seems little doubt that, in the opinion of overseas respondents, standards in British hotels and restaurants have improved substantially over recent years. However, it seems equally clear that standards elsewhere have risen too and that Britain has, at best, just about kept pace. While, on most attributes, the most common evaluation of British hotels and restaurants was that they are 'about average,' the balance is weighted more towards a 'below average' than to an 'above average' rating. Particular concern was expressed about the sheer physical shortage of accommodation, especially at peak times and in certain areas, as well as at the lack of good quality accommodation. It was felt, by travel agents[1], that these shortages inhibit travel to the U.K."

264. The Economic Development Committee is pursuing ways in which the hotel and catering industries themselves may be induced to raise their standards and their efficiency. The Committee on Invisible Exports was concerned to examine what the Government might do to help. The starting point, it was decided, was the E.D.C.'s own assessment: "It can only be concluded that unless the rate of hotel construction is accelerated, and existing capacity utilised more efficiently, Britain will fail to realize some part of the potential increase in foreign currency that may be earned from the growth of world tourism." Against this background, in the opinion of the Committee, official help is not over-generous. Only at the beginning of 1967 did the Government announce a scheme to provide loans to hotels "for selected hotel development projects." The commitment was for £5 million. The scheme was to operate as an experiment to run throughout 1967. To be eligible for a loan a project must satisfy three conditions: the Board of Trade must be satisfied that it will provide accommodation acceptable to overseas visitors and to result in new or increased earnings from overseas guests; the project must involve capital spending of not less than £20,000; and work must not have begun on the site before 20 July, 1966. The amount of such loans will not normally exceed 50 per cent of the full costs of the development. Repayments can stretch up to 15 years. The rate of interest will be the Exchequer lending rate, which at the time of the

1. The Committee concerned itself with this problem of getting visitors to Britain, in particular whether enough is being done by travel agents to provide package tours of Britain for foreign visitors. Though British travel agents appear willing to do more, they naturally complain that promoting traffic to Britain is not as profitable for them as sending British people abroad. The Committee believes that this problem, clearly a financial one, deserves further investigation by the British Travel Association.

initial announcement was 7 per cent or $7\frac{1}{8}$ per cent, according to the term of the loan. An Hotel Loans Advisory Committee was set up to advise the Board of Trade on applications.

265. In comparison with the corresponding aid given to hotel industries in other countries, this kind of help appears to the Committee to have been both belated and marginal. Both the Irish Republic and Portugal provide outright subsidies. In Ireland cash grants up to 20 per cent of construction costs are available for new hotels and extensions and similar grants for structural work, staff accommodation and guest entertainment facilities. In addition state guaranteed loans are available over an extended period with facilities for an early interest free period. There are tax allowances for spending incurred on extensions or improvements. In the case of Portugal grants of capital are available through the Tourism Fund. In addition the Government makes loans of 40 per cent of costs over 20 years, some with reduced interest rates, others interest free. There are also tax concessions. Although other countries do not provide subsidies, official help is extensive. In France there is a Development Fund under the French National Plan to provide financial help for modernization of existing hotels and construction of new ones. Loans, which are granted through approved credit institutions subject to guarantee, amounted to about £13 million in 1965. In Spain, although no subsidies or tax exemptions are granted to the hotel industry, Government help consists of credit from a Revolving Fund. In 1965 loans of about £7 million were granted at a fixed rate of interest. The Italian Government provides credit for a maximum of 20 years at 5 per cent for up to 50 per cent of the cost of new buildings and up to 25 per cent for the cost of new internal furnishings. In addition special loan facilities at 3 per cent are available in Southern Italy. Total short and long term credit allocated had reached £112 million in 1965.

266. In addition the hotel industry has had to contend with further burdens imposed on it by the Government in recent years. The main new taxation burden was the selective employment tax which is dealt with in some detail in Chapter XVIII. The financial effect on the hotel industry was clear: in contrast to manufacturing industry it received neither refund nor premium. Secondly, early in 1966, the industry lost the investment allowances allowed on its equipment (as distinct from the buildings) and was not regarded as eligible for the Government's new cash grants. The severity of these measures and their impact on the hotel industry are open to debate. If they are taken in conjunction with the help now being given to hotel industries in several countries abroad, however, one conclusion emerges: that the Government is not providing sufficient help to enable this country to derive the maximum benefit from its tourist potential.

267. In contrast to the relative lack of Government support for the travel industry (and particularly for the core of this complex industry—the hotels catering for overseas visitors), recent official efforts have been concentrated on the other side of the overseas account by restricting individual travel allowances. The tourist allowance has been reduced to £50 per person and

business allowances strictly controlled. This action is in sharp contrast to that of most other western countries. For example the United States, Canada, Western Germany, Belgium, Denmark, Luxembourg, and Switzerland all have unlimited tourist allowances; Portugal has an allowance limit of £625 for each journey, Sweden £415, France £365, Austria £361, Holland £300, Italy £300 and Spain, Norway and Eire £250.

268. The Committee has come to the conclusion that while short-term measures may have been necessary to cope with Britain's immediate economic situation in the summer of 1966, the present combination of restrictions on Britain's own tourist spending abroad and insufficient financial help to the hotel industry should not serve as the long-term solution to Britain's continuing travel deficit. Britain may enjoy less sunshine than other countries but, as the inflow of American visitors demonstrated in 1966 (more came to Britain than to any other European country), she can still hold her own in the wider field of cultural and historical interests. She can also be expected to benefit from the rising living standards throughout Europe, from the expansion in long distance air travel (from North America and the Commonwealth) and from the continuation of law and order in contrast to recent events in the Middle East, Far East, parts of Africa and even some parts of the Mediterranean. Thus prospects are good. The Committee is also convinced that the opportunities will be lost unless the emphasis of Government policy is reversed.

RECOMMENDATION

269. The Committee, therefore, recommends that the Government should significantly increase its financial help to the hotel industry. The Committee's view on the selective employment tax and the export rebate scheme are set out in Chapter XVIII.

APPENDIX A: CHAPTER X
INTERNATIONAL PASSENGER SURVEY
Sampling Method

The sample is designed to be representative of international traffic on all main routes into and out of Great Britain with the exception of routes to the Irish Republic and sea routes to Scandinavia.

1. Air Traffic

This is sampled at London (Heathrow) and London (Gatwick), Manchester, Prestwick, Southend and Lydd all the year round. In alternate summers, commencing in 1964, other airports have been covered during the third quarter of the year only. These have been Birmingham, Luton, Lympne and Manston. The sampling fractions in use at each airport vary widely as do the hours worked. These differences arise from attempts to relate sampling to the incidence of traffic and so to secure the utmost economy in interviewing time.

At all airports the same method is used for selecting passengers for interview. Interviewers use mechanical counters to count passengers passing a fixed point, usually near the Immigration control and approach every 10th passenger for interview. At London No. 1 Building, which carries most European traffic, interviewers work alternate mornings (7 a.m.-2.30 p.m.) and afternoons (2.30-11 p.m.). In the two summer quarters they select every 50th and in winter every 25th passenger. A night-shift from 11 p.m.-7.30 a.m. is worked every eighth night from May-September.

At No. 3 Building, which carries most long haul traffic, interviewers work from 7 a.m.-11 p.m. every day, and select for interviewing every 15th departing passenger and every 25th arriving passenger. These sampling fractions are maintained all the year round. At Manchester and Prestwick interviewers work from 7 a.m.-11 p.m. every day of the week. At Prestwick the sampling intervals are the same as at London No. 3. At Manchester one passenger in 50 is selected for interview in the two summer quarters and one passenger in 25 in the winter quarters. At Gatwick every 50th passenger is selected for interview on sampled days in the second quarter of the year and on sampled days plus every weekend in the third quarter. Night shifts are worked on two out of every three weekend nights. In the winter quarters one day a week is worked using a sampling interval of 25. At Lydd and Southend every 50th passenger is interviewed in the summer quarters, usually between 7 a.m. and 11 p.m. and every 25th on one day a week in the winter quarters. At airports sampled in alternate third quarters only a random day is selected in each week of the quarter and every 50th passenger is interviewed.

2. Short Sea Traffic

The sample of short sea routes is restricted to Harwich-Hook, Dover-Ostend, Dover-Calais, Dover-Boulogne, Folkestone-Calais, Folkestone-Boulogne, Newhaven-Dieppe and Southampton-Cherbourg. On each route a fixed sample is drawn on a crossing (for example, 30 interviews on the Dover-Ostend, 20 on the Dover-Calais), and crossings are sampled from the previous year's passenger figures. (The numbers are fairly stable from year to year with the exception of the car ferries.) In winter the same is 1 per cent. As 30 is 1 per cent of 3,000, a crossing on the Dover-Ostend route is selected which occurs at intervals of 3,000 passengers on a cumulative list of crossings. As this figure is related to traffic more crossings are drawn at the height of the traffic. In the summer quarter the percentage of passengers selected for interview is cut by half to make it practicable to man the greatly increased number of crossings. Passengers on a crossing are selected for interview at the head of the gangway in the same way as at the airports and are interviewed during the crossing.

3. LONG SEA TRAFFIC

All vessels embarking 100 or more passengers at British ports are sampled, as are all vessels arriving at British ports to disembark 200 or more. One in two of departing vessels with 13-99 passengers are sampled as are one in two of arriving vessels with 13-199 passengers. No vessels with 12 passengers or less are sampled. The sampling intervals used are the same as on the long haul air routes. Individual passengers are selected for interview by the same method as at the airports and are interviewed as they board a vessel or as they disembark.

CHAPTER XI

OVERSEAS INVESTMENT

270. Overseas investment, and the return on it in terms of invisible earnings, is divided in the balance of payments into three main categories: portfolio, direct[1] and "other." As clearly pointed out in the introduction, it was understood when the Committee began its work that, since the role of direct investment was being investigated independently by Mr. W. B. Reddaway on behalf of the Confederation of British Industry, the Committee would not duplicate that inquiry. Attention was directed, therefore, to portfolio and "other" investment activities. But first the Committee considered the way in which balance of payments statistics of overseas investments were collected.

STATISTICAL COVERAGE
(a) *Income from direct investment*
(i) *Other than oil*

271. The regular Board of Trade annual inquiry covers earnings from all forms of direct investment overseas apart from those of the oil industry. The earnings include branch earnings, interest payments in respect of loans granted and the remitted dividends from subsidiaries, together with the parent companies' share of the unremitted profits which is retained for reinvestment. Though conducted on a voluntary basis, the Board of Trade reckons that the firms contacted account for over 95 per cent of the total U.K. direct investment overseas[2], and that the response rate in respect of any particular inquiry varies from 75 to 85 per cent.[3]

272. The results of these inquiries are presented in the *Board of Trade Journal* (the latest article was published on June 30, 1967), and provide a breakdown of income by type, by geographical area and by broad industrial groups. As far as the *total* earnings recorded in the *U.K. Balance of Payments*, 1966, Table 13/14, these are probably as comprehensive as can be reasonably expected.[4]

(ii) *Oil*

273. Information of the earnings of oil companies is supplied by the industry to the Bank of England and the overall results are passed to the Central

---

1. The Board of Trade makes this distinction between portfolio and direct investment:
    "Broadly speaking, direct investment is investment by companies in branches, subsidiaries and associates, collectively described as 'affiliates'; and portfolio investment is other investment in stocks or shares of companies or in the bonds or issues of public authorities."
    Board of Trade Journal, June 30, 1967.
2. Though the Board of Trade contacts all firms known or believed to have overseas interests, some companies inevitably slip through the net.
3. A quarterly sample survey is also conducted. This covers firms accounting for about 35 per cent of foreign earnings.
4. Checks with statistics published by the more important partner countries, viz. U.S., Canada, Australia, etc. reveal a very close proximity with the Board of Trade estimates.

Statistical Office and Ministry of Fuel and Power. Such earnings as are published represent the surplus on the current transactions of U.K. companies from their operations overseas and include the value of services rendered between parents, overseas subsidiaries and associated companies.

    (b) *Income from portfolio investment*
      (i) *On private account*

274. For the past six years, the Board of Inland Revenue has supplied data to the Central Statistical Office on most kinds of income earned by or remitted to U.K. residents on portfolio investments abroad.[1] Details of the information collected by the Inland Revenue are given on pp. 64-67 of the *Inland Revenue's* 1965 *Report*. This is set out in full in Appendix A and TABLE 42. The reconciliation of the *Inland Revenue* and *U.K. Balance of Payments*, 1966, data is given in TABLE 43 in Appendix B.

      (ii) *On official account*

275. Exchequer income incorporates interest and dividend payments received on securities held in the Exchange Equalization Account (which is known from Treasury records). In 1964, it was estimated that such securities were worth $1,250 million but during the past two or three years most of them have been sold and a large part of the proceeds has been taken into the reserves.

    (c) *Other investment income*
      (i) *Interest on certain claims in sterling*

276. This information is supplied by the Bank of England and is computed from returns made by over 200 U.K. banks and other financial institutions. It is worked out by applying the appropriate rates of interest to three main forms of claims: (a) advances and overdrafts, (b) certain commercial bills and promissory notes, (c) acceptances outstanding[2] and represents the earnings of U.K. banks on loans made (or credits given) to foreigners. The monies received on claims in non-sterling currencies are treated as a form of financial arbitrage and is classified under financial and allied services.

      (ii) *Interest received by financial institutions, manufacturers and exporters on trade credit extended to foreign importers*

277. This is estimated by the Central Statistical Office by applying appropriate rates of interest to the estimated amount of trade credit outstanding, wherever such credit is granted to non-related companies and is for more than 180 days (i.e. medium or long-term credit). Table 32 of the *U.K. Balance of Payments*, 1966, gives the results of the latest Board of Trade inquiry into trade credit. (See also *Board of Trade Journal* of June 17, 1966.) Interest on trade credit extended to related companies is included as part of the earnings on overseas direct investment.

      (iii) *Annuities and income from trust funds held abroad and accruing to U.K. persons or institutions; income from real estate owned by individuals, etc.*

---

1. Of which it is estimated that 60 per cent is earned by companies and the balance by individuals and partnerships.
2. For details see Table 26 of *U.K. Balance of Payments*, 1966.

278. Data on this item is supplied by the Inland Revenue: the income is running currently at some £20 million a year.

HISTORICAL BASIS

279. As the statistics set out in Chapter II show, it was not until the second half of the nineteenth century that the complex machinery of British overseas earnings attained its full momentum, and investment revenues began their most powerful growth. Until 1870, these moved in parallel with the income from shipping. From that point on they rose sharply, and by 1913 had left shipping returns at a third of their level, far behind. It is clear that by the last decades of the nineteenth century the cycle of investment and income had become a self-generating process and had achieved a momentum of its own. In each year investment yields were devoted where necessary to the coverage of deficits in the overall current account and were then fed back into the pool of capital assets abroad. Thus augmented, the investment reservoir yielded a greater return in the following year, and the pattern was again repeated. A "revolving" fund seemed to have taken shape. The combined efforts of traders and investors had led to the creation of a financial mechanism of apparently immense durability and of crucial value to the balancing of the country's external accounts. Nothing less than a catastrophe, it seemed, could have torn this great structure down.

280. The catastrophe occurred. In the First World War of 1914-18, and in the ensuing 20 years of economic blight, at least £1,000 million of the 1913 stake of £4,000 million net capital, was lost, sold, sequestered or destroyed during the war, or dissipated in the economic disarray of the 1920s and 1930s. By 1939 it had proved possible to restore the net asset position to the £4,000 million holding of 26 years before. In the Second World War which immediately followed, a further £1,000 million was sacrificed, and unquantified disinvestment continued into the 1950s. In addition, capital debts of £3,000 million, in the shape of the sterling balances, sprang up.

281. Re-investment started fairly soon. It is clear that by the late 1950s private long-term investment abroad (net of disinvestment) was proceeding at a rate of about £300 million a year, and this rhythm of build-up was maintained in the 1960s. In 1964 the amount rose to £406 million, although it reverted to £356 million in 1965[1]. The foregoing does not take account of the inflow of capital funds, which at times exceeded the sums leaving the country (e.g. in 1961 and 1962), or of the official position which was certainly included in the net asset figure of £4,000 million estimated for 1913 and 1939. In 1962 and again in 1964 the Bank of England made the first official post-war estimates of the country's total net capital worth abroad. This showed total assets in 1964 at £15,540 million, against liabilities of £13,390 million, a net favourable position of £2,150 million. This assessment included short as well as long-term capital. Counting long-term capital only, private and official, the balance was struck at £10,715 million assets (of which £9,420 million

1. Table 2, "Overseas Investment", *Board of Trade Journal*, June 30, 1967.

were private) and £5,970 million liabilities (of which £3,384 million were on private account), leaving the U.K. as a net creditor to the extent of £4,745 million. (i.e. her long-term creditor position is bigger than her short-term debtor position.) Since 1945 the emphasis has been on direct investment which, by the Bank of England's calculations, accounted for about £6,000 million out of the U.K.'s total overseas private investment of £9,400 million mentioned above.

282. The effect of these changes in capital flows on revenue is apparent. Yearly net returns (i.e. income received from overseas investment less income paid to foreigners) rose steadily throughout the nineteenth century, amounting to some £5 million in 1825 and culminating in the rate of £188 million in 1913. Their growth then virtually stopped. Apart from a brief run at the £250 million level in 1925-29, they remained around £200 million until 1938. Starting again from a very low level after 1945, they then returned, in the greatly depreciated values of the post-war period, to a general average of £250 million during the 1950s. In the last few years they have risen somewhat further, reaching £396 million and £416 million in 1963 and 1964, and topping the £450 million mark in 1965. It was only in the early 1950s that these incomes exceeded even the nominal value of those received in 1913. In real values, they were worth, even in 1965, less than half the 1913 income. Measured against the objective yardstick of gross national product, they equalled 8·5 per cent of the latter in 1913 and no more than 1·5 per cent in 1965.

TABLE 40

INTEREST, PROFITS AND DIVIDENDS: 1958–1965

£ million	1958	1959	1960	1961	1962	1963	1964	1965
Portfolio:								
Debits	55	49	56	51	52	64	69	70
Credits	115	121	133	133	142	141	148	160
Net	+ 60	+ 72	+ 77	+ 82	+ 90	+ 77	+ 79	+ 90
Direct:								
Debits	95	136	137	128	134	168	203	221
Credits	195	238	258	249	274	330	375	403
Net	+100	+102	+121	+121	+140	+162	+172	+182
Other:								
Debits	239	211	245	243	232	203	212	239
Credits	373	304	289	304	338	360	377	440
Net	+134	+ 93	+ 44	+ 61	+106	+157	+165	+201
Total:								
Debits	389	396	438	422	418	435	484	530
Credits	683	663	680	686	754	831	900	1,003
Total "Interest, profits and dividends" Net	294	267	242	264	336	396	416	476

283. The changes within these totals of overseas investment income have been equally significant. Portfolio income, once the mainstay of Britain's invisible earnings, is now the smallest category of the total item "interest, profits and dividends." Details are set out in TABLE 40. Although the

statistical breakdown between direct and portfolio investment income has only been available since 1958, it seems clear that portfolio investment has been of declining importance since 1914. In recent years receipts from portfolio investments rose by 28 per cent between 1958 and 1964 when, at £148 million, they represented 17 per cent of total investment income receipts. Payments from foreign portfolio investment in the U.K. were stable at around £50 million until 1962 but increased sharply in 1963 and 1964 to £64 million and £69 million. Yet, although this is the smallest item of foreign investment it does yield a net surplus which helped the balance of payments by £79 million in 1964. In 1958 the surplus was £60 million; by 1966 it had reached £94 million.

CAPITAL VERSUS INCOME

284. Overseas investment influences the balance of payments accounts in different ways and in considering methods of improving invisible earnings the Committee has been conscious of these various cross-currents. They can be set out in a simple way.

285. An *inflow* of capital funds to the U.K. can lead to (*a*) an improvement in the capital account; (*b*) a subsequent payment of interest overseas; and (*c*) earnings of foreign exchange from commissions (particularly relating to an inflow of portfolio investment).

286. On the other hand an *outflow* of capital funds can lead to (*a*) a deterioration on capital account and (*b*) subsequent receipts of dividends or profits. Thus in recent years attention has been focused on the net outflow of capital. It is understandable that at a time when the visible trade account was in significant deficit (e.g. from 1964 onwards), more consideration was given to the effect of a net outflow of capital on the central gold reserves, even though investment financed by free exports or by borrowing abroad has no immediate impact on the reserves. Yet any outflow should be taken into account with the yield in terms of "interest, profits and dividends." This is done in the case of the three categories of overseas investment in TABLE 41.

TABLE 41

CAPITAL AND INTEREST FLOWS

£ millions	1961	1962	1963	1964	1965	1966
Portfolio (Net)						
Capital	+143	+100	+ 15	− 43	+ 43	+ 65
Interest	+ 82	+ 90	+ 77	+ 79	+ 90	+ 94
Direct (Net)						
Capital	+ 10	− 79	− 76	−101	+127	− 90
Interest	+121	+140	+162	+172	+166	+210
Other (Net)						
Capital	− 40	− 15	+ 10	−109	− 71	− 24
Interest	+ 61	+106	+157	+165	+194	+113
Total (Net)						
Capital	+113	+ 6	− 65	−252	−155	− 49
Interest	+264	+336	+396	+416	+451	+417

Sources: Direct interest and capital element from *Board of Trade Journal*, June 30, 1967.
Other items from *Economic Trends*, June, 1967.

287. As the table brings out, there has been a growing return from overseas investment since the beginning of the 1960s. Even in 1963, 1964 and 1965, when the flows of capital led to a *net* outflow of funds from the United Kingdom, the return on overseas investment more than offset this net outflow. This was so in the case of direct investment. It was particularly so in the case of portfolio investment.

288. The Committee has come to two tentative conclusions from its brief examination of the statistics of overseas investment:

1. It believes that the United Kingdom is probably unique in generating such a large two-way traffic in capital movements and in the consequent returns from such capital investments. Whereas the U.S. is a bigger exporter of capital and the developing world a bigger importer of capital, no other country so plainly combines both roles as the United Kingdom.

2. In formulating exchange control policy, the Committee believes it essential to consider the *net* effect of all these flows of capital, interest and profits and not to concentrate on one to the exclusion of the others.

RECOMMENDATIONS

289. 1. The Committee, therefore, recommends that a detailed study be made of the role of the United Kingdom in the international flow of capital—direct, portfolio and "other"—and of the impact of this, and of the returns flowing from it, on the U.K.'s balance of payments.

2. The Committee, in the belief that obstructions to both the inflow and outflow of portfolio investment are likely to undermine earnings of invisible income, recommends that the Government should consider policies aimed at eliminating or reducing such obstructions, for example:

   (i) The removal of stamp duty.

   (ii) An increase in the number of fixed interest securities free of tax at source to non-residents.

   (iii) The negotiation of further double taxation relief agreements with the minimum possible rate of withholding tax.

   (iv) Introduction of shares of no par value.

   (v) Bearer share issues by U.K. companies.

   (vi) Removal or adjustment in the case of investment trusts of the 25 per cent surrender of exchange to the Treasury arising from sales of foreign securities.

   (vii) Adjustment of death duty provisions relating to the foreign ownership of U.K. securities.

APPENDIX A

INCOME FROM ABROAD:
EXTRACT FROM INLAND REVENUE REPORT

The following extract is taken verbatim from the Inland Revenue Annual Report for 1965.

In the following paragraphs estimates are given of the income arising abroad and accruing to British residents so far as it can be identified. The estimates represent the income for income tax purposes, and must not be confused with the total receipts from overseas which are the figures of direct importance for the purpose of the international balance of payments; nevertheless the connection between the two sets of figures is indicated where possible.

Income arising abroad to residents in the United Kingdom falls into eight different classes according to the nature of the income and the way it is taxed. Thus (i) to (iii) below distinguish the interest and dividends from overseas paid through paying agents here or collected from overseas through bankers, coupon dealers, etc. Income tax on such income is charged on the agent or banker concerned, and in general the assessments made in a financial year relate to the income paid by such agents in the same year. Classes (iv) to (vi) distinguish the identifiable income from abroad assessed to income tax on the recipient under the normal rules of Schedule D. Except for assessments on O.T.C. distributions ((vi) below) the amounts assessed in a year are normally related to the income of accounting periods ending in the previous year. Finally (vii) and (viii) relate to income which cannot be separated from United Kingdom income taxed in the same way—(vii) to assessments based normally on the income of the previous year and (viii) to assessments on income of the current year.

The classes of income from abroad for taxation purposes are:

(i) Interest on overseas government and municipal securities, paid through paying agents in this country. The amounts assessed to income tax are the gross amounts of interest actually paid by the agents.

(ii) Interest and dividends from overseas companies paid through paying agents in this country. In many cases some double taxation relief is allowed at the time of payment. In such cases the amount assessed is the amount of interest and dividends received by paying agent plus the amount of overseas tax for which relief is given. Income tax at the standard rate is charged on this amount and the relief to be allowed is set against the tax. The amount of money actually received by the paying agent is therefore the total amount assessed less the double taxation relief allowed. (The relief allowed at this stage may be too large or too small in the case of a particular individual ultimately receiving the income and the necessary adjustment is made then by his local Inspector of Taxes.)

(iii) Interest, dividends, and other annual payments within the meaning of section 187 of the Income Tax Act, 1952, not payable in this country but collected from overseas through bankers, coupon-dealers, etc. This income includes a certain amount of overseas government interest not distinguishable from company interest and dividends, and further small amounts of annuities, etc., paid annually. As in (ii) some double taxation relief is allowed on most American dividends and Canadian interest and dividends.

(iv) Income from foreign securities and possessions taxed under Cases IV and V of Schedule D (which are usually not separable). Assessments usually include the amount of overseas tax for which relief is given, but tax relief granted in a year often includes tax relief for earlier years, and so the income net of foreign taxation cannot be readily identified as it can be in the previous categories. The normal basis of assessment is the income of the previous year.

(v) Income arising from businesses with their assets situate abroad controlled in this country but carried on mainly abroad. The profits of such concerns are normally assessable on the preceding year basis under Case I of Schedule D, except for companies which have qualified as Overseas Trade Corporations for 1957-58 and later years (see (vi)). The income assessed is that remaining after deduction of capital allowances but, as for (iv), it includes the amount of overseas tax for which relief is given.

(vi) Overseas Trade Corporations have formed a special class of companies since the Finance Act, 1957, before which their profits would have fallen into category (v). Since then, they have not been taxed on their trading income, but have been assessed instead only to income tax under Case VI of Schedule D on distributions made out of their exempt trading income. The following numbers of companies qualified for and adopted Overseas Trade Corporation status for each year:

1957–58	829	1961–62	960 (estimated)
1958–59	915	1962–63	975 (estimated)
1959–60	915	1963–64	975 (estimated)
1960–61	960 (estimated)		

Apart from these, the only annual figures are those of the aggregate assessments on distributions shown in Table 42, but these on the one hand include substantial distributions made to other Overseas Trade Corporations within the same group of companies and on the other hand (especially in the earlier years) exclude distributions made out of profits earned before they became exempt trading income. Moreover, they are the assessments made in the year and not those for the year, so that on the admission of a claim to Overseas Trade Corporation status any adjustments for a previous year (the vacation of the original assessment on profits and its replacement by an assessment on distributions) is in general reflected in the figures for the assessment year in which the claim was allowed.

A special survey in 1963 showed that whilst the total distributions for 1962 were about £114 million (before deduction of tax), the amount remaining after excluding distributions to other Overseas Trade Corporations was only about £85 million, which was paid out of a net total exempt trading income of about £130 million (estimated on normal commercial lines and before deduction of foreign tax). The cost of the scheme to the Revenue was shown to be in the neighbourhood of £10 million a year, after allowing for relief that would otherwise have been due in respect of foreign tax.

(vii) Income earned abroad by concerns which, though trading abroad, have their main business at home. The overseas component of profits of such concerns cannot be identified because the total profits are assessed to income tax in one sum under Case I of Schedule D. The principal concerns in this category are shipping, banking and insurance companies having branches abroad; it also includes manufacturing and trading concerns with works or branches abroad.

(viii) Emoluments from an office or employment received in the United Kingdom by a United Kingdom resident for duties performed overseas are taxed under Case III of Schedule E, but they cannot be separated from other Schedule E earnings. Also, pensions from overseas are often taxed under Schedule E (see below).

Most of the income in (i), (ii) and (iii) is portfolio investment income from abroad, though (iii) in particular may also include income from foreign trusts where the interest and dividends from securities held by the trust are paid directly to the United Kingdom beneficiary. Since in all cases the assessments are made on the paying or collecting agent, no information is available centrally about the ultimate recipient of income, unless he is a non-resident. In these cases such income is normally excluded from assessment. Some income of non-residents, however, suffers deduction of tax that is later repaid and this income, which is estimated at about £5 million a year, is included in the table below. The total income exempted from assessment on the paying agent under Schedule C and Schedule D in 1963-64 for any reason amounted to £27 million and £56 million respectively, of which the greater part was income of non-residents, although some of it was income of exempt persons or bodies in this country.

Since the income in (iv) to (vi) is assessed on the recipient the amounts received by companies and by individuals and partnerships can be shown separately. The most important component of the income of companies in (iv) is the distributions and other income received from overseas subsidiaries. Class (iv) also contains a substantial amount of portfolio investment income falling outside (i) to (iii), as well as all portfolio investment income from the

Republic of Ireland (even if paid through paying agents, etc.), which is always taxed in this manner owing to the special terms of the Irish double taxation relief agreement. The rest of (iv) is miscellaneous types of income from abroad, such as foreign bank interest and other loan interest; foreign trust income; rents and royalties from abroad; and (for individuals) annuities and some pensions from abroad. However, in many cases pensions from dominions and colonies are remitted in a lump sum to the Commonwealth Relations Office or Crown Agents, and thence distributed to the individual pensioners; these pensions, taxed under Schedule E, are included in (viii), the amount being of the order of £10 million.

Dividends in groups (ii), (iii) and (iv) are from companies not resident in the United Kingdom for tax purposes; payments by overseas subsidiaries to United Kingdom parent companies are usually in (iv) but some are included in (ii). Some non-resident companies are nevertheless registered in the United Kingdom; the total of dividend payments by this class of non-resident companies is estimated at about £3 million for 1963-64. For balance of payments purposes, such companies are treated differently from the majority of the companies in this group (which are both non-resident for tax purposes and registered overseas); not only the remitted dividends, but the whole of the profits arising overseas go on the credit side of the balance of payments current account.

The following table gives classified details of the identifiable income from abroad received in the years 1954-55 to 1962-63 for classes (i) to (vi) and that in 1963-64 for all these except (iv) and (v). For these two classes the income forms the basis for the 1964-65 assessments, which have not yet been analysed.

APPENDIX A: CHAPTER XI

TABLE 42

INCOME FROM ABROAD

Taken from Inland Revenue Annual Report, 1965

£ million

Year	Interest on overseas government and municipal securities (i)	Company interest and dividends paid through U.K. paying agents (ii)		Interest and dividends received through encashment of coupons (iii)		Income from abroad assessed Cases IV and V in the following year (iv)		Net trading profits from abroad assessed Case I in the following year (v)		Distributions by O.T.C.'s assessed Case VI in the year to 30th Sept. (vi)
		Gross assessment	Net income received	Gross assessment	Net income received	Individuals and partnerships	Companies	Individuals and partnerships	Companies[1]	
1954–55	24·4	42·5	35·6	32·6	30·0	28·5	64·7	·4	293·3	—
1955–56	22·7	42·8	36·8	47·4	44·0	29·5	77·7	·3	315·2	—
1956–57	21·7	51·5	43·8	51·0	46·9	30·0	95·0	·4	217·3	—
1957–58	21·6	45·0	38·7	47·4	42·8	32·0	127·3	·2	177·6	9·3
1958–59	21·5	46·4	40·0	45·9	41·5	31·4	234·1	·2	209·2	22·5
1959–60	23·1	47·0	41·7	50·7	45·8	31·0	154·7	·1	128·9	54·1
1960–61	22·8	57·0	49·3	56·7	51·6	30·8	202·0	·1	185·3	98·7
1961–62	22·3	51·6	44·5	58·4	53·2	31·3	206·9	·4	160·4	111·0
1962–63	21·8	48·7	41·6	60·2	55·0	32·0	253·5	·8	156·5	152·1
1963–64	21·4	51·7	44·1	62·1	56·7	32·0	253·5	·8	156·5	126·9
1964–65	22·8	55·8	47·5	68·8	63·1	32·0	253·5	·8	156·5	126·9

1. For 1956-57 and later years the figures exclude O.T.C.'s; see paragraph (vi).

TABLE 43

RECONCILIATION OF INLAND REVENUE AND BOARD OF TRADE DATA ON PORTFOLIO INVESTMENT EARNINGS (1964)

£ *million*

	Table in Inland Revenue Annual Report 1964–65	*Balance of Payments Figures 1964–65*	*Balance of Payments Figures 1964*
1. Government and municipal interest	22·8	22·6	22·4
2. United Kingdom paying agents	47·5	47·7	43·8
3. Coupon dealers	63·1	63·1	60·6
Deduct payments to non-residents	—	−6·0	−6·0
Deduct income from Trust (^{1}) funds held abroad	—	−9·0	−9·0
Add Cases IV and V	22·0²	22·0	22·0
Add income on E.E.A. dollar portfolio	—	14·0	14·0
Total		154·4	147·5

1. Included in the Inland Revenue figures under categories (1) to (3) above. Classified in the balance of payments as "other" income, together with a further £8 million assessed under Cases IV and V.
2. Inland Revenue estimate—£30 million in all; assessed at £32 million in 1962-63. £8 million classified in the balance of payments as "other" income.

CHAPTER XII

MISCELLANEOUS SERVICES

290. The Committee has been impressed, in the course of its investigations, by the variety of services that bring in a foreign income. In some cases details of these earnings are well known and collected regularly; in others the Committee has undertaken a special inquiry to discover the size of earnings; in others again the Committee has suggested areas for future investigation[1]. In this chapter such miscellaneous services are examined and set out separately.

1. MARKET IN ANTIQUES AND WORKS OF ART

291. Interviews were held with representatives of Christie, Manson and Woods Ltd. and Sotheby & Company who between them do virtually all the auction business, and with representatives of the Antique Dealers' Association, the Society of London Art Dealers and the Antiquarian Booksellers' Association. All stressed the importance of the art market in attracting overseas visitors to London and leading to expenditure here. Such earnings, however, are recorded by the travel survey.

292. Sources of invisible income, however, seemed to be mainly the following:

> Profits and commissions on overseas business.
> "Expertising."
> Repairs and restoration.
> Catalogues.

"Expertising" arises only in the antique trade, where fees accrue to the Association. The following figures were supplied by the Association:

1963	£10,800
1964	£14,000
1965	£14,500

Fees are paid by the shipper and should, therefore, be included in the f.o.b. values declared to customs.

293. The Society of London Art Dealers said that members received fees for repairs and restoration, but believed they would be small. The Society eventually decided that their earnings were not large enough to warrant the work of collecting figures.

294. Sotheby & Company gave their income from overseas sales of catalogues at £45,000. Christie's overseas sales of catalogues is approximately £18,000. Again, however, it seems that these receipts are included in the returns of visible trade.

---

1. An overall allowance is at present made in the balance of payments estimates for earnings from the miscellany of services which are not separately recorded.

295. Profits and commissions are much more substantial, but there are serious problems both in estimating their total amount and in determining how much of it is covered by the visible trade figures.

296. Sotheby's gave their commissions from overseas clients at between £350,000 and £400,000. Christie's were unable to give a figure, but their business is somewhat smaller than Sotheby's and a smaller proportion of their sales are on behalf of overseas clients—they estimated around 10 per cent whereas Sotheby's said "between a quarter and a third." On this basis their earnings could not be much more than £100,000. None of the Associations was able to provide figures, though in each case the earnings of individual firms were believed to be small. One might, therefore, guess the total, including the auction firms, at between £500,000 and £750,000. It seems likely, however, that a large part of this is reflected in the valuation of "visible" trade.

297. Overseas trade in this field may be divided into three categories:
  1. Exports of works formerly in the possession of British residents.
  2. Imports of foreign owned works sold to British residents, and
  3. Re-export of works consigned to London for sale and sold to overseas buyers.

298. In principle, the third category should be recorded as re-exports in the trade accounts but it is very difficult to draw a hard and fast line between 1 and 3. As already mentioned, the auction firms know the proportion of their sales which originate abroad, but they very frequently do not know the destination of works sold. These may be bought by a British dealer acting as agent for an overseas client, or by a dealer acting as principal, but who subsequently sells to an overseas buyer.

299. Trade in antiques and works of art, as recorded in the monthly trade accounts, is:

	£ million	
	1965	1966
Imports	23·4	23·8
Exports	29·1	26·8
Re-exports	4·6	3·4

The small value of re-exports strongly suggests that some works recorded as exports are in British ownership for only a very short time.

300. It was generally agreed among those interviewed that exports were normally declared at their sale value, which would include the profit or commission of the auctioneer or dealer. One firm, however, mentioned that some overseas buyers probably under-valued goods in order to evade customs duties in their own countries.

301. There is much more doubt about the valuation of imports. Christie's stated that imports from America were normally entered at insured value, which tended to exceed the price actually realized, while imports from Europe were under-valued. Sotheby's thought that imports were sometimes entered at a "very modest" value.

302. The outcome of all this appears to be that commissions earned by the

sale of foreign owned works to overseas buyers are included in the visible trade figures, as are also commissions and profits from the sale of British owned works to overseas buyers. If imports were correctly valued, they would overstate payments due on foreign works retained in Britian by the amount of dealer's commissions, and this should be entered as an invisible export. However, there seems no possibility of separating this element from commission on other business. Moreover, in so far as imports are under-valued, the trade accounts over-state our credit position both in regard to retained imports and to re-exports. This may well exceed the amount of commissions omitted.

2. FILMS AND TELEVISION

303. Particulars of receipts from overseas in respect of production and exhibition of cinematograph films and television material are published in the *Board of Trade Journal* (the issue of 6 January, 1967, contains revised 1964 figures). They also form part of the items "Films and television" in Table 11 of the *U.K. Balance of Payments* Pink Book, though the 1964 figures have been revised since the 1966 edition of the Pink Book was published. The components of this item for 1964 now published by the Board of Trade are as follows:

Receipts in respect of films	£20 million
in respect of television and radio	£2 million
	£22 million
Less overlap estimated at 50% of exports of films and television, included in the "visible" accounts[1]	£3 million
	£19 million

304. The data is obtained by the Board of Trade from some 250 film companies. These include a number of U.K. owned companies, each set up to produce a single film, production of which is almost always financed by United States capital; the film *Tom Jones* for example, was made this way. By this method the U.S. backers obtain the benefit of payments from the U.K. production fund which is restricted to companies' both registered and controlled in the U.K. The important American rights in general belong to the U.S. backers and the U.K. rights to the U.K. company, but arrangements vary. Of other foreign rights, much may depend on which company, U.S. or U.K., can best exploit them: quota arrangements may favour one or the other, e.g. for some European countries U.K. owned rights receive a more liberal treatment.

305. The film figures exclude any rights restricted solely to television, but these are thought to be insignificant. The television figures include all sales, of rights by the B.B.C. and the Independent Television Companies.

3. ROYALTIES

306. This item includes amounts received by U.K. residents in return for

1. These represent the cost of the films plus carriage *per se* as opposed to the royalties earned on the films.

the right to use British processes[1] and other information (e.g. licences to use patents, trade marks, designs, copyrights, etc.) excluding film royalties, but including literary and artistic royalties. Once again the data is collected each year by the Board of Trade and published in its *Journal* (the latest article is contained in the issue of 21 July, 1967). Separate details are given for transactions between related and non-related concerns, overseas, for technological and other kinds of royalties and for individual countries and industries. The inquiry is a voluntary one and still in its early stages: though every effort is made by the Board of Trade to contact all firms known to have overseas connections of one kind or another, in 1964 only 5,000 U.K. companies completed returns.

307. The breakdown of royalty[2] transactions in 1964 (in rather more detail than is published in the *Board of Trade Journal*) was as follows:

	£ million 1964	
Total Royalties, etc.	U.K. Credits	U.K. Debits
Transactions with related concerns overseas*	20·4	26·6
Transactions with other concerns overseas	38·5	23·7
*An estimated breakdown of these figures would be:		
Transactions with overseas parent companies	0·5	24·3
Transactions with overseas branches, subsidiaries etc.	19·9	2·3

308. In considering the payments between related companies, one of the difficulties is to assess how much the U.K. company is subsidizing, or being subsidized, by its foreign subsidiaries. From the viewpoint of the investing firm, one of the aims may be to minimize its international tax burden. This could mean that it pays the investing company to bear the cost of providing technical expertise and managerial services to its overseas subsidiaries (assuming the U.K. to be the high tax country) thus allowing higher profits to be earned abroad (net of tax) than might be the case if such services had been charged at normal prices. But this could be to the disadvantage of the balance of payments: for remittance of royalties plus profits earned (less tax) is likely to be greater than the remittance of no royalties but a higher profit. To some extent at least then, the published figures of royalties, taken in conjunction with the earnings of direct investment, may reflect the struc-ture of international fiscal arrangements.

4. ADVERTISING

309. Advertising activities may earn foreign currency for the U.K. in two quite distinct ways. First, foreign companies may buy, either directly, or through advertising agencies, the services of particular advertising media in

1. One particularly significant earner of foreign income from royalties is the National Research Development Corporation. Its income from abroad arises almost wholly from royalty payments, options on licences and sales of patent rights. These earnings in recent years were: £217,000 in year to June, 1965; £163,229 in nine months to March, 1966; and £468,890 in year to March, 1967. Expenses are incurred aboard in running an office in Washington and also in negotiating licence agreements. These are subject to sharp fluctuations but N.R.D.C. believes that they have probably ranged between £20,000 and £40,000 in recent years.
2. In the case of both films and television and royalties, there are debits to be offset against U.K. earnings. In both cases they are smaller than the credits.

the U.K., e.g. the press, TV, films etc. In this case, it is the *total advertising* receipts which accrue to the U.K. as foreign currency. Second, U.K. advertising agencies may earn income from foreign clients by work undertaken on their behalf in overseas countries. In this case, it is the *commission* earned by the agencies on the advertising which accrues to the U.K. as foreign currency.

310. These two sources of income can be examined in turn:

(a) Home advertising

311. The main source for these figures is the Statistical Review of press and TV advertising. This document gives particulars of the advertising expenditures of the leading advertisers according to media and agency (if employed), from which it is possible to pick out the advertising directly commissioned by foreign companies. This expenditure includes the commission of U.K. agencies where such agencies are used, but excludes that of other than the leading advertisers and that directed to non press and TV advertising services. Allowing for missing coverage and advertising on other U.K. media (e.g. posters), the total is believed to have been between £6 million and £8 million in 1964.

(b) Foreign advertising

312. The earnings from foreign advertising accrue to advertising agencies from three kinds of activity:

     (i) a U.K. agency can buy, on behalf of a foreign client, the services of a foreign advertising media, direct from that media.

    (ii) it can buy such services, indirectly, via the U.K. representatives of a foreign media.

   (iii) it can operate its foreign activities through a branch or subsidiary company overseas.

313. Earnings in respect of (i) and (ii) represent a commission but present indications, though only rough, are that they are small. They may have been between £3 million and £4 million in 1964. Earnings in respect of (iii) are earnings of direct investment and thus shown in a separate part of the balance of payments.

314. In view of the unsatisfactory nature of some of these estimates of advertising earnings, the Committee discussed the position with the Institute of Practitioners in Advertising. The Institute has subsequently agreed to undertake a survey among members of their overseas earnings.

5. MANAGEMENT CONSULTANTS

315. This growing new profession has expanded its foreign earnings in recent years. The Committee approached the Management Consultants Association for information about such earnings. The Association, which was founded by four consulting firms in 1956, now comprises 17 members whose consulting staff numbers over 2,000 representing an estimated 70 per cent of professional management consultants in the United Kingdom. The Association reported that during 1966 member firms earned £2,600,000 gross in fees from foreign clients. When overseas expenses are deducted from

this total, the Association estimates, net invisible earnings of member firms amounted to £304,000 for 1966.

6. Casinos

316. It became clear to the Committee that a growing amount of foreign income was being attracted by the leading casinos in London and elsewhere. It is estimated that over 1,000 casinos are in existence, but only a few attract large numbers of foreign visitors and most of these are in London. The Casino Association of Great Britain, which represents five of the best known gaming casinos in London, made an estimate of its members' invisible income on behalf of the Committee. Net direct foreign exchange earnings (i.e. the sums held in foreign exchange after payment of any winnings in foreign exchange) for each member of the Association worked out as follows:

> (a) *Clermont* (year to April, 1967)   £228,000
>   1 blackjack, 1 roulette, 1 baccarat and
>   2 chemin-de-fer tables.
>
> (b) *Crockford's* (year to April, 1967)   £301,000
>   2 blackjack, 2 roulette, 1 baccarat and
>   3 chemin-de-fer tables.
>
> (c) *Playboy* (year to June, 1967, estimated)   £280,000
>   1 craps, 6 roulette, 7 blackjack tables.
>
> (d) *Curzon House* (year to April, 1967)   £118,000
>   1 baccarat, 1 chemin-de-fer, 1 chemmy/
>   Baccarat, 3 blackjack, 4 roulette, 1
>   craps tables.
>
> (e) *Palm Beach* (year to October, 1966)   £302,000
>   1 baccarat, 2 chemin-de-fer, 6 black-
>   jack, 7 roulette, 1 craps tables.

317. The Association believes that these earnings in most cases should be doubled in order to allow for the fact that most foreign players will change half of their "gambling" foreign currency before entering the premises. (The exception is Clermont's where virtually all foreign business is on credit.) On this basis the earnings of these five casinos work out at £2,230,000. What proportion of the country's total foreign earnings from gaming accrue to these five casinos is not known, but if they account for just under 50 per cent of the total, total foreign earnings from gaming in the United Kingdom may now be approaching £5 million. These earnings should, of course, be included under "travel" earnings.

7. Accountants, Solicitors and Other Professions

318. Investigations in the City of London convinced the Committee that some of the large firms of accountants and solicitors earned a significant amount of money from foreign clients. It was accordingly decided to ask several professional associations for help in undertaking pilot surveys among their members. Details were asked of accountants, solicitors, actuaries, surveyors etc. for the year 1965. The results of these investigations were as follows:

> (a) *Institute of Chartered Accountants in England and Wales:* £1,052,000.

184

319. Some 3,700 replies were received out of a possible total of 5,500-6,000. Sixteen firms contributed 75 per cent of the total.

(b) *Institute of Chartered Accountants of Scotland:* £32,345.

320. Some 363 replies were received out of a possible 632. The earnings were accounted for by 39 members.

(c) *Association of Certified and Corporate Accountants:* £35,000.

321. Members were also asked what they expected to earn in the next few years. The results were: 1967, £40,000; 1968, £45,000; and 1969, £54,000.

(d) *Institute of Cost and Works Accountants*:

322. The majority of the Institute's 9,500 members work in industry and public service and some are in teaching. A few members are in practice— either as partners or employees of management consultants or as consulting cost accountants. The former are covered by another part of this inquiry; the latter earn little from abroad. Accordingly it was decided not to undertake a special inquiry.

(e) *Law Society:* £870,000.

323. Some 2,700 replies were received from solicitors[1] out of a possible total of 6,000-7,000.

324. (It is clear from replies that many members excluded sterling receipts from non-residents. This strongly suggests that the total foreign earnings in balance of payments terms may have been substantially understated.)

(f) *Royal Institution of Chartered Surveyors:* £360,878.

325. Membership exceeds 20,000. Accordingly the survey was confined to 50 large firms. Of these nine replied in time to be included in this report. They accounted for the £360,878.

(g) *Institute of Actuaries:* £60,000 (approx.).

326. The majority of members are employed in full time service with insurance companies and other institutions. The earnings shown are of members employed in whole time professional practice.

327. It has not been possible, within the time available, for the Committee to examine closely and in any detail the obstacles preventing the various professions and commercial concerns dealt with in this chapter from earning additional invisible income. But the Committee believes that several difficulties faced by such earners of foreign income need to be aired:

(a) There is said to be a growing tendency on the part of European Governments to place restrictions on the freedom of British firms of chartered accountants to practice in their territories. The Committee received complaints concerning the following countries: Belgium, Denmark, Holland, Malta, Norway, Portugal and Spain.

(b) The Committee received evidence from the Royal Institute of British Architects that U.K. architects frequently face competition from foreign architects "whose fees are subsidized by their governments." There seems to be a case for a thorough inquiry into the

1. Barristers invariably act only on the instructions of a solicitor and are paid for their services by the solicitor. Thus in the case of foreign clients, the solicitor would invariably receive the foreign currency and pay counsel in sterling.

practices of foreign architects and governments in relation to over-seas projects. The Code of Professional Conduct of the R.I.B.A. is also a clear inhibiting factor in discouraging British architects from cutting their fees. Here also, in the view of the Committee, there is a case for a re-examination of the Code of Professional Conduct in relation to the meeting of overseas competition.

(c) The Committee received evidence from consulting engineers, architects and management consultants of the difficulties encoun-tered in financing feasibility studies for overseas projects. It was said that foreign competitors were subsidized in carrying out these studies sometimes to the extent of offering them free. In spite of the Feasibility Fund, already in existence, the Committee believes that there is sufficient substance in these complaints for them to be examined by the inquiry into major overseas capital projects being undertaken by Lord Cromer.[1]

The ground to be covered by Lord Cromer's inquiry is:
1 (1) The procedures and problems involved for British Industry in:
    (a) Setting up Consortia to compete for large overseas capital project business.
    (b) Associating such Consortia where necessary with Consulting Engineers, Construction and Civil Engineer-ing Contractors and Financial Institutions (including E.C.G.D.).
(2) The distinctions in organisation and approach within Industry which may be desirable:
    (a) Where a feasibility study of the overseas project has already established a framework within which Consortia have to compete.
    (b) Where, in the absence of any feasibility study, there is need or opportunity to develop, sell and execute a project, whether on a turnkey or other basis.
(3) The Government's role in the capital project export field and the relationships between Government, the Financial Institutions and Industry, with particular reference to:
    (a) Collection and dissemination of export intelligence.
    (b) The desirability of prompt, effective action by Industry in organising whatever approach is best adapted to secure and handle a prospective project.

CHAPTER XIII

OVERSEAS EARNINGS OF THE CITY

328. In this context, "the City" must be interpreted as a group of commercial and financial institutions, not as a geographical place. The institutions concerned are located very largely within the City of London, and account for a very large proportion of the economic activity that goes on there. However, some of the institutions included are located outside the City, e.g. some insurance companies, while some overseas earnings generated within the City are not included, e.g. tourism, earnings of accountants etc. The four main items traditionally included are:

Insurance: Comprising British insurance companies, Lloyd's underwriters and the insurance brokers.

Merchanting: Including the earnings of the organised commodity markets, and some other merchanting earnings.

Brokerage: Comprising the earnings of the Baltic Exchange (other than its commodities section), the Stock Exchange and a number of smaller items, and

Banking: Including earnings of interest on lending to overseas clients, profits on foreign exchange dealing and various commissions for services rendered by these banks to overseas clients.

329. The latest official estimate of earnings from the four sources (£200 million) refers to 1965, and was given by Lord Cromer, when still Governor of the Bank of England, in a speech to the Confederation of British Industry, reprinted in the June 1966 issue of the Bank of England's *Quarterly Bulletin*. An earlier estimate of £150 million for the year 1961 was given by the Central Statistical Office to the Committee of Inquiry on Decimal Currency.[1] Neither of these figures was broken down into its constituent parts. The only such breakdown was in answer to a Parliamentary question of 19 December, 1957. The figures (for 1956) are shown below.

	£ *million* 1956
Insurance	40[2]
Merchanting	30
Brokerage	30
Banking	25
	125

330. Unfortunately these estimates are not necessarily comparable with all

1. Report of the Committee Cmnd. 2145.
2. Excluding income from portfolio investments

the information made available to, or collected by, the Committee. The following paragraphs, therefore, discuss this new information in regard to each of the main categories.

INSURANCE

331. The estimate of insurance earnings is complicated by the fact that underwriting profits fluctuate violently from year to year—a bad hurricane, for example, can make a big difference to the figures. This has to be borne in mind in considering details for any particular year.

332. Figures given to the Committee for the year 1965 were as follows:

Companies:	£ million
overseas branches, subsidiaries and agencies	19
marine and other "home-foreign" business	2
head office overseas portfolio investment income	25
	—
	46
Lloyd's (underwriting and interest)	13
Brokers	22
	—
	81
	—

333. One question immediately arises from these figures. Should the figure of £25 million for income from foreign securities held in U.K. portfolios be included as an invisible earning of the City? It is not related to overseas business, but to the ordinary investment activity of individual insurance companies. If it is included, it would be difficult to exclude similar income earned by investment trusts, pension funds and other financial institutions.

MERCHANTING

334. The official estimates refer to the earnings from "scheme" commodities and to other forms of merchanting within the limited area of re-export and third country trade only. Merchanting profits on imports to the U.K. are shown in the balance of payments figures under a different item, "commissions on imports" (see appendix to Chapter V). Merchanting profits on British exports and re-exports are assumed to be included in the price at which "visible" goods are sold and so are not counted in invisible earnings at all.

335. Figures supplied to the Committee report earnings for the organized markets in coffee, cocoa, grain, rubber, sugar, copper, tin, lead, zinc and cattle foods of between £12 and £13 million (Chapter VI, TABLE 28). These figures are based on the response to questionnaires circulated by the various markets associations to their members and will not be complete. Nevertheless this is only a sample of the commodities being handled and excludes such items as wool, tea, spices, fibres, etc.; the total earnings on commodities might be reasonably guessed at between £25 million and £35 million of

which an indetermined proportion will be in respect of U.K. imports. However, such guesswork is extremely hazardous and in view of the fact that large firms tend to be very co-operative, the smaller figure is much more likely to be right.

336. On the basis of official figures the earnings in re-exports and third country trade excluding scheme commodities is estimated at between £15 and £20 million a year. Our figure for the mid-sixties, on the basis most nearly comparable with past estimates, might be put at £35-£45 million compared with £30 million of the 1956 official estimate. How far the higher figure is due to real growth, and how far to the inadequacy of the information previously available, it is impossible to say.

337. This estimate, however, does not cover by any means all of the mercantile earnings of the City. Commissions on British imports are, as already stated, included in the official estimates of invisible earnings, and it is only logical to credit the City with its share of these. The difficulty is to estimate what this share should be. There is no information on which to base a direct estimate. One possibility is to assume that the City's share of total commissions is proportionate to the Port of London's share of total imports. About 30 per cent of retained imports come through the Port of London, and commissions in 1965 were estimated at £82 million. On this basis, therefore, the City's share could be put at roughly £25 million. Looked at in another way this figure would represent $2\frac{1}{2}$ per cent on only £1,000 million, out of over £2,500 million imports of food and raw materials in 1965.

338. Finally, there are commissions on exports. These are assumed to be included in the prices at which goods are entered in customs records, though this may not always be so. In so far as it is not so, the official estimates will, of course, under-estimate total overseas earnings from visible and invisible trade together. Regardless of the manner in which they are (or are not) recorded, the services of export merchants are a contribution to the balance of payments and, so far as it is known, the payment for them should be included in an estimate of merchanting earnings. The British Export Houses Association has submitted to the Committee an estimate of commissions earned by export houses of £26$\frac{1}{4}$ million, 75 per cent of which is assumed to come from British trade and 25 per cent from third country trade. Since earnings from third country trade have already been included, it is the figure of approximately £20 million earned on British exports that is relevant.

339. The total earnings of mercantile activities carried on mainly, though not wholly in the City may, therefore, be estimated very roughly, as follows:

	£ *million*
1. Re-exports and third country trade	
(a) Commodity markets[1]	20–25
(b) Other markets	15–20
	35–45
2. Imports	25
3. Exports	20
TOTAL	80–90

1. This allows up to £15 million for the commodity market's earnings on U.K. imports.

340. As already explained, the estimates are subject to large errors, but it is probably safe to say that the total is not less than £80 million and may be more than £90 million. This total is very much higher than that of any previous estimates, partly because these have not included items 3 and 4, above, but also because item 1 has almost entirely been under-estimated.

BANKING

341. The results of inquiries made by the Committee into the earnings of banking are fully described in Chapter IV. The figures are based on replies from about three-quarters of all the banks concerned, holding about 89 per cent of all deposits with commercial banks in London. These show earnings of £17½ million from foreign exchange dealing and various services performed in London, and £34 million from the profits of overseas branches and subsidiaries and from charges for services provided to them. The first of these figures is closely in line with previous estimates.

342. On interest account, the Committee's inquiry produced results that are in sharp contrast with those of earlier inquiries. These may be summarized as follows:

	£ million
Interest received from overseas	
Loans and discounts in sterling	32·3
Loans etc. in foreign currencies	73·5
	105·8
Interest paid overseas	
On sterling deposits	48·0
On foreign currency deposits	77·9
	125·9
Debit balance	20·1

343. This, however, does not present a fair picture of the activities of the banks. A considerable part of the short-term claims generally known as "sterling balances" are held by overseas residents on deposit with British banks or London offices of overseas banks. Some of these deposits are, of course re-lent overseas but a considerable part are lent to British borrowers, so that the banks' loans to non-residents are consistently smaller in total amount than the deposits received from them. Because a large part of the funds placed on deposit with the banks are on-lent by them in the U.K.—for example, to local authorities—it is doubtful whether it would be accurate to take this type of banking activity into account when assessing the earnings of the City. The difficulty lies in deciding what proportion of the total interest paid on the sterling balances it is proper to include here. There are, of course, several ways of calculating this, and none can be considered significantly better than the others. The Committee have decided in favour of regarding interest paid on "working balances"—i.e., the level of balances which overseas traders and banks need to maintain in London in order to conduct their day-to-day business—as deductible from the banks' total

interest earnings. The remainder of the sterling balances may be regarded as a form of investment in the U.K., and it would not be appropriate for interest paid on them to be included.

344. The problem is to decide the size of the working balances, what proportion bear interest, and what rate of interest should be applied. Any calculation of this kind is of necessity only approximate. Assuming that working balances comprise 25 per cent of "Other holders'" current and deposit accounts in the Bank of England's External Liabilities and Claims Series (averaging in 1965 some £1,500 million), and that 50 per cent are interest bearing, a rough figure of interest paid in 1965 would be £10½ million.

345. Figures of sterling interest reported to the Committee are thought to have covered about 90 per cent of all deposits with commercial banks, so that total sterling interest earnings might be £36 million. Deduction of the £10½ million interest on working balances gives net sterling earnings of £25½ million.

346. The working balances concept cannot be applied to foreign currency deposits, which are mainly Euro-dollars. Because these deposits frequently pass from bank to bank before being ultimately either on-lent abroad or employed in the U.K., it could be argued that the entire net debit of £4½ million should be counted against the banks. At the other extreme it could also be argued that the debit arises only because funds borrowed in foreign currencies are switched into sterling and lent in the U.K. The banks make a profit on foreign currencies borrowed and on-lent abroad and it might be said that this should be regarded as part of their overseas earnings while the payments on funds switched into sterling should be regarded as a liability of the ultimate U.K. borrower and not of the banks. This concept would produce an addition of several millions to the banks' overseas earnings. Finally, of course, on the grounds that the debit is the result of high interest rates prevailing in the U.K. in 1965, the funds could be regarded simply as investment attracted to this country by the prospect of a high return. Thus, depending upon which of these three concepts is chosen, the banks' total net interest earnings, both sterling and foreign currency, appear to have been (a) £21 million (i.e. £25½ million minus £4½ million) or (b) several millions over £25½ million or (c) simply £25½ million. The Committee decided to avoid the first two cases and to consider that such funds were investments in this country. This produces a figure of £25½ millions for bank interest earnings.

347. If the earnings reported from services and overseas subsidiaries are also grossed up, the total earnings of banking can be estimated as follows:

	£ million
Services	19½
Overseas subsidiaries	37½
Interest	25½
	82½

348. Returns submitted by about 25 per cent of members of the Baltic Exchange in response to an inquiry on behalf of the Committee showed earnings from shipping (including second-hand ships) of £6·8 million. The Baltic also does a similar business in aircraft, which earned £175,000 for the firms replying to the Committee's questionnaire, and possibly about three quarters of a million over-all.

349. Information forwarded to the Committee by the Stock Exchange showed earnings of £2½ million. For reasons given in Chapter VII this does not include jobbing income, so that the total earnings of stockbrokers and jobbers may well be between £3 and £4 million. A number of other activities, including underwriting, the management of overseas securities, and the services of Lloyd's Register of Shipping probably bring in at least another £5 million. Total earnings from brokerage and related activities are, therefore, estimated at £30-£35 million.

It is now possible to bring together the Committee's estimates for the four major categories of earnings:

	£ million	
Insurance		
Including income from foreign securities held in U.K.	81	
Excluding such income		56
Merchanting		
Including U.K. import and export trade	85	
Excluding such trade		40
Banking	82½	82½
Brokerage	35	35
	283½	213½

350. The figures are not, of course, accurate to anything like the nearest million, but the Committee is satisfied that the earnings of the group of activities are between £275-£295 million on the basis shown in the left-hand column and between £205-£225 million on that shown in the right-hand column. Even the lower of these figures, the definition for which the Committee prefers to be adopted in future, is higher than any previous estimate, official or unofficial. The previous estimates and those now presented by the Committee are not closely enough comparable to establish the rate of growth of earnings.

351. The Committee feels it necessary to stress that the estimate of £205 million to £225 million for the City's earnings in 1965 is a conservative one. In the first place the year 1965 was a bad one for insurance earnings. Secondly, the estimates take no account of the earnings of accountants, solicitors etc. in the City which, as is shown by the results of the Committee's new inquiries set out in Chapter XII, clearly account for several millions a year. Thirdly, the interest earnings included in the total City estimate

(largely through the banks) has been restricted to the amount *known* to be earned in the City.

352. As indicated at the beginning of this chapter, the earnings measured are those of a group of activities predominantly located in the City, not those actually accruing within the "square mile." Finally, it must be noted that they are a mixture of income from services performed by the institutions concerned and income from property owned by those institutions overseas. It would, therefore, be misleading to regard them as an indication of the productivity either of labour or capital actually employed in the City.

353. The Committee suggests that in future corresponding estimates of the "City's" earnings should be made and published annually by the Bank of England or the Central Statistical Office, separately from the official balance of payments statistics.

CHAPTER XIV

STATISTICAL CONCLUSIONS

354. In examining the invisibles sector of the balance of payments, the Committee has had two aims constantly in mind: to discover how reliable the statistics are and whether policy decisions can and should be based on them; and to judge whether new information or a re-arrangement of existing figures would help to stimulate earnings by creating a better understanding of the problems. It is little use forming a view about banking or insurance, for example, without knowing what exactly they earn in terms of foreign exchange.

355. In undertaking this detailed scrutiny of the balance of payments statistics, the Committee has come to certain broad conclusions, as well as the more detailed ones outlined in earlier chapters. But before setting them out, the Committee feels it right to emphasise two points. One is that it is convinced that both the scope and the presentation of U.K. data on invisible exports compare very favourably with those published by other countries and have been greatly improved in the last decade or so.[1] The other is that certain deficiencies of some importance still exist and, indeed, are well recognised by Government departments. These deficiencies are quite varied in character; the Committee deals with each of them in turn.

1. DEFICIENCIES OF COVERAGE

356. The coverage of individual items on invisible account varies considerably; in some cases it is quite comprehensive; in other cases inadequate. In general, the coverage is good as far as most of the more important items are concerned, but there are deficiencies in the "other services" category. (See TABLE 44 for a summary of the Committee's assessment of the main deficiencies.) In recent years, there has been a marked improvement in coverage (e.g. in respect of direct investment income, royalties, trade credit and travel earnings). Inadequacies still, however, remain due not so much to lack of knowledge of the sources of information but to practical difficulties in eliciting the data required.

2. DEFICIENCIES OF SAMPLING AND VALUATION

357. Where other than a complete census is taken some form of estimation procedure is necessary. This may be achieved by taking a sample and/or using related sources of information.

    (a) *Sampling procedure*

        Wherever sampling is used there are two problems involved: first the method of sampling and second the technique of "grossing up."

---

1. See Appendix A for Treasury evidence on "the preparation of statistics" submitted to the Estimates Committee, session 1966-67. This outlines the progressive improvements.

Table 44

COVERAGE OF STATISTICS ON INVISIBLE EARNINGS AND
PAYMENTS

A. BROADLY ADEQUATE
   1. BASED ON NEAR COMPLETE COVERAGE
      (a) *Direct reporting method*
      Direct investment income
      Trade credit
      Forces expenditure
      Crown agents' fees
      Pensions, etc.
      Foreign receipts of U.K. airlines
      U.K. shipping industry (full census)
      Films
      Telecommunications
      Lloyds' underwriting and brokerage earnings
      Insurance company earnings, except as noted below

      (b) *Indirect estimation method*
      Expenditure by overseas students
      Expenditure by overseas journalists
      Earnings of banking

   2. BASED ON GOOD SAMPLE

      (a) *Direct reporting method*
      Royalties
      Expenditure by foreign airlines in U.K.
      Travel earnings
      U.K. shipping industry (annual sample)

      (b) *Indirect estimation method*
      Package tours (part of "travel earnings")

   3. BASED ON PERIODIC INVESTIGATIONS

      (a) *Direct reporting method*
      Disbursements of foreign ships in U.K. ports

      (b) *Indirect estimation method*
      Commissions on imports

B. GENERALLY INADEQUATE
                 Insurance (i) Earnings of life insurance companies
                           (ii) Insurance of mutual indemnity companies
                          (iii) Foreign business (excluding marine) underwritten by
                                insurance companies in London
      Stock Exchange earnings
      Brokerage and merchandising earnings
      Earnings of advertising agencies
      Market research
      Service charges
      Architects' and consulting agencies' fees
      Miscellaneous and other credits (entertainers' earnings, etc.)
      Commissions earned on export trade

In some cases, the total *number* of observations is known but not the *value* of each (e.g. the expenditure by tourists in the U.K.): in others both have to be computed. Sometimes the sample consists of the larger firms in a particular sector (as in civil aviation figures); in others it is based on a random spread. It is acknowledged by Government departments that there is some room for improvement in sampling procedure, but in general this would not appear to be a major deficiency in the presentation of invisible exports.

(*b*) *Estimation procedure*

There are various forms of estimation procedure and often a combination of two or more of these are used for any one item. Each, in the view of the Committee, has its own dangers. First, there is the "grossing up" of sample data. Secondly, in some cases, where the behaviour patterns of some but not all of the observations are known, the rest are assumed to behave in like manner, e.g. in the travel inquiry it is assumed that the pattern of spending in the U.K. of visitors on packaged tours is similar to that of other visitors. Thirdly, the provisional shipping estimates made by the C.S.O. for the current year are based on projecting forward past trends and these are followed up by estimates based on the results of the Chamber's sample inquiries. Fourthly, where little data is available in this country, estimations have to be based on partner country information, e.g. as in the case of various types of private transfers.

(*c*) *Valuation procedure and definitions*

This is partly a question of classification, but methods of valuation and definitions used in respect of a number of items in the balance of payments need to be looked into further. These include direct investment income, certain shipping earnings, commission on imports and exports.

3. Deficiencies of Classification

358. Any classification is largely a matter of convenience, and in general the U.K., in line with other countries, adopts a *functional* rather than *sectional* approach to the classification of invisible earnings. In some cases, the breakdown is not detailed enough, e.g. the industrial split up of direct investment income and the different types of "financial and allied services" income, but as the collection of statistics is improved this should be remedied. A recent example is the new table giving more details on "other services" income (Table 11 in *Balace of Payments Pink Book*, 1966). There is, however, in the view of the Committee, a case for presenting supplementary information on invisible earnings (and payments) by sectors to assess the contribution of particular sectors of the economy to the U.K. balance of payments and to assist policy making in general. Several recommendations have already been made in earlier chapters. Three examples will suffice here:

(a) *Travel earnings*

It is considered that the international fare payments and purchase of goods bought by foreign tourists in U.K. might be estimated, and published, separately. This would enable significant comparisons to be made of U.K. travel earnings with those of some other countries and would help policy decisions here.

(b) *Insurance earnings*

At present these are spread over four separate headings in the balance of payments accounts. Since this is an important item, the Committee is convinced that a regular annual attempt should be made to assess its contribution separately.

(c) *Earnings of banking*

A similar point applies here: there is no way, at present, of assessing the contribution of the banking sector to the balance of payments. The Committee believes that an annual assessment should be made in future.

359. The Committee realizes that this raises an important point relating to the use of official balance of payments statistics. The information, as presented, naturally needs to be in line with international usage, usually that suggested by the International Monetary Fund. In principle the Committee does not wish to change or to recommend any change in the presentation of the basic statistics (a potential exception is discussed in the chapter on shipping). But it believes that more could be done and ought to be done in enabling those wanting to make policy decisions to compile statistics on what might be termed an "industrial" basis, i.e. showing the payments contribution (gross and net) of insurance, banking, tourism, merchanting, etc., etc. The Committee believes that this can be done, without interfering with the accepted form of the balance of payments. It has indicated what might be done in individual chapters. Banking figures, for example, can still be divided up into different sectors of the balance of payments: what is now essential is that the different elements should be capable of being brought together by anyone wishing to do so. The Committee believes that official statistics are a tool to be used. In the case of the invisible sector, they still require fashioning to meet the needs of the policy makers, including those in the private sector of the economy.

4. SUMMARY

360. How important are these various deficiencies? The answer to this question must depend primarily on the value of the particular items in question and the cost of improving the statistics. Obviously, in recent years, attention has been focused on improving the more important components on invisible account—notably direct investment income and travel earnings. Measured in terms of the marginal improvement in statistics, *vis à vis* the cost of conducting an inquiry, a state of diminishing returns may soon be reached. But previous chapters have shown that there may be scope for improvement particularly in two directions of great importance, i.e. shipping

and "other services." Here it may be desirable that new inquiries should be launched or the coverage of existing inquiries greatly improved; in other cases (e.g. travel, investment and aviation income) it is more a case of refining existing methods.

361. The Committee has also been aware, throughout its inquiry, of the complex relationships between gross invisible earnings and certain corresponding expenditures abroad. The relationships are both statistical and organic. For example, certain U.K. earnings from shipping or airlines lead directly to expenditure abroad, for refuelling and other servicing. Other relationships are not so directly connected yet, because of reciprocal agreements between governments, for example, U.K. earnings also naturally lead to foreign earnings from us. In other cases again U.K. invisible earnings are simply a by-product of world trade. Thus while the Committee has inevitably been concerned with ways of stimulating Britain's invisible earnings (in line with its original terms of reference), it has had to bear in mind that certain stimuli could also increase Britain's invisible payments.

RECOMMENDATION

362. The Committee believes that these relationships deserve to be explored more thoroughly than has been possible with the time and resources at its disposal. It recommends, therefore, that the detailed correlations between invisible earnings and invisible payments should be closely analysed, where possible, sector by sector, either by individual trade associations or by the appropriate government department.

PRESENTATION OF INVISIBLES

363. The Committee has also become increasingly aware of deficiencies both in the frequency with which the official invisible figures are published and in their presentation. In particular, it has become clear that the visible trade figures, published monthly by the Board of Trade, are in danger of giving a distorted view of Britain's true payments position.

364. The Committee, therefore, has considered the form of the visible trade figures published by the Board of Trade and has examined what might be done, month by month, as well as less frequently, to show the valuable contribution of Britain's invisible earnings from banking, insurance, financial and commercial services, tourism, shipping, etc. As earlier chapters have shown this contribution has been consistently in surplus for as far back as official records go, the total having reached over £550 million annually in 1962–65.

365. The Committee has examined how often this overall picture, revealing the full contribution of invisibles, is presented in official publications. The answer is quarterly and annually: four times a year, when the quarterly balance of payments estimates are published in *Economic Trends* and once a year in *United Kingdom Balance of Payments* by the Central Statistical Office. In contrast, the more frequent details of visible trade, published *monthly*

by the Board of Trade, made no reference, until a few months ago, to the important contribution from invisibles.

366. These monthly trade figures (usually published in the second week of every month) include crude figures of visible imports, exports and re-exports, representing recorded values of goods entering or leaving the United Kingdom as well as corresponding figures making an allowance for *seasonal* influences. The Board of Trade also publishes in the same monthly press release a monthly visible trade balance worked out on a payments basis[1] and also seasonally adjusted. On this basis the visible trade balance for March, 1967, for example, emerged as a deficit of £12 million. In previous months, according to the March statement, the balance had been —£1 million (February); — £6 million (January); — £7 million (December); and + £92 million (November). These figures, therefore, provide only a partial view of Britain's total current payments position because of the absence of the contribution from invisible earnings. Regular emphasis is given to a continuing deficit, while the persistent surplus on invisibles is largely hidden from view. The Committee, therefore, considered what might be done to fill this gap.

367. Statistics on invisible transactions in the balance of payments suffer in four ways in comparison with visible transactions: they are published with a longer time-lag; they are less reliable; they appear less frequently; and they are given less publicity. These four problems are worth considering separately.

1. DELAYS IN PUBLICATION

368. The first intimation of quarterly invisible earnings (and payments) appears about $2\frac{1}{2}$ months after the end of the quarter in question and is published in brief summary form by the Government.[2] The first detailed estimates are contained in *Economic Trends* which appears at the end of the third month following the quarter in question. (Estimates of the October/December, 1966, invisibles payments and receipts, for example, were published in the March, 1967, issue of *Economic Trends*.) There is thus a two and a half to three month time lag after the last month of the previous quarter before publication. According to the official statisticians it is extremely unlikely that this time lag could be much reduced, using the present method of collecting data. Moreover, there is no reason to suppose that monthly figures (even if they could be calculated) could be assimilated any more speedily. Thus the January invisible payments and receipts would not be known until mid-April, the February payments and receipts not until mid-May and so on.

2. RELIABILITY OF THE QUARTERLY STATISTICS

369. The quarterly figures (as initially published) vary in their accuracy from fairly firm estimates based on quarterly surveys to informed guesses. Each sector of invisibles varies:

1. The main adjustments are (a) the addition of details of second-hand ships and aircraft, of new ships delivered abroad and of atomic energy materials, and (b) the deduction of the costs of insurance and freight from the crude import figures.
2. Only four items are included: (1) Government, (2) Interest profit and dividends, (3) Private transfers, (4) Other.

(*a*) *Government*

Figures are provided on a quarterly basis by relevant Government departments. These figures are believed to be reasonably accurate.

(*b*) *Transport*

    (i) *Shipping*. The provisional quarterly figures produced by the Central Statistical Office are based on those given in the previous annual inquiry *plus* related indicators (e.g. statistics of overseas trade and shipping movements), plus estimated trends. The yearly inquiry is a full one every four years and about a 50 per cent sample in the intermediate years. There have been errors because it is extremely difficult to estimate the change in U.K. shipping performance *vis à vis* that of other countries. Informal talks have taken place between the Board of Trade and the industry about ways of improving the quarterly estimates.

    (ii) *Aviation*. Figures are provided by the air corporations and most airport authorities.

(*c*) *Travel*

The return of passenger movements supplied to the Board of Trade is again a quarterly one and there is, at present, some time lag—about three months—in providing the data for the last quarter. This means that the initial estimates have to be revised subsequently. Some improvement is expected in the speed with which figures of passenger movements become available and this should cut down the time-lag in providing travel figures. It is, however, unlikely that if monthly data were collected (using the same sample as the quarterly survey) that the time lag could be reduced below $2.2\frac{1}{2}$ months.

(*d*) *Interest, Profits and Dividends*

    (i) Direct investment income. At present the quarterly return is based on a sample of about 30 per cent of investing firms, and although questionnaires are despatched each quarter, the Board of Trade, in effect, runs this inquiry by telephone. The income recorded, however, is only as good as the accounting system of the respondent firms allows.

    (ii) Portfolio investment income. Data on this are provided on a quarterly basis by the Inland Revenue. The time pattern of dividend and interest receipts is important here and this item fluctuates considerably between quarters and would do so even more on a monthly basis.

    (iii) The earnings of oil companies. This income is a residual figure in the sense that it represents a cash surplus over payments and includes such items as royalties and fees paid on inter-company account. There are extremely complicated problems here in calculating meaningful figures on a quarterly basis, not least the fact that the timing of income and costs varies so considerably from quarter to quarter. The figure provided is often revised quite substantially when the annual data are known.

(iv) Other income. Trade credit figures are collected quarterly and there is also an annual survey. In estimating income earned on short term assets, details of the latter are provided by the banking system.

(e) *Other services*

Here the value of the data varies considerably. In some cases information is available on a quarterly basis, e.g. data on the flow of funds of insurance companies, foreign forces expenditure, foreign earnings of U.K. banks, telecommunications income, etc. In others, movements in income are based on movements in visible trade, e.g. commissions on imports and exports, or on related data on the debit side of the balance sheet, e.g. that obtained from Exchange Control Records. Then there is a miscellaneous section where the previous annual figures are simply divided by four and some allowance made for the trends of earnings.

370. Thus there are three types of errors and omissions inherent in the quarterly figures:

1. Errors and omissions due to incomplete information at the time the figures are published.
2. Errors and omissions due to the fact that no quarterly data are obtained by the direct reporting method and the value of the items in question have to be based on annual surveys, etc. (e.g. shipping inquiry).
3. Errors and omissions due to deficiencies in estimation procedures which are put right when new investigations have been completed (e.g. revisions of estimates of interest on trade credit and of royalty payments consequent upon the findings of these inquiries).

Revised[1] figures for 1 are given in *Economic Trends* as and when appropriate. Revised figures for 2 appear first in *Economic Trends* following the publication of the *Balance of Payments Pink Book* (in September of each year). Revised figures for 3 appear as and when such errors are revealed.

3. POSSIBILITY OF MONTHLY INVISIBLE FIGURES

371. One way of emphasizing the contribution of invisible earnings, in the view of the Committee, would be to publish monthly figures at the same time as the monthly visible trade figures. The Committee examined this possibility and discussed the matter with various government departments. One fact was immediately clear: accurate monthly figures of invisible earnings are not at present available. Some figures are collected quarterly, some annually, others not at all.

372. The method of collecting statistics, it was found, had a strong bearing on the prospects of obtaining monthly figures. That used in the United Kingdom (i.e. the direct reporting and estimation method rather than the

1. An analysis of the size of the revisions in the quarterly statistics is shown in Appendix B.

so-called "ticket" system) is time consuming and cannot be undertaken much more quickly than it is at present. The Committee noted that no country which uses the direct reporting and estimation method of recording its invisible earnings and payments (including the U.S.) publishes monthly estimates. Some countries, however, which use the so-called "ticket" system, notably Germany, do produce such monthly estimates. The Committee thus considered whether the "ticket" system, whereby individual transactions are recorded by the banks and other institutions, might not be used in this country. But it became clear that, for special reasons relating to British conditions, such a system might prove both burdensome and highly complex. The major difficulty facing British banks would be that of identifying receipts or payments which represent transactions between residents and non-residents. This would be extremely difficult given the lack of exchange control on remittances to and from the sterling area and given the complex nature of the United Kingdom banking network. Problems of this kind are not met in Germany.

373. An alternative approach considered by the Committee was to extend present methods selectively to produce monthly figures. Some of the information on private invisibles collected by direct inquiry (e.g. travel and Lloyd's underwriting) is essentially collected *seriatim* and could perhaps be tabulated monthly, and without undue delay. The indirect estimates used elsewhere might perhaps be extended to a monthly basis eventually (this is particularly true of some sections of the City's earnings). Yet, the Committee was informed, major gaps might still remain particularly where information was based on company accounts, which are rarely, if ever, produced more frequently than quarterly.

374. Beyond the problems of collecting the information, it was represented to the Committee, there were difficulties arising from delays in collection and from the sharp monthly movements in some of the items, such as for example oil royalties and parts of "interest, profits and dividends." Thus, in the first place, even if monthly figures were possible, they would not correspond to the same month as the latest visible trade figures because of the different time-lag in collection. Secondly, the sharp changes in the monthly totals, reflecting the "lumpiness" of certain items, might seriously mislead the public about the true trend of invisible earnings.

375. After considering these factors the Committee came to two conclusions: that the "ticket" system was inappropriate for introduction into the United Kingdom; but, that, in spite of the obvious difficulties in attempting to produce monthly figures, some further effort ought to be made.

RECOMMENDATIONS

376. 1. The Committee, therefore, recommends that the Central Statistical Office, along with the appropriate government departments, should undertake a specific inquiry into the feasibility of producing monthly estimates of invisible earnings and payments, and, if thought appropriate, should publish its findings.

2. The Committee also recommends that every effort should be made, within the resources of government departments and of the industries concerned, to improve the quarterly estimates of invisible earnings and payments.

4. PUBLICITY FOR INVISIBLES

377. In addition to the annual and quarterly publication of invisible transactions, the press release on visible trade, published monthly by the Board of Trade, now[1] contains a reference to invisible earnings. In "notes to editors" at the end of the press release the following sentence is included:

"The total current account in the balance of payments comprises two main components, the visible trade account and the invisibles account. The latter is usually in significant surplus, over the five years 1961-66 it averaged £150 million a year."

In view of the size of this contribution, and of its persistence over centuries, outlined in detail in chapters II and III, the Committee regards this reference, inserted among the technical notes at the end of the monthly press release, as quite inadequate. It certainly does little to dispel the impression which seems to be widely held at home, and still more widely abroad, that the balance of visible trade figures are the only pointer of any significance to our balance of payments, an impression which can, in certain circumstances, obviously be very dangerous.

RECOMMENDATIONS

378. 1. The Committee, therefore, recommends that the Board of Trade should reconsider the form of its monthly press release relating to visible trade, with a view to including the following improvements:

(a) It is recommended that the table published monthly in the press release should in future include columns showing private invisible trade figures, Government spending and Britain's total payments position. An example of this is set out in TABLE 45.

(b) It is recommended that, after the first sentence setting out the latest monthly visible trade figures in the press release, a reference to invisibles should be included, along the following lines:

"In addition to visible trade, net invisible earnings produce a regular surplus, which, in the year to (say) June 30, 1966, averaged £11 million a month."

379. 2. The Committee also recommends that the Central Statistical Office should consider whether it could produce a monthly moving average of invisible transactions (taking into account the latest quarterly figures) so that the suggested monthly reference to invisibles might be brought close to recent experience.

1. The first reference of this kind appeared in March ,1967.

TABLE 45

UNITED KINGDOM TRADE

Seasonally adjusted values
£ million per month

	Exports f.o.b.	Re-exports f.o.b.	Imports c.i.f. Total	Imports c.i.f. Excluding U.S. military aircraft, etc.	Visible Trade Balance[1]	Government Expenditure (net)	Other Invisibles (net)	Net Invisible Earnings	Total Current Payments Balance
1964	368	13	475		−45	−36	+44	+13	−33
1965	394	14	479		−22	−37	+51	+14	+10
1966	420	16	496		− 9	−38	+46	+ 8	− 5
1965 1st quarter	384	13	457		−12	−34	+44	+10	− 2
2nd quarter	381	13	484		−41	−38	+55	+17	−24
3rd quarter	399	15	487		−25	−39	+53	+14	−13
4th quarter	412	16	489		−11	−38	+52	+14	− 1
1966 1st quarter	416	16	507		−24	−36	+48	+12	−15
2nd quarter	395	16	495		−34	−40	+42	+ 2	−35
3rd quarter	426	16	513		−20	−37	+43	+ 6	−17
4th quarter	444	17	470	470	+41	−40	+50	+10	+47
1967 1st quarter	450	15	524	523	− 6	−36	+63	+27	+14
1967 January	471	18	550	550	− 6	n.a.	n.a.	n.a.	n.a.
February	453	15	522	522	− 1	n.a.	n.a.	n.a.	n.a.
March	424	14	501	499	−12	n.a.	n.a.	n.a.	n.a.
April	441	15	556	549	−44[2]	n.a.	n.a.	n.a.	n.a.
May	438	15	531[3]	525[3]	−24[2][3]	n.a.	n.a.	n.a.	n.a.
June[2]	418	14	524	522	−39[2]	n.a.	n.a.	n.a.	n.a.
1st quarter	450	15	524	523	− 6	−36	+63	+27	+14
2nd quarter[2]	432	15	537	532	−36[2]	n.a.	n.a.	n.a.	n.a.
1st half[3]	441	15	531	528	−21[2]	n.a.	n.a.	n.a.	n.a.

[1]Excluding transactions relating to U.S. military aircraft financed by Exim Bank credit.   [2]Provisional estimates.   [3]Revised estimates.

The entries in the last four columns (surrounded by the double line) are the suggested additions referred to in the Committee's recommendations.

U.K. BALANCE OF PAYMENTS STATISTICS

The following brief extract on the recent development of U.K. balance of payments statistics is taken from a memorandum submitted by the Treasury to the Estimates Committee, session 1966-67. (Fourth Report from the Estimates Committee: Government Statistical Services, H.M.S.O., £1 17s. 6d.)

"Comprehensive balance of payments accounts began to be compiled by the Bank of England from the end of the Second World War. The statistics were derived largely from Exchange Control records and returns from the banking system, but other sources were also used, e.g., the trade accounts and the periodic census of shipping transactions carried out by the Chamber of Shipping. From 1948 half-yearly figures were published by the Treasury in White Papers issued in April and October of each year. From 1958 summary quarterly figures were issued by Treasury Press Notice.

"By the late 1950's the gradual relaxation of Exchange Control regulations had seriously reduced the value of this source of statistics and it was imperative that new, wider-ranging, sources should be developed. Also, the need was felt to construct the accounts more completely on a 'flow of resources' basis than on the 'cash payments' basis provided by Exchange Control and banking figures. This was desirable both for better understanding of the economic developments taking place and for a better integration of the statistics of international transactions into the national income accounts. In conjunction with the launching of several major new inquiries, in particular on private direct investment from and into the U.K., responsibility for compiling the accounts was transferred in 1960 to the Central Statistical Office. Publication continued to be by half-yearly White Paper and quarterly Press Notice but in 1963 the system was changed to publication of full quarterly figures in *Economic Trends* and the issue of an annual publication (known familiarly as the 'Pink Book') giving detailed figures for a run of years and a description of sources and methods. Preliminary figures for the latest year are given jointly with national income figures in a White Paper before the Budget.

"With information drawn from a large number of different kinds of source there are considerable problems of obtaining complete and consistent coverage and valuation of transactions. Timing differences between the measurements of transactions in goods and services and the making of payments for them which are reflected in the monetary sector of the accounts are one aspect of this. The further extension of the Bank of England's system of returns from the banks and the launching of a regular inquiry into export and import trade credit have narrowed the gaps, but some remain. Measurement of some invisible services is still only rough. One witness to the imperfection of the statistics is the 'balancing item' which measures the extent to which the accounts as a whole fail to fit consistently together. Although small in relation to the gross amount of transactions (generally much less than 1 per cent) the balancing item is larger relative to the surplus or deficit in the balance of payments and tends to fluctuate erratically; it therefore causes a problem in interpreting the results.

"The past few years have seen a big extension in the amount of detailed information collected and published. Improvement of the quality of the figures by scrutiny of the coverage, basis of valuation and consistency of treatment between different items is a continuing process. The main emphasis in developing new inquiries is at present in the field of invisibles. A new series of travel figures based on the passenger interview scheme has recently been introduced; an inquiry into royalty payments and receipts is nearly complete and its extension to other forms of service transactions by companies is being considered. Overseas holdings of British securities through United Kingdom nominees are a known source of errors in measuring portfolio investment; it may be that the new withholding tax on interest and dividends will lead to better identification of these holdings. Attention is also being given to the form in which the accounts can be best presented to promote understanding of balance of payments developments."

APPENDIX B: CHAPTER XIV

REVISIONS IN QUARTERLY STATISTICS

The extent to which the quarterly payments figures published by the Central Statistical Office are revised is illustrated in TABLE 46. In this table data for two quarters (the first and second quarters of 1964) are examined and revisions are shown which have taken place since the first estimates were published. As can be seen, in each quarter there were four revisions (although not all items were revised each time). The variations of the individual credits and debits, in general, do not seem very significant: but in the case of the balance on total invisible account, the percentage of error is quite considerable. TABLE 47 presents the initial and final estimates of the *total* invisible earnings and payments and the net balance of total invisibles for the period from the first quarter of 1962 through to the fourth quarter of 1965. While the percentage revision on both total debits and credits rarely exceeds 5 per cent the percentage revision on the balance ranges very widely indeed. In absolute terms, in the year 1962 the first estimate of the net credit of the four quarters (added together) was revised upwards by £67 million; in 1963 by £39 million; in 1964 it was revised downwards by £20 million and in 1965 downwards by £19 million.

No detailed information is published on a quarterly basis about the components of the main items on (private) invisible account except for interest profits and dividends, where separate data are recorded for income earned by direct, portfolio and other (including oil) investments. There are often quite substantial revisions made to the original estimates of earnings of direct and other foreign investments.

It should be added that these problems of revisions to earlier estimates are shared by all countries.

TABLE 46

REVISIONS OF STATISTICS ON INVISIBLE ACCOUNT FIRST AND
SECOND QUARTERS 1964

£ million

	Government			Transport Shipping			Aviation			Travel		
	Debits	Credits	Net	Debits	Credits	Net	Debits	Credits	Net	Debits	Credits	Net
1. First qtr., 1964												
June 1964	135	15	−120	175	163	−12	17	18	+1	30	32	+ 2
September 1964	135	15	−120	172	163	− 9	20	25	+5	31	33	+ 2
December 1964	144	22	−122	171	163	− 8	20	25	+5	31	33	+ 2
March 1965	143	22	−121	173	164	− 9	21	25	+4	31	33	+ 2
September 1965	139	16	−123	177	171	− 6	21	25	+4	27	24	− 3
2. Second qtr., 1964												
September 1964	111	8	−103	176	175	− 1	28	34	+6	67	52	−15
December 1964	115	8	−107	176	175	− 1	27	33	+6	65	52	−13
March 1965	115	8	−107	177	175	− 2	27	33	+6	64	52	−12
September 1965	117	8	−109	184	179	− 5	26	34	+8	65	49	−16
March 1966	115	8	−107	184	179	− 5	26	34	+8	65	49	−16

APPENDIX B: CHAPTER XIV

TABLE 47

ORIGINAL AND REVISED FIGURES OF TOTAL INVISIBLE DEBITS AND
CREDITS 1962–1965

£ million

	Debits		Credits		Balance		Change from A to B	
	A	B¹	A	B	A	B	Absolute	Percentage
1962								
1st quarter	538	504	591	581	+53	+77	+24	+ 45·3
2nd quarter	553	532	612	603	+59	+71	+12	+ 20·3
3rd quarter	604	589	623	623	+19	+34	+15	+ 78·9
4th quarter	576	540	583	563	+ 7	+23	+16	+228·6
1963								
1st quarter	529	514	574	590	+45	+76	+31	+ 68·9
2nd quarter	553	554	603	614	+50	+60	+10	+ 20·0
3rd quarter	622	638	655	664	+33	+26	− 7	− 21·2
4th quarter	583	579	604	605	+21	+28	+ 7	+ 33·3
1964								
1st quarter	566	580	617	653	+51	+73	+22	+ 43·1
2nd quarter	607	632	632	678	+25	+46	+21	+ 84·0
3rd quarter	684	697	688	694	+ 4	− 3	− 7	−175·0
4th quarter	586	609	636	645	+50	+34	−16	+ 32·0
1965								
1st quarter	588	626	668	684	+80	+58	−22	+ 27·5
2nd quarter	657	678	741	730	+84	+52	−32	+ 38·1
3rd quarter	751	756	725	755	−26	− 1	+25	+ 96·2
4th quarter	622	629	666	683	+44	+54	+10	+ 22·7
Arithmetic Mean error (plus or minus) 1962–1965							17.3	64·7
Median error 1962–1965							+11	+ 28·0

Source: Economic Trends.
1. A = Original estimates.
   B = Revised estimates.

REVISIONS OF STATISTICS ON INVISIBLE ACCOUNT FIRST AND SECOND QUARTERS 1964

£ million

	Other services			Interest, Profit and Dividends			Private Transfer			Total Invisibles			
	Debits	Credits	Net	Debits	Credits	Net	Debits	Credits	Net	Debits	Credits	Net	
													1. First qtr., 1964
	76	139	+63	98	223	+125	35	27	−8	566	617	+51	June 1964
	72	*130*	*+58*	*101*	*241*	*+140*	*37*	*26*	*−11*	*568*	*633*	*+65*	September 1964
	72	*134*	*+62*	*95*	*238*	*+143*	*38*	*26*	*−12*	*571*	*641*	*+70*	December 1964
	72	*135*	*+63*	*97*	*237*	*+140*	*37*	*30*	*−7*	*574*	*646*	*+72*	March 1965
	70	135	*+65*	*104*	*241*	*+137*	*38*	*31*	*−7*	*576*	*643*	*+67*	September 1965
													2. Second qtr., 1964
	76	139	+63	113	196	+ 83	36	28	−8	607	632	+25	September 1964
	77	*142*	*+65*	*113*	*207*	*+ 94*	*37*	*29*	*−8*	*610*	*646*	*+36*	December 1964
	78	*144*	*+66*	*115*	*219*	*+104*	*37*	*30*	*−7*	*613*	*661*	*+48*	March 1965
	76	*144*	*+68*	*121*	*221*	*+100*	*38*	*30*	*−8*	*627*	*665*	*+38*	September 1965
	76	*144*	*+68*	*127*	*229*	*+102*	*38*	*30*	*−8*	*631*	*673*	*+42*	March 1966

Figures in italic are those which have been amended since the previous publication of *Economic Trends*.
Source: Economic Trends.

CHAPTER XV

EFFICIENCY OF THE CITY

380. In examining ways in which invisible income might be expanded the Committee has been obliged to look at the efficiency of individual services and trades. As previous chapters have already shown, such an examination has immediately raised fundamental questions. How can efficiency be measured in most service trades? What exactly is meant by efficiency in the City, for example? Is it the efficient use of the country's resources; the efficiency of a firm or industry; or the efficiency of the market? The Committee came to the conclusion that some exploratory examination of these three aspects of efficiency was called for, with a view to making recommendations about future inquiries and studies.

1. Efficient Use of Resources

381. This is a particularly economic concept and the Committee did not feel itself competent to pass judgement on the question whether, if the resources used in the City, in the tourist trade, in shipping, in civil aviation etc., etc., were used elsewhere in the economy, the results would be more or less productive. But from an examination of evidence presented to it, the Committee concluded that far less was known about this aspect of the service trades than about that of the main manufacturing industries. It accordingly asked Professor John H. Dunning to prepare a paper about it, with particular reference to the financial and commercial activities within the City of London. This is attached as Appendix A to this chapter. As will be seen, it attempts to compare the productivity of the City (measured in different ways) with that of the country as a whole. It comes to two main conclusions. One is that the service trades show a higher (crude) labour productivity than manufacturing industries (largely because they utilise a higher percentage of skilled labour) and a higher capital productivity. The other is that such comparisons are still highly unsatisfactory because insufficient academic work has been done in this field.

2. Efficiency of Individual Firms

382. Is a bank or an insurance firm more or less efficient than another? Profitability and the return on capital employed may be compared, but this is not quite the productivity measuring rod so often used in manufacturing industry. As already mentioned in earlier chapters, there are many different ways of comparing output in these service trades. The banks, for example, submitted 18 different indicators of their activity to the Prices and Incomes Board when asked for ways of measuring their output. The same problem

arises in insurance, in shipping and elsewhere. But certain evidence is available in a more general way. For one thing several service trades have been becoming more capital intensive. To take just one example, between 1959 and 1965 the average growth of gross fixed capital formation in U.K. manufacturing industry was 58 per cent; in insurance, banking and finance it was 189 per cent. It is also clear from evidence supplied to the Committee from several City industries that investment in fixed assets by the financial sector is likely to expand even more rapidly in the future than in the past and that this, in due course, should result in a higher labour productivity.

383. The trend towards larger units or co-operative ventures is also accelerating in the service industries. The British Insurance Association can point to several important mergers in the last decade (particularly around the 1959-61 period). The same trend is at work in other branches of the insurance world, though at Lloyd's the introduction of a central accounting system, which has removed the necessity for individual accounting between many Lloyd's syndicates and Lloyd's brokers, has been a more significant institutional innovation. The "pooling" of certain services may well be expected to increase in the years to come in this and other financial sectors in the City. In shipping, two new consortia have been formed by shipping companies to take advantage of containerization; and the movement towards larger units in shipping, civil aviation, the hotel industry, etc., is proceeding apace. Increasing use is also being made of consultancy services to improve productivity. The B.I.A. has engaged McKinsey & Co. to assist them by studying ways and means of improving efficiency in certain aspects of the insurance industry. The banks are well advanced in their introduction of computers.

384. Most of the service industries, except shipping, are essentially labour intensive. In addition, since many operate large office premises in the City, they are often space intensive as well. The cost of space in Central London and labour in general has risen considerably faster than that of capital equipment, while, at the same time, the opportunities for renting expensive machinery have expanded. This has led to a substitution of capital for labour, wherever possible, and some change in the location of business away from Central London to other parts of the country. The net result of these trends has been a rise in the labour productivity in many Central London offices, as these have become increasingly specialized in their functions.

385. Yet, although these trends seem to point in the right direction, it is dangerous to be complacent. The Committee was continuously aware of the overall world trends shown in the analysis in chapter III. While the United Kingdom still maintained a dominant position in invisible trade, her share of the total invisible credits in the world had dropped from 17·7 per cent in 1952 to 14·9 per cent in 1964. And it can be argued that, *ceteris paribus*, a declining share of the market may be an indication of lower (relative) efficiency.

386. In the face of this slightly conflicting and rather unsatisfactory evidence, the Committee came to the conclusion that it was difficult to be precise

about the productivity of individual service industries. Comparatively little work has been done on the subject and it is only recently that the service trades themselves have really attempted to get to grips with measuring efficiency. Even now there is no consensus of opinion among, for example, insurance companies, stockbrokers, commodity brokers, bankers, shipping firms etc., as to how efficiency can best be assessed in their particular trade— though the need to find such a measure is becoming more and more recognized.

3. Efficiency of Markets

387. By its nature any examination of the efficiency of markets is relevant only to part of invisible earnings, mainly those from the financial, insurance and commodity marketing activities of the City, though certain art markets have similar characteristics. These activities can be looked at from two points of view: Could the organisation of the various markets, as distinct from individual firms, be altered in ways which would increase efficiency, and, secondly, could export earnings be increased by devoting more resources to these activities?

388. A detailed review by the Committee of the organisations of each market was clearly impossible, but it felt it useful to suggest certain criteria of efficiency, which might be put to representatives of the individual markets.

1. Does the market establish a true (world) price?
2. Can deals be made with complete confidence in the fulfilment of bargains?
3. Does the market provide speed of dealing?
4. Has it the capacity to handle both small and large deals?
5. Can it provide appropriate types of contract, e.g. appropriate grades of commodities or futures for an appropriate date?
6. Is it adaptable?
7. Are its services cheap?

389. The price established in an efficient market ought to be sensitive enough to reflect all economically significant changes in supply or demand yet stable enough not to oscillate violently in response to rumours or to changes that are so small or so short-lived as to be insignificant. Moreover, if the market serves a considerable area it should establish a price that is uniform. This ability depends, of course, partly on influences outside its control, e.g. bulk trading agreements at national prices or legal price controls would be major obstacles. But it also depends on the organization of the market and the conduct of its members. An obvious requisite is a high standard of commercial honesty and efficient rules to prevent the "rigging" or "cornering" of the market. London markets pride themselves, and with justice, on their very high standards. Where the members of a market deal as principals and not just as brokers, price stability requires that they should have enough capital to iron out short-run fluctuations by "taking a position." Finally, the establishment of uniform prices between different places requires active arbitrage dealings.

390. From the point of view both of maintaining an efficient service and promoting the long-term growth of invisible earnings, the capacity to adapt to changing circumstances is of great importance. Here opinions differ. Some people are inclined to reproach the City with conservatism, yet there have been notable examples of adaptability, mentioned in earlier chapters, such as the growth of the Euro-dollar and Euro-bond markets, the development of the foreign exchange market, the successful introduction of an air-broking market and several new commodity markets.

391. One significant point has struck the Committee in considering the efficiency of the country's commercial and financial markets. The associations representing the various services, and responsible for the administration of the markets, vary considerably both in their structure and efficiency. Some have the financial resources and staff to carry out their functions. Others, in the experience of the Committee, are under-staffed and far from being a true reflection of the institutions they represent. The Committee was particularly concerned at the lack of financial resources available to promote and publicize City markets. Moreover, although many activities in the City of London are closely allied, there is no established mechanism for promoting their services as an entity in overseas markets. In a broader sense, too little attention seems to be given to the structure of the City of London as a financial and commercial centre *vis-à-vis* other similar centres abroad. No strong rival centre has emerged overseas, in spite of the recurrent sterling crises, though international activity on the New York market has broadened considerably over the past five years. Yet, at the same time, little attention seems to have been paid to the City's overall structure or its fitness for the future.

RECOMMENDATIONS

392. 1. The Committee recommends that further practical studies should be encouraged into the efficiency of the main service trades earning invisible income.

2. The Committee recommends that individual trade associations in the City should consider some criterion for measuring the efficiency of their members.

3. The Committee recommends that City associations should consider both a joint effort to promote their combined services in overseas markets on a continuing basis, and an examination of the City's future role *vis-à-vis* other financial and commercial centres abroad.

APPENDIX A: CHAPTER XV
EFFICIENCY OF THE CITY
By Professor John H. Dunning

To the economist, the *real* cost of using resources to produce any given amount of goods and services is the output which those resources could have alternatively produced. Looked at from the individual firm's viewpoint, the *money* cost of using resources comprises four main components:

(i) payments made to other firms for the purchases of materials, components, semi-finished goods and services;

(ii) wages and salaries;

(iii) interest on loan capital;

(iv) profits (before tax) to shareholders (including undistributed profits).

The total money value of these payments is equal to the gross output of the firm; but the value actually created by that enterprise, which excludes purchases from other enterprises, is equal to items (ii) to (iv) above only, i.e., its net output.

Net output (Op) then represents the actual contribution of a firm to the output of the national economy. Whether or not this is as valuable a contribution as it could be, depends on whether the resources used (mainly labour and capital) could have created more output had they been used differently. Let us assume we know what these resources could have earned in their next best use, i.e. their *opportunity cost*. Let $w*$ be the opportunity cost of labour (L) and $q*$ the opportunity cost of capital (Kpk) (this includes both profits and interest). While the *money* cost of producing Op is then $wL + qKpk$ (where w and q = the actual wages and salaries paid and the actual return earned on capital), the real cost is $w*L + q*Kpk$. It follows that $\dfrac{Op}{w*L + q*Kpk}$ defines the efficiency of producing Op in terms of the "next best" way of using the resources actually used in producing that output. The big assumption in all this is that it is possible to put a reasonable evaluation on $w*$ and $q*$ and that the "p" component of Op is determined by competitive forces. If one assumes labour and capital are reasonably mobile, then the actual wages paid by a firm may be a good proxy to $w*$; for $q*$ one could impute the average rate of return earned by the industry in which the firm operates.

This particular measure is useful only for evaluating the *comparative* performance between firms, industries or regions. It cannot tell us whether, at a given moment of time, a particular firm, industry, or region, is operating at *maximum* efficiency. For example, out of 100 firms in (say) the brewing industry—one will be the most efficient *relative* to the others. But our measure can give no indication whether that firm itself could improve its efficiency.

What then can we say about the efficiency of the City, using efficiency in this particular sense of the word? Let us first look at the data which are published on the subject. In an article published in the *District Bank Review* in March, 1967, G. D. N. Worswick and C. G. Fane computed the following data on labour productivity (i.e. Op/L) for the main S.I.C. categories, for the U.K. as a whole, in 1964.

LABOUR PRODUCTIVITY IN 1964

All U.K. industry

(a) Individual Trades	£	(b) Summary	£
Agriculture	1,080	(a) All goods (less agriculture)	1,122
Mining	1,108	(b) All goods	1,119
Manufacturing	1,117	(c) All services (less distribu-	
Construction	1,151	tive trades)	1,129
Gas, Electricity and Water	2,238	(d) All services	1,096
Transport and Communi-		(e) Total	1,108
cation	1,480		
Distributive Trades	982		
Insurance, Banking and			
Finance	1,467		
Public Administration	962		
Various Services	957		

Now if it is assumed that the productivity of each individual trade is the same in the City as in the U.K., then applying this data to the distribution of employment in the City as given in the Census of Population for 1961, we can make a rough estimate of the labour productivity (i.e. Op/L) of the City for categories (a) to (e). The results are as follows:

Op/L	(£)	National Average = 100
(a) and (b)	1,119	100·0
(c)	1,317	116·7
(d)	1,268	115·7
(e)	1,239	111·8

It would be possible to look into the breakdown of (a) separately as data are available on both the Op/L of individual manufacturing trades and the numbers employed in the City, but since manufacturing industry only accounts for about one-fifth of the labour force in the City, we did not pursue this further.

From a purely *structural* viewpoint, then, the City's productivity is seen to be above average—at least when productivity is assessed in terms of Op/L. However, when one relates net output to employee compensation (i.e. takes into account the *quality* of labour employed), the situation is somewhat different. The national figures of Op/wL in 1964 are given below.

(a) Individual Trades		(b) Summary	
Manufacturing	1·36	(a) All goods (less agriculture)	1·36
Construction	1·34	(b) All services (less distributive	
Gas, Electricity and Water	1·96	trades, public adminis-	
Transport and Communica-		tration, etc.)	1·37
tion	1·31	(c) All services (less public	
Distributive Trades	1·55	administration, etc.)	1·41
Insurance, Banking and		(d) Total	1·39
Finance	1·22		
Other Services	1·44		

Applying the same "weights" to the City as before (i.e. its employment distribution) we arrive at the following summary figures of Op/wL for the City.

	Op/wL	National Average =100
(a)	1·36	100·0
(b)	1·24	90·5
(c)	1·28	90·0
(d)	1·30	93·5

On this criterion, the economic structure of the City appears to be rather less favourable than that of the U.K. as a whole.

So far no account has been taken of the use of capital. It would thus be quite wrong to conclude that a higher labour productivity in a particular industry implied that resources were more efficiently utilized in that industry than elsewhere. Only if it was known that the *same* or *less* capital was used could one be sure this was the case. Unfortunately, the data on capital employment are practically non-existent and we have been forced to make a "guesstimate" of its importance. This we have tried to do in the following way. First we computed the gross fixed investment in manufacturing and the individual service industries for the ten year period 1955/64. Using this as a proxy for the capital *stock* (Kpk) of these industries, we then related this figure to the wage-bill (wL) of these same activities in 1964. The capital stock/wage bill ratio (Kpk/wL) is given below for the U.K. as a whole.

(a) Individual Trades		(b) Summary	
Manufacturing	1·47	(a) All goods (less agriculture)	1·47
Construction	0·48	(b) All services (less distributive	
Gas, Electricity and Water	11·49	trades and public ad-	
Transport and Communi-		ministration)	1·93
cation	2·63	(c) All services (less public ad-	
Distributive Trades	1·26	ministration)	1·77
Insurance and Banking	1·28	(d) Total	1·64
Other Services	0·96		

If we now calculate Kpk/wL for the City, weighting the above indices by their employment distribution in the City (again in 1961) we arrive at the following results:

	Kpk/wL	National Average =100
(a)	1·47	100·0
(b)	1·57	81·3
(c)	1·53	86·4
(d)	1·51	92·1

The fact that these ratios are *less* for the City than for the U.K. as a whole suggests that the City is (structurally) of below average capital intensity. To test this, we calculate the various *output/capital* ratios (Op/Kpk) for the U.K. and the City. Kpk is defined as gross fixed capital formation 1955/64.

216

(a) Individual Trades	
Manufacturing	1·01
Construction	2·76
Gas, Electricity and Water	0·20
Transport and Communication	0·54
Distributive Trades	1·33
Insurance, Banking and Finance	1·03
Other Services	1·47

(b) Summary	
(a) All goods (less agriculture)	1·01
(b) All services (less distributive trades and public administration)	0·74
(c) All services (less public administration)	0·84
(d) Total	0·91

The appropriate Op/Kpk's for the City work out as follows:

	OP/Kpk	*National Average* = 100
(a)	1·01	100·0
(b)	1·07	144·5
(c)	1·11	132·2
(d)	1·09	119·8

These indices suggest that the capital productivity of the City is higher than that of the U.K. as a whole.

In summary then, the economic structure of the City is such that it has a lower labour but higher capital productivity than the average for the U.K. The combined productivity ratio will obviously depend on the labour/capital ratio which, in turn, depends on the imputed *cost* of capital. For the purposes of this exercise, we have assumed that labour costs are three times as important as capital costs and have taken a three-to-one wL/qK ratio for each of our global calculations.[1] The results are as follows:

Productivity in City/Productivity in U.K.

(a) All goods	1·00
(b) All services (less distributive trades and public administration)	1·06
(c) All services (less distributive trades)	1·01
(d) All goods and services	1·00

$$\text{(e.g. for } (d) \quad 3\left(\frac{1\cdot30}{1\cdot39}\right) + \frac{1\cdot09}{0\cdot91} = \frac{2\cdot80 + 1\cdot20}{4} = 1\cdot00)$$

This conclusion would suggest that resource allocation in the City is contributing to the national output about the same output per unit of input as the rest of the country. Though the service industries show a higher labour productivity than manufacturing industries, they utilize a higher proportion of highly paid labour, and hence on balance, yield a lower output-labour *cost* ratio. On the other hand, such industries use less capital per unit of output.

The situation is rather different if one wants to evaluate the contribution of the City to the national output, assuming that the differences in employee compensation between the City and the national economy directly reflect

1. $\dfrac{Op_C}{w^*L_C + q^*Kpk_C} \div \dfrac{Op_{UK}}{w^*L_{UK} + q^*Kpk_{UK}}$

differences in labour productivity. It then becomes legitimate to take Op/L rather than Op/wL as one's real cost per unit of output measure. If this is done, the combined productivity indices for the City *vis à vis* the U.K. as a whole work out as follows:

Productivity in City/Productivity in U.K.

All goods	(*a*)	1·00
All services (less distributive trades and public administration)	(*b*)	1·24
All services (less distributive trades)	(*c*)	1·20
All goods and services	(*d*)	1·14

What this means is that the value of output produced in the City, per unit of (homogeneous) capital and labour, assuming productivity to be the same in each industry, is between 14 per cent and 24 per cent higher than in the U.K. as a whole.

But what of the comparative productivity in the various individual industries? Here, it is difficult to make even an intelligent guess. We *do* know, however, from Inland Revenue data that the differential between the average (taxable) income of people working in the City and that for the U.K. as a whole is very considerable. In 1959 it was also more than one-fifth higher than one would expect from purely structural considerations. This would suggest that these earlier measures very considerably underestimate the true efficiency of the City; and intuitively it would seem reasonable to suppose that, e.g., banking and insurance in the City yield higher returns than these same activities elsewhere in the country.

AVERAGE EMPLOYMENT INCOMES IN THE
CITY OF LONDON ANALYSED INTO STRUCTURAL
AND EFFICIENCY EFFECTS 1959

	City of London	England and Wales
Average employment income (Schedule E) 1959–60	952	645
"Assumed" employment income (given the industrial structure of employment in 1961) 1959	704	631
"Assumed" difference in employment incomes	$\frac{704-631}{631}$ or	11·6%
Actual difference in employment incomes	$\frac{952-645}{645}$ or	47·6%
Therefore differential advantage of employment incomes in the City of London as opposed to England and Wales	47·6—11·6 =	36·0%

Sources: Average employment income 1959/60: Inland Revenue.
    Average income from employment by industrial group: National Income Blue Book and Annual Abstract of Statistics, 1959.
    Employment structure 1961: Census of Population.

Viewed in a dynamic context the following two tables attempt to show the growth in output per man in the City, between 1949 and 1964, assuming, as in previous paragraphs, that for each industry or trade, the City's growth of productivity is the same as the national average. The "weights" chosen are again those of employment distribution in 1961.

PERCENTAGE NATIONAL GROWTH IN LABOUR PRODUCTIVITY

AVERAGE RATES PER ANNUM
(at Constant Prices)

	1949–59	1959–64
Agriculture	3·6	6·5
Mining	0·4	4·3
Manufacturing	2·3	3 8
Construction	1·6	2·0
Gas, Water and Electricity	4·0	4·3
Transport and Communication	2·5	4·2
Distributive Trades	1·3	1·4
Insurance, Banking and Finance	1·9	1·0
Public Administration	6·6	1·6
Various Services	1·0	0·6

	National Rates of Growth		City Rates of Growth	
	1949–59	1959–64	1949–59	1959–64
(a) All goods	2·2	3·4	2·3	3·3
(b) All services	1·6	1·8	1·7	1·7
(c) All services (less distributive trades)	1·7	1·9	1·8	1·7
(d) Total	1·9	2·7	1·8	2·0

These figures would suggest that the real (labour) productivity of the City is probably not increasing as fast as that of the U.K. as a whole. However, taking into account increases in capital input, the relative position of the City is probably quite different—but we have no means of really putting this hypothesis to the test.

These broad conclusions are also supported by U.S. evidence. Victor Fuchs has shown[1] that in the period 1939/63 (a) there is a strong correlation between output per man and growth of output (or employment) in the service industries, (b) the rate of increase in productivity in the service sector is less than in the manufacturing sector. Details are given in the table below.

AVERAGE ANNUAL PERCENTAGE CHANGES IN OUTPUT PER MAN AND RELATED VARIABLES 1939–63
(The United States)

	Real Output Per Man	Real Output	Employment	Average Employee Compensation
Service sector	1·45	3·75	2·30	5·62
Goods sector	3·03	3·94	0·91	6·83
Total economy	2·23	3·84	1·61	6·22

In conclusion, it might be of interest to look at the changes in the numbers employed in main S.I.C. groups in the City between 1951–61,

1. *Review of Income and Wealth, No. 3,* 1966, pp. 211/247.

compared with those of the national average. Both the following tables would seem to confirm the tremendous "built in" growth potential of the City.

EXPECTED AND ACTUAL CHANGES IN EMPLOYMENT BY INDUSTRIAL ORDERS

Industry	(I) Actual Change 1951–61 City of London %	(II) Actual Change 1951–61 England and Wales %	(I) Minus (II)
TOTAL EXTRACTIVE	—79	—20	—59
TOTAL MANUFACTURING	+10	+6	+4
Of which:			
Paper, Printing and Publishing	+23	+18	+5
TOTAL SERVICES	+17	+9	+8
Of which:			
Transport and Communications	+12	—2	+14
Distribution	—5	+20	—25
Insurance, Banking, Finance	+29	+31	—2
Professional Services	—2	+40	—42
Miscellaneous Services	+83	—1	+84
Public Administration	+27	—17	+44
TOTAL: ALL INDUSTRY	+16	+6	+10

Source: Censuses of Population 1951 and 1961.
Note: Only the larger industrial groups are shown in the table because, as the 1961 Census is based on a 10 per cent sample, the application of this comparison to industrial groups with small employment in the City is liable to a high degree of error.
General conclusion: This table goes some way to pinpointing the source of the advantageous differential shift in the City between 1951 and 1961 (see following table). The prodigious growth rate of miscellaneous services is the prime cause but employment has also increased, relative to the National average in the Transport and Public Administration Sectors. The large category of Insurance, Banking and Finance has grown at about the National average for employment in that order.

DIFFERENTIAL AND PROPORTIONALITY SHIFTS IN THE CITY OF LONDON 1951–1961

	Actual Growth of Employment 1951–61 %	"Expected" Growth of Employment 1951–1961 %	Proportionality Shift	Differential Shift
City of London	15·7	11·8	+6·0	+3·9
G.L.C.	4·4	9·6	+3·8	—5·2
South-East England	9·3	8·3	+2·5	+1·0
England and Wales	5·8	5·8	—	—

Source: Census of Population Industry Tables 1951 and 1961.
'Expected growth' = growth of employment if employment in each industry grew at the national growth rate for employment in that industry.
Proportionality shift = 'expected' sub-divisional growth rate MINUS national growth rate.
Differential shift = actual sub-divisional growth rate MINUS 'expected' sub-divisional growth rate.
Conclusions: The faster the average growth of employment in the City can be regarded as reflecting its advantageous initial structure and its differential advantages roughly in the ratio 3 : 2.

220

CHAPTER XVI

POLICIES OF DEVELOPING COUNTRIES

393. It has already become clear that one of the main foreign threats to Britain's invisible earnings will arise from restrictions placed on these activities by foreign governments, primarily in an effort to encourage similar domestic enterprises. These actions and intentions have found particular expression in the recent United Nations Conference on Trade and Development (U.N.C.T.A.D.). The first full meeting took place in Geneva in May, 1964, where the combined voice of the developing nations was strongly in evidence. Several important resolutions and decisions, affecting Britain's invisible earnings, have already been reached. This new permanent body on the international scene will meet in full session for the second time in New Delhi early in 1968. The Committee, therefore, decided to examine the work of U.N.C.T.A.D. and to consider how far its decisions were likely to affect Britain's main earners of invisible income.

394. The basic factor behind the work of U.N.C.T.A.D. is that the gap between the import requirements of the developing countries and their export earnings is widening. The United Nations Secretariat has estimated that if the 5 per cent a year growth target set for the so-called Development Decade (largely the 1960's) is to be achieved, this gap, on the basis of recent trends, might reach $20,000 million by 1970. The first U.N.C.T.A.D. Conference in Geneva in 1964 agreed that a considerable increase in aid and other capital flows to the developing countries was necessary but it also recommended that studies should be undertaken to examine ways by which the developing countries could make greater efforts to mobilize their own resources. One area where it was considered foreign exchange earnings might be increased, or net savings achieved, was on invisibles, and item 13 on the agenda of the U.N.C.T.A.D. Conference was as follows:

"Improvement of the invisible trade of developing countries:

(a) Role of invisibles in the balance of payments of developing countries;

(b) Measures for improving the invisible trade of developing countries through increasing receipts from services such as tourism and reducing payments for transportation, insurance and similar charges."

395. A Committee of the Conference discussed these problems and it made a number of recommendations which were accepted by the Conference and incorporated in the Final Act and Report as recommendations A.IV. 21 to 26. The Committee on Invisibles and Financing related to Trade, within the Trade and Development Board established by the Con-

ference, is responsible for examining these recommendations, with a view to implementing suitable policy measures to carry out the broad outlines agreed by the Conference and to investigating ways of improving and standardizing international statistics on invisibles' transactions.

396. The information presented to the U.N.C.T.A.D. Conference showed that the net deficit on services[1] of the developing countries represented more than three-quarters of their total deficit balance on goods and services, and that earnings from services accounted for only 60 per cent of outgoings for services. It was assumed, therefore, that there was a great deal of scope for improving the developing countries' net position on services by raising foreign exchange earnings from shipping and tourism and by reducing the foreign exchange cost on these items and other services such as insurance.

TABLE 48

GROSS RECEIPTS FROM MERCHANDISE EXPORTS AND "INVISIBLES" OF 41 DEVELOPING COUNTRIES

($ million)

	Annual average 1956–1963	1963
Exports of Merchandise and non-monetary gold	16,357	19,109
Gross receipts from services:	3,335	3,820
Travel	878	1,066
Government	652	718
Investment income	231	216
Freight insurance and other transportation	760	952
Other services	814	864
Total goods and services	19,692	22,929
Private transfers	598	827
Total gross receipts from merchandise exports and invisibles	20,290	23,756
Total Invisibles	3,933	4,647

Source: I.M.F. Balance of Payments Year Books; prepared by World Bank.
N.B. In 1961, the payments by these same 41 countries for services totalled $7,545 million and receipts for services totalled $3,431 million.

397. In order to assess prospects the World Bank analysed recent data on invisibles, covering the invisible earnings of 41 developing countries for the period 1956-63 (TABLE 48). In this period, total receipts from invisibles accounted for 19·4 per cent of total current account earnings (exports plus invisibles). Earnings from services only represented 20·4 per cent of merchandise exports and, therefore a slightly lower proportion of merchandise imports. Although developing countries' earnings from invisibles grew much less quickly than earnings by developed countries during this period, their average rate of growth was higher than that for merchandise exports—4·3 per cent a year compared with 3·4 per cent a year. The most rapidly growing item in invisible earnings by developing countries

1. Services include all invisible items as defined by the I.M.F. *except* private transfers; i.e.—freight, insurance, other transportation, travel, investment income, Government services and other services.

222

was private transfers which represents around 15 per cent of their total earnings from invisibles. Earnings from freight and travel, which each account for around one-fifth of total earnings from invisibles, increased at slightly lower rates.

398. The relative weights of invisibles in the total current account receipts of developing countries show wide variations. A few countries obtain 50 per cent or more of their current account earnings from invisibles while many others obtain less than 5 per cent of their earnings from this source. These wide discrepancies indicate the scope for development of services by developing countries, especially since those countries where invisible earnings are important normally rely on incomes from one or two particular items, such as tourism and emigrants' remittances for Mexico and Spain, "other services" for Panama and "private transfers" for Israel.

399. To this end the U.N.C.T.A.D. Conference agreed a number of recommendations[1] with regard to invisibles which provide a broad policy outline for the promotion of invisible earnings by developing countries; in particular with respect to shipping, insurance, tourism and the transfer of technology. The objectives of these specific recommendations, which are discussed more fully below, were summarized by resolution 31 (iv) of the fourth session of the Trade and Development Board which reads:

> "1. *Invites* the United Nations Development Programme and the Secretary-General of the United Nations to give all due consideration to requests from the developing countries for technical assistance in the fields of export promotion and invisibles, including shipping, insurance and tourism;
>
> 2. *Welcomes* the statements of the Secretary-General of U.N.C.T.A.D. that the secretariat is ready to play an effective role in technical assistance activities by providing substantive support to such activities and not by adding further machinery to what already exists;
>
> 3. *Recommends* to the Secretary-General of the United Nations and to the U.N.D.P. to ensure that the services available in U.N.C.T.A.D. are so utilized in the consideration of requests from developing countries, and in the execution of such requests, in the field of export promotion and invisibles including shipping, insurance and tourism."

400. The types of policy for improving the developing countries' position on invisibles fall into three basic categories, although there is considerable overlap between them. One suggested method of helping the developing countries is through various forms of international co-operation which would enable these countries to have more impact in such fields as shipping freight rates, the introduction or improvement of legislative and administrative measures governing the operations of national and foreign insurance and re-insurance and the removal of unnecessary impediments to international travel. Secondly, the developing countries are encouraged to

1. U.N.C.T.A.D. Final Act and Report: annex A.IV. 21 to 26.

co-operate on a regional basis to develop earnings from certain sectors and to maximize returns from a given outlay—i.e. to avoid duplication of efforts. Finally, efforts are made to encourage development of national resources and potential by means of technical, financial and training facilities available from international agencies, and from governments and from private sectors in advanced industrial countries. Under all these categories the U.N.C.T.A.D. seeks to increase all means of assistance offered by developed countries to ease the foreign exchange burden on invisibles account of the developing countries, including technical and financial assistance, measures to facilitate the transfer of technology and know-how on favourable terms and guidance in the expansion of earnings from services. Specific policies which fall under these categories are examined below.

1.   SHIPPING

401. The cost and efficiency of shipping services are said to be of great importance to the expansion of merchandise trade of the developing countries because their exports consist mainly of primary commodities which have low value to volume ratios and have to be transported in bulk over long distances. Those countries, therefore, have strong interests in developments in freight rates and the total tonnage of world shipping in relation to growth in the volume of world trade. The share of developing countries in the volume of world seaborne trade is tending to increase; it rose from 54·3 per cent of export goods loaded in 1958 to 57·2 per cent in 1965.

402. Throughout the 1960's, it has been argued, the rising trend in world freight rates has been greater than the increase in price of manufactures imported by developing countries and contrasts strongly with the price index of the principal primary commodities exported by the developing countries which has been falling. The purchasing power of commodities in terms of freight services indicates a sharper decline than suggested by the trend in developing countries' terms of trade.

403. The income from shipping services goes mostly to developed countries because most of the present shipping tonnage is owned by residents of these countries. The developing countries own only 7 per cent of the world's shipping fleet and judging by their share of orders for new ships some decline in this proportion can be anticipated.

404. These developments in freight rates, shipping tonnages and trade volume indicate that on present trends the developing countries can expect no relief on their trade balances from smaller debits on transportation. At its first session the Trade and Development Board established a Committee on Shipping, "to promote understanding and co-operation in the field of shipping, and to study and report on economic aspects of shipping that might be referred to it." (U.N.C.T.A.D. Final Act annex A.IV.21). This Committee has initiated preparatory work on a number of topics outlined in Annex A. IV. 22 of the Final Act but so far has only reported on the problem of setting up consultation machinery to promote co-operation between shippers and Liner Conferences.

224

405. Although Liner Conferences have existed for many years, shippers in many parts of the world remain unorganized. The Committee on Shipping recommends that shipping councils should be established at national or regional level and that closer co-operation between shippers and conferences should be achieved through organized consultation machinery. It is stressed within U.N.C.T.A.D. that in many developing countries such machinery could only be effectively run by government authorities which could safeguard nations' interests in bargaining with the Conference. The Committee on Shipping recommended general guide lines for the consultation machinery in its report (see TD/B/C.4/20; November 29, 1966).

406. The Committee on Shipping has also initiated the following work as within the terms of reference:

    i. A research programme has commenced to establish minimum standards and to exchange information on port facilities in developing countries. The modernization of ports is an important element in the chain of ocean transport which might be considered with regard to ship design, sailing schedules, inland transport systems, etc.

    ii. A number of studies by the U.N.C.T.A.D. Secretariat have been endorsed by the report committee to examine levels and structures of freight rates, conference practices and the adequacy of shipping services. An annual review of current and long-term aspects of maritime transport will also be undertaken.

407. There remain many points in the recommendations of the U.N.C.T.A.D. Conference that still require action from the Committee on Shipping. Some developing countries, for example, do not believe that "commercial viability" (as laid down in recommendation A.IV.22 para. 3) should be the main consideration in deciding whether to expand or establish a national merchant marine since, for some of them, shipping is in their view an important means to economic unification. This and other points will be raised again at the second session of the U.N.C.T.A.D. Conference.

2. INSURANCE

408. Insurance services, measured in terms of premium income, have expanded in recent years at a faster rate than national income in developed countries and in some developing countries, although the volume of insurance transactions in many of the latter countries is small. It is estimated that the ratio of insurance premium receipts to national income in most developing countries is below 1 per cent, and seldom reaches 2 per cent even where the insurance system is relatively advanced, whereas in some developed countries it can reach $8\frac{1}{2}$ per cent. Consequently, out of an estimated world insurance premium income of $57·7 billion in 1962, the share of developing countries was $2·7 billion or 4·7 per cent.

409. The extent of direct operations by foreign companies in developing countries varies greatly according to the policy of individual governments. The governments of many developing countries are adopting legal and supervisory measures to obtain greater control over the insurance market in

order to protect policy-holders, limit foreign exchange liabilities and generally to promote what they regard as a healthy and efficient insurance market. A further important aim is to mobilize insurance funds (especially life insurance reserves), for domestic investment in public or private projects. These efforts are likely to be circumscribed, however, by the highly technical and complex nature of insurance, which requires planning and efficient organization, and in early stages of growth of national markets there continues to be a considerable need for international reinsurance protection.

410. The Committee on Invisibles and Financing related to Trade recommended a programme of work which included the establishment of an expert group to study reinsurance questions arising from Recommendation A.IV.23 of the Final Act. In its report this group recommended that where the contribution of reinsurers in the setting up of the technical reserves by the direct insurer is not based on an agreed percentage of the actual figures of the reinsurers' proportion in the technical reserves, it should be 60 per cent of the re-insurance premiums; this arrangement might assist in reducing the outflow of reinsurance funds from developing countries. The expert group also recommended that the Secretariat should report upon current developments in the field of regional reinsurance arrangements and should study in a few selected developing countries conditions and problems relating to the establishment of national and regional reinsurance institutions. A questionnaire on insurance legislation, supervision and markets has been sent to all developing countries to enable studies to be made of terms and conditions in reinsurance, to improve international statistics on insurance, and to assist with plans for co-ordinating insurance legislation and supervision in developing countries.

411. In all matters related to insurance U.N.C.T.A.D. call for a high level of co-operation from the developed countries, in the form of technical assistance and training facilities and encouragement to developing countries to strengthen their insurance markets.

3. TOURISM

412. World expenditure on foreign travel has risen by around 12 per cent a year in the sixties and it is estimated to have reached about $13,000 million in 1966. With the exception of countries close to the rich industrial areas of North America and North-West Europe, such as Mexico, the West Indies, Spain and North Africa, the share of world receipts going to the developing countries is low; in 1966 Africa's share was around $2\frac{1}{2}$ per cent and that of Asia was less than 5 per cent. Only in recent years as incomes in the industrial countries have continued to rise and faster, cheaper and more reliable travel services have become available has the tourist potential of the more distant developing countries begun to be exploited.

413. In view of the strong expansionary forces that exist for tourism there is room for "newcomers" from among developing countries to attract more visitors and to increase their foreign earnings, without prejudice to traditional tourist centres. The Trade and Development Board has drawn up a pro-

gramme of work on tourism in accordance with the recommendations of the U.N.C.T.A.D. Conference (Final Act Annex A.IV.24). The initial research involves a review of present and prospective patterns of world travel, the collections of statistics relating to tourism and a study of activities in the field of tourism by other organisations. In the initial phase the Secretariat is collecting and examining source material and relevant documentation in search of appropriate methodology for country studies on tourism.

414. The U.N.C.T.A.D. Conference made a number of proposals to facilitate the expansion of earnings from tourism from developing countries which are contained in Annex A.IV.24 to the Final Act but little attempt has so far been made to implement measures to further these policies.

415. An important factor in the expansion of travel to the more distant and remote places is the cost of travel. The U.N.C.T.A.D. Conference recommended that the "Governments and organizations concerned with international travel, explore the possibilities for further reductions of passenger fares which will result in the promotion of tourist travel to developing countries, and it drew attention to the ultimate responsibility of Governments for the level of air fares. The U.N. Conference on International Travel and Tourism in 1963 recommended certain steps to Governments to facilitate travel and the development of tourism which have been endorsed by U.N.C.T.A.D.

416. In most developing countries that have so far benefited from expansion in world travel there has been little planned development of tourism in its relationship with the rest of the economy, the potential market or national investment decisions. The work programme of the Committee on Invisibles and Financing related to Trade pays particular attention to the possibility of exchanging information and experiences between developing countries to achieve planned development of tourism. The developing countries are also recommended to organize regional co-operation for the promotion of travel to and within regions. Regional co-ordinating bodies have been set up in Central America and East Asia and several studies are in process to review tourist problems for specific regions in Africa and Latin America.

417. Developing countries are urged by U.N.C.T.A.D. to take advantage of technical assistance for tourism available from U.N. agencies and other international organizations. Technical advice is available for specific projects in development of tourism or for comprehensive surveys of a country's tourist programme. It has also been recommended by the Committee on Invisibles and Financing related to Trade that the Secretary-General of U.N.C.T.A.D. should give "substantive support" to technical assistance and investments in infra-structure related to tourism.

4. TRANSFER OF TECHNOLOGY

418. It was agreed at the U.N.C.T.A.D. Conference for "developed countries, developing countries and competent international bodies to undertake appropriate measures to facilitate the transfer of technology to develop-

ing countries." Specific recommendations on the subject are contained in Annex A.IV.25 and 26 to the Final Act.

419. The developing countries are primarily users rather than producers of scientific information and they have the greatest interest in the development of a system which will make such information most efficiently and economically accessible. The patented and unpatented know-how needed to establish and operate modern industries is particularly important for economic development, yet even if the relevant technical information is published it may not be possible to use it without operating experience. The acquisition of both those is costly. No attempt has been made so far to estimate the burden on the balance of payments of developing countries of the transfer of technology—i.e. payments for licences, direct technical training, technical documents etc.

420. Developed countries are requested in Annex A.IV.26 of the Final Act to "encourage the holders of patented and unpatented technology to facilitate the transfer of licences, know-how, technical documents and new technology in general to developing countries, including the financing of the procurement of licences and related technology on favourable terms." Little work has so far been undertaken on this subject by the Committee on Invisibles and Financing related to Trade but "in due course a programme of work should be drawn up covering the consideration of measures for improving the balance of invisible trade of developing countries in relation to the transfer of licences, know-how, technical documents and technology in general."

BROAD IMPLICATIONS

421. The work programme for the Committee on Invisibles and Financing related to Trade as outlined in the recommendations of the U.N.C.T.A.D. Conference (Final Act A.IV.21 to 26) is extensive and the above outline indicates that work has only begun in a few fields. The initial phase of research for each subject involves collection of statistics and information, and the examination of methodology in a number of case studies based on the experience of a few developing countries. Only two export committees have so far reported to the Committee on Invisibles; the Committee on Shipping has made certain recommendations on consultation machinery between shippers and shipowners, and the Expert Group on reinsurance has made certain recommendations on technical reserve ratios. Many other studies have been initiated but until these are completed there can be no recommendations for policy instruments and so U.N.C.T.A.D. policy can only be described and assessed in the broadest terms with respect to the original recommendations of the U.N.C.T.A.D. Conference.

422. An important problem that is mentioned either implicitly or explicitly in the U.N.C.T.A.D. Conference recommendations on invisibles concerns improvements to international statistics. Until adequate data becomes available it is difficult to assess the problems of raising the earnings from invisibles of developing countries. The U.N.C.T.A.D. Secretariat has

228

initiated a number of studies on statistics, often in collaboration with other international bodies, and has circulated a questionnaire on insurance statistics and legislation. No results are yet available, however, and work must, for the time being, proceed on a basis of existing material.

CONCLUSIONS

423. Since only two of the U.N.C.T.A.D. Committees have so far made specific recommendations, on shipping and insurance, it is too soon to draw final conclusions. But they illustrate some of the potential dangers that may lie ahead for Britain's invisible earnings in general. The Committee has thus come to the following tentative conclusions:

1. In the case of *insurance*, both the recommendations and the programme of work include features which
   (a) will tend to interfere with private contracts between insurers and reinsurers.
   (b) suggest lines of action which are contrary to the general concept of freedom for insurers to operate on an international basis.
   (c) show a growing emphasis on Government influence and interference, sometimes to the detriment of commercial interests.

2. In the case of *shipping* the actual and potential threats from U.N.C.T.A.D. policies fall under two main heads:
   (a) certain pressures to reduce or regulate freight rates, sometimes regardless of the cost to shipowners.
   (b) the stimulation by U.N.C.T.A.D. of government intervention and participation in the commercial aspects of shipping.

3. The Committee is assured by the Chamber of Shipping, the British Insurance Association and Lloyd's that the co-operation and liaison between them and the Board of Trade (the department concerned with the U.N.C.T.A.D. conferences) is now extremely close and has improved considerably since the first U.N.C.T.A.D. meeting in Geneva in 1964 (for example, an insurance representative was attached to the Government delegation at this year's meeting of the Committee on Invisibles and Financing Related to Trade in New York).

4. The United Kingdom's policy at U.N.C.T.A.D., in the view of the Committee, should continue to pursue two objectives:
   (a) To support general policies in trade and aid designed to raise the trading opportunities and living standards of the developing nations.
   (b) To support policies designed to encourage the expansion of invisible earnings in the developing countries, while resisting artificial stimuli and Government interference, both of which would undermine commercial interests and thus overseas commercial help.

424. With these conclusions in mind the Committee also considered a recent specific example of the kind of international agreements that involve

both developing countries and Britain's invisible earnings. This was the revised text of the Berne Copyright Convention agreed at the Stockholm conference on intellectual property which ended on July 14 this year. The United Kingdom Government did not sign the revised text, which contained a protocol permitting member countries which are "developing" by United Nations standards, to issue compulsory licences to translate and publish works, on payment to the copyright owner, but without his prior consent. It is understood that developing countries which are members of the Berne Convention cannot apply this protocol to works whose country of origin is the United Kingdom unless the U.K. Government either accede to the Convention or agree, without acceding, that they should do so. Nevertheless there are growing fears among British publishers that pressure may soon be brought to bear to persuade the U.K. Government to accede to the revised Convention. The Committee was told by the Publishers' Association that such a decision could well lead to a loss to British publishers and authors of some £10 million. This would include the loss on both sales of books and on the sales of rights. The latter are strictly invisible earnings and the potential loss in this case are put at about £1½ million (out of the £10 million) by the Publishers' Association.

425. The Committee recognizes the needs of the developing countries to obtain the books they need as cheaply as possible; educational help is one of the main elements of aid required. But it also believes that (as in the case of the policies to be pursued at the U.N.C.T.A.D. Conference) this kind of aid should (*a*) go through the proper channels (i.e. the appropriate Government department in London) and (*b*) should not be misappropriated from private industry or private individuals by undermining the entire principle of copyright which has taken so long to establish and plays such a vital part in international publishing.

RECOMMENDATION

426. The Committee recommends that Britain's main invisible trades concerned with U.N.C.T.A.D. should liaise more closely among themselves in order to formulate a more coherent policy. There is a clear need for a continuing analysis outside the Government departments of the policies of the developing countries in general and of U.N.C.T.A.D. policies in particular, as they are likely to affect Britain's invisible earnings.

CHAPTER XVII

INTERNATIONAL OBLIGATIONS

427. In its report the Committee has set out specific recommendations both about possible tax changes, with a view to increasing invisible earnings, and about the removal of tax and other obstacles. It is important, however, to consider how far tax incentives, designed to increase invisible receipts, are likely to transgress Britain's international obligations. This is examined in this chapter.

428. In considering any change in British fiscal or administrative policies affecting "invisible" transactions Britain is limited by certain international obligations. These arise mainly from the following organizations and treaties to which the U.K. has already adhered: (1) The International Monetary Fund (I.M.F.); (2) The General Agreement on Tariffs and Trade (G.A.T.T.); (3) The Organisation for Economic Co-operation and Development (O.E.C.D.); and (4) the European Free Trade Association (E.F.T.A.). If Britain joins the (5) European Economic Community, or Common Market (E.E.C.) we shall also have to pay regard to the provisions of the Treaty of Rome and to the regulations, decisions, directives and recommendations issued under it.

429. The first part of this chapter summarizes the obligations involved in these various links, present and potential, in so far as they relate to British law and practice in invisible transactions. It will consider in particular how these obligations would affect any British effort to remove obstacles to invisible earnings, or to introduce incentives to stimulate these earnings. In practice each organization has concentrated on a different aspect of commercial and financial policy, though some of them overlap.

430. Certain principles are common to all these agreements except the Rome Treaty. They are concerned largely with the removal of obstacles to international trade and payments—the reduction of tariffs, liberalization of current payments and, with more caution, of capital movements, and the easing of exchange restrictions. An associated principle is to secure as much non-discrimination as possible, in the belief that policies applied universally tend to encourage expansion while policies applied selectively tend to divide trade patterns into compartments and thereby to restrict expansion.

431. Further, a principle to which Britain has given support in the postwar period is to ensure that international trade should not be distorted by artificial Government aids. It is this principle which leads to protests when a government favours the business of its nationals to the disadvantage or exclusion of non-residents, as in subsidies or fiscal rebates.

432. The Treaty of Rome and the work of the E.E.C. has in a sense less general objectives: moving away from the idea of world-wide non-discrimination the E.E.C. aims at the gradual harmonization of policies, and eventual integration, of the member economies. This implies ultimately complete freedom of trade, services, establishment, current and capital transactions within the Common Market area—and at the same time uniform rules of commercial policy for dealing with other countries. In its efforts to create a Common Market the Brussels Commission is critical of any national measure, such as aids to specific industries, which is "likely to distort intra-Community competition." This principle of establishing free and fair competition throughout the community is likely to be pressed with increasing force upon member governments.

433. We turn now to the practical implications of each agreement for British policy relating to invisible transactions:

1. INTERNATIONAL MONETARY FUND

434. The two most important of the bodies to be considered—I.M.F. and G.A.T.T.—have little direct bearing on invisibles. The Fund has not formulated any particular views regarding measures to stimulate invisible earnings, or to restrict activities of non-nationals, by fiscal measures. However, under Article IV, Section 3 of the Fund's Articles of Agreement the rates for spot exchange transactions must not differ from the par value of a member's currency by more than 1 per cent. The Fund will examine, therefore, whether any particular fiscal measure affects exchange transactions and, if so, whether the resultant exchange rate differs from parity by more than 1 per cent. Thus, for instance, encouragement of tourism by means of a special exchange rate would be subject to Fund approval under Article VIII, Section 3, as a multiple currency practice if the rate were in excess of the prescribed margin. On the other hand, incentives such as (1) tax exemption to encourage investment in hotels etc., or (2) rebate on purchase tax for tourists, would not run counter to I.M.F. obligations so long as these measures did not affect the exchange rate. Similarly, fiscal measures which favoured nationals but discouraged activities of non-nationals—this has in some countries been done by a special tax—would not raise any Fund problem so long as the tax were not applicable to exchange transactions.

435. In general, the I.M.F. is concerned with the progressive removal of restrictions on all types of payments arising from current transactions, services as well as trade. The U.K. has accepted the obligations of Article VIII which requires us to make sterling formally convertible and prohibits the introduction of restrictions on current payments without the Fund's approval. This would limit Britain's freedom to restore former restrictions on certain invisible transactions, or to impose new ones. But it does not seem to limit our freedom to encourage services by fiscal or other devices, provided these cannot be interpreted as creating in effect a special exchange rate (as the investment currency provisions do, and the security sterling rules did until the 1967 Budget). Deviations from Article VIII

undertakings may be permitted, subject to consultation with the Fund, in the event of serious balance of payments difficulties, though only for strictly limited periods.

2. General Agreement on Tariffs and Trade

436. G.A.T.T. is concerned with merchandise trade. Part II of the agreement contains some broad reference to services linked with trade, such as shipping and insurance, liberty of transit, customs valuation, treatment of films etc. There has been no discussion of these or allied subjects since the 1950's. The well-known prohibition of export subsidies and other financial stimulants applies only to trade in goods, as distinct from services and monetary transfers. The G.A.T.T. secretariat has made no study of invisibles and has left the field, in practice, to other organizations, notably the I.M.F. and O.E.C.D.

3. European Free Trade Association

437. E.F.T.A., like G.A.T.T., is mainly concerned with trade in goods. The Stockholm Convention does not lay down explicit policies for the treatment of invisibles. But certain lines of conduct are implied in the broad decision to co-operate, and, as import duties are finally abolished within the group, "non-tariff" obstacles may attract growing interest.

4. Organisation for Economic Co-operation and Development

438. It is the O.E.C.D.[1] which deals, in practice, with the liberalization of invisible transactions among the principal advanced countries. This situation goes back to 1950, when within the old O.E.E.C. (Organisation for European Economic Co-operation) a twofold decision was taken to break out of the restrictive network of postwar bilateral agreements. The European Payments Union was established to make the currencies of member countries more interchangeable, and a Code of Liberalization was approved which required members to remove quantitative restrictions on imports from other members and also, gradually, to liberalize current invisible transactions and —much later—capital movements.

439. When the O.E.C.D. was set up (30 September, 1961) to take over and extend the work of the O.E.E.C. it adopted the previous policy of calling for the removal of restrictions on "current invisible operations" between members. (Other aspects of the liberalization policy are omitted for the purpose of this report.) A Committee for Invisible Transactions was appointed which agreed on a new "Code of Liberalization of Current Invisibles" and thus obtained specific obligations as well as new commitments from member governments to pursue policies of liberalization. The Code as agreed in 1961 is still largely operative (latest printed edition December 1964) and some relevant sections of it are attached to this chapter as an appendix. At the time each member country had the opportunity of making reserva-

1. Members include Austria, Belgium, Canada, Denmark, France, Germany, Greece, Iceland, Ireland, Italy, Japan, Luxembourg, Netherlands, Norway, Portugal, Spain, Sweden, Switzerland, Turkey, United States, United Kingdom.

tions, and a number were made. After that, any member country that went back on an undertaking to permit payments or transactions within the limits of the Code had to give notice of a "derogation." This may be done on balance of payments grounds, but only for limited periods.

440. In order to show how the O.E.C.D. procedure works it may be useful to mention how it dealt with the U.K. decision, in July 1966, to introduce a foreign exchange allowance for British tourists at £50 per year. The decision was taken in default of a specific undertaking in the Code to allow a minimum of 700 dollars' worth per person per journey automatically and supplements on justification. In 1961 the U.K. had not raised any reservation on this clause. In 1966 the O.E.C.D. recognized that the balance of payments crisis justified the British "derogation" but expressed the hope that this would be one of the first crisis measures to be rescinded. The matter will come up every six months in the O.E.C.D. Committee on Invisibles, and reminders will be sent periodically to the British government.

441. The emphasis of the Code is towards the removal of obstacles. But the promotion of free and fair competition is also recognized as a relevant principle. Thus the main obligation on member governments is to work towards liberalization and not to impose new restrictions. The Code does not explicitly deal with fiscal policies affecting invisible transactions. But in Article 16 of the Code it is provided that any member government may lodge a complaint on the ground that some measure taken by another member "tends to frustrate the progress of liberalization." O.E.C.D. is then required to consider the matter and may make representations to the member concerned with a view to the removal of the offending measure.

442. That is general policy. In addition, as has been shown in some of the cases mentioned, questions are frequently raised by individual member governments which consider that their nationals are suffering damage. In fact generally policy and complaints procedure interact. To explore the working of the system further it may be helpful to look at some hypothetical questions. If, for instance, there were a broad change in the U.K. tax system,[1] such as a shift to a Tax on Value Added, no difficulty would probably arise unless the new tax were to offer some kind of rebate for particular industries or services. Then an element of subsidy might well be suspected, and a complaint might be raised in O.E.C.D.

443. Again, a British decision to apply investment grants in a graduated manner, raising the grants according to results in invisible exports, might not arouse comment if it were kept in general terms. But if it came to be regarded as a deliberate subsidy to specific trades or services opposition would be raised, and the U.K. might be pressed to modify the policy.

444. Officials experienced in the working of the system stress that this is a matter of degree. Much depends on the form in which any measure is introduced and presented. Some services, too, are more sensitive than others. A tax advantage to British hotels related to the number of foreign visitors they

---

1. The Code, being essentially directed towards promoting the liberalization of exchange control, does not bear on questions of general fiscal structure.

attract might not offend against the Code. Equally, it is possible that the reaction evoked by measures favouring invisible earnings by British banks and insurance companies, would be much less than that by similar measures relating to shipping or civil aviation.

445. These differences are relevant to any suggestion of an outright export subsidy for British service industries, according to the size of their invisible earnings in foreign exchange. This would not offend against the Code in principle. But complaints relating to specific services would have to be expected, and in the end the O.E.C.D. might take action on the ground of preserving free and fair competition.[1]

446. In short, the tendency within O.E.C.D. is to look beyond the topics defined in the Code to any condition or measure which hampers the movement towards liberalization, or which introduces an element of discrimination. The O.E.C.D. committee can be induced by any member to take up a wide variety of subjects, and if it decides to pass a disapproving comment the offending member is placed in an uncomfortable position. Beyond the Committee for Invisible Transactions stands the full organization itself and it is this, not merely the Committee, which is primarily interested in internal measures designed to act as incentives or disincentives to international transactions.

5. European Economic Community

447. Many new problems will arise if Britain joins the E.E.C. The Treaty of Rome[2] lays down several relevant principles in a number of Articles, dealing particularly with the right of establishment (52-58), the progressive abolition of restrictions on the supply of Services (59-62), the progressive liberalization of capital movements (67-73) and the limitation and ultimate abolition of "aids" for particular activities, with important exceptions (92-94).

448. In addition to the Treaty there are two Directives dating from 1960 and 1962 laying down in detail how member states are required to abolish restrictions on the movement of capital and of current payments connected with movements of capital. A list of activities is attached, dealing largely with banking and security subjects.

449. The E.E.C. has its own list of current invisibles, and the Commission is charged with continuing scrutiny of member states' policies and conduct. It makes recommendations for action to the Council of Ministers; in some directions member states are required to consult the Commission before taking any action that might conflict with the Treaty or Directives.

450. There are two basic principles: the removal of restrictions between member countries, and the avoidance of any measure "which distorts or threatens to distort competition by favouring certain enterprises or certain

1. Shipping is a special case. In this case only, the Code includes a statement that the shipping policy of member governments is based on "the principle of free circulation of shipping in international trade in free and fair competition." In consequence, non-residents should not be hampered by exchange control, by laws favouring the national flag, by preferential shipping clauses in trade agreements, etc. While the enforcement of this obligation in the field of maritime transport has not been very successful, efforts have recently been made to cite the terms of Note 1 of the Code in connection with quite different subjects. At present this attempt is confined to a "study".

2. Quotations in this report are from the English translation which has no legal standing.

products." The latter relates particularly to "aids" granted by the State or by means of public resources. It would appear, therefore, that Britain would not be permitted, once inside the E.C.C., to take certain fiscal or other steps to stimulate invisible earnings. In practice, however, "aids intended to facilitate the development of certain activities or of certain economic regions" may be permitted, provided that they do not alter trading conditions to such a degree as would be contrary to the common interest (Article 92 3 (c)).

451. Tax reliefs against indirect taxes may be allowed—for exporters of both goods and services—but reliefs against direct taxes are specifically forbidden (Article 98).

452. While the power of the Commission to examine and recommend must not be underrated, its efforts to eliminate all national policies which are "incompatible with the Common Market" (Article 92) are not invariably successful. The strength of the Commission's reaction varies, too, with the subject. In the case of tourism, for instance, a good deal is permitted, and is being done. But any new measure that looks like a straight export subsidy, whether for goods or services, must be submitted to the Commission for consultation, and is liable to be strongly criticized. (While existing policies might be provisionally sanctioned, any *new* steps tend to meet strong opposition.)

453. In the case of stimulants for investment—tax allowances, investment grants, credit at specially low interest rates, etc.—member governments are required to consult with the Commission. Usually there is no strong objection provided the timing is approved.

454. It should be remembered that the E.E.C. is a developing group and it is not possible to predict exactly how far or how fast the policy of economic integration will be carried, or how the powers of the Commission will develop. As customs duties are finally abolished next year attention is certain to switch to other obstacles to a Common Market. Pressure for the further remolikely restrictions on capital movements, on the right of establishment, etc., is val of to grow. Efforts to reduce and finally to remove discriminatory treatment of nationals and non-nationals within the E.E.C. may be intensified. In the field of fiscal policy the pending harmonization of turnover taxes may well be followed by attempts to harmonize the structure of direct corporate taxation among the Six. In short any measure that might be permissible at present, although conflicting with Treaty principles, may well be resisted as time goes on.

455. To sum up: if the U.K. joined E.E.C. it would not be permissible to give an outright export subsidy to her service industries according to the size of their foreign exchange earnings, except in a highly selective manner where a case could be made out for support of depressed regions or activities. Any such arrangement that existed well before our entry might be allowed to stand, at least for some time. Tourism may be regarded as outside these rules. Investment incentives (for hotels, service premises, etc.) would probably be permitted subject to consultation.

456. The Committee feels the need to stress that the significant increase in Britain's invisible earnings from financial and commercial services over the past 10 to 15 years has been associated with the removal of restrictions rather than with the provision of positive incentives. It was the relaxation of exchange control rules which permitted the progressive reopening of the London commodity markets, of the London gold market, and of the London banks' large transactions in foreign exchange, spot and forward, and in foreign currency loans, short and long. Any further removal of restrictions, far from offending against any international obligations, would be in line with their objectives of liberalization.

457. As has been pointed out in earlier chapters, present and potential restrictions in other countries are one of the most important obstacles to the growth of British invisible earnings. It is, of course, British policy to press for the removal of such restrictions through the various international organizations. But the Committee believes that there may be scope for improving the mechanism by which the experience and difficulties of British firms overseas is passed on to the official bodies which are able to take such matters up in the proper forum.

APPENDIX A: CHAPTER XVII

O.E.C.D. CODE OF LIBERALIZATION OF CURRENT INVISIBLE OPERATIONS

Undertakings with Regard to Current Invisible Operations

Article 1: *General Undertakings*

(*a*) Members shall eliminate between one another, in accordance with the provisions of Article 2, restrictions on current invisible transactions and transfers, hereinafter called "current invisible operations." Measures designed for this purpose are hereinafter called "measures of liberalization."

(*b*) Where members are not bound, by virtue of the provisions of this Code, to grant authorizations in respect of current invisible operations, they shall deal with applications in as liberal a manner as possible.

(*c*) Members shall use their best offices to ensure that the measures of liberalization are applied within their overseas territories.

(*d*) Members shall endeavour to extend the measures of liberalization to all members of the International Monetary Fund.

(*e*) "Member" shall mean a Member of the Organization which adheres to this Code.

Article 2: *Measures of Liberalization*

(*a*) Members shall grant any authorization required for a current invisible operation specified in an item set out in Annex A to this Code.

(*b*) A member may lodge reservations relating to the obligations resulting from paragraph (*a*) when:
  (i) an item is added to Annex A to this Code;
  (ii) obligations relating to an item in that Annex are extended; or
  (iii) obligations relating to any such item begin to apply to that member.

Reservations shall be set out in Annex B to this Code.

Article 3: *Public Order and Security*

The provisions of this Code shall not prevent a member from taking action which it considers necessary for:
  (i) the maintenance of public order or the protection of public health, morals and safety;
  (ii) the protection of its essential security interests; or
  (iii) the fulfilment of its obligations relating to international peace and security.

Article 4: *Obligations in Existing Multilateral International Agreements*

Nothing in this Code shall be regarded as altering the obligations undertaken by a Member as a Signatory of the Articles of Agreement of the International Monetary Fund or other existing multilateral international agreements.

Article 5: Controls and Formalities

    (*a*) The measures of liberalization provided for in this Code shall not limit the powers of members to verify the authenticity of current invisible operations nor to take any measures required to prevent evasion of their laws or regulations.

    (*b*) Members shall simplify as much as possible all formalities connected with the authorization or verification of current invisible operations, and shall co-operate, if necessary, to attain such simplification.

Article 6: Execution of Transfers

    (*a*) A member shall be deemed to have complied with its obligations as regards transfers whenever a transfer may be made:

        (i) between persons entitled, by the exchange regulations of the State from which and of the State to which the transfer is to be made, respectively, to make and/or to receive the said transfer;

        (ii) in accordance with international agreements in force at the time the transfer is to be made; and

        (iii) in accordance with the monetary arrangements in force between the State from which and the State to which the transfer is to be made.

    (*b*) The provisions of paragraph (*a*) do not preclude members from demanding payment of maritime freights in the currency of a third State, provided that such a demand is in conformity with established maritime practice.

Article 7: Clauses of Derogation

    (*a*) If its economic and financial situation justifies such a course, a member need not take the whole of the measures of liberalization provided for in Article 2 (*a*).

    (*b*) If any measures of liberalization taken or maintained in accordance with the provisions of Article 2 (*a*) result in serious economic disturbance in the Member State concerned, that member may withdraw those measures.

    (*c*) If the overall balance of payments of a member develops adversely at a rate and in circumstances, including the state of its monetary reserves, which it considers serious that member may temporarily suspend the application of measures of liberalization taken or maintained in accordance with the provisions of Article 2 (*a*).

    (*d*) However, a member invoking paragraph (*c*) shall endeavour to ensure that its measures of liberalization:

        (i) cover, twelve months after it has invoked that paragraph, to a reasonable extent, having regard to the need for advancing towards the objective defined in sub-paragraph (ii), current invisible operations which the member must authorize in accordance with Article 2 (a) and the authorization of which it has suspended since it invoked paragraph (c), and, in particular current invisible operations relating to tourism if, in whole or in part, their authorization has been suspended; and

(ii) comply, eighteen months after it has invoked that paragraph, with its obligations under Article 2 (a).

(e) Any member invoking the provisions of this Article shall do so in such a way as to avoid unnecessary damage which bears especially on the commercial or economic interests of another member and, in particular, shall avoid any discrimination between other members.

CHAPTER XVIII

TAX AND OTHER OBSTACLES

458. So far as domestic obstacles are concerned the Committee felt obliged to examine two aspects of indirect taxation criticised generally by virtually every sector of Britain's invisible exporters, the selective employment tax and the export rebate scheme. In addition, in considering how to broaden the export drive to embrace invisible earnings, the Committee looked closely at the Queen's Award to Industry. All three issues are considered in this chapter.

459. The Committee examined the Selective Employment Tax (S.E.T.) to consider whether (and how) it might be amended in the interests of invisible earnings. Introduced in the 1966 Budget, it is effectively a polltax on all employees (with partial exemption for certain categories of part-timers) levied through the National Insurance system, and with varying rates for men, women, boys and girls. The tax is "selective" because manufacturing receives a matching refund of tax paid together with an additional payment (7s. 6d. per week for each adult male), which will be supplemented by a substantial additional premium for manufacturing in development areas. Certain categories of employer, notably the public sector and some transport undertakings, have the tax refunded but receive no premium. Other sectors, largely the service industries, pay the tax without refund.

460. Broadly speaking, therefore, those who earn foreign exchange through invisible trade are put at a relative disadvantage to those who earn it through visible trade in the form of manufactured goods. This is because insurance, banking and finance, the export houses and major tourist facilities (e.g. hotel accommodation, theatres, etc.) pay the tax without refund. A substantial invisible earner less affected by the tax is the transport sector—shipping, airlines, and so on. Even here there are important variations, particularly in the shipping industry. The shore establishment of shipping companies operating seagoing ships can fall into the refund category (which involves the time and trouble of collection and delay in repayment); shipbrokers, freight agents, shipping agents cannot do so. In addition, shipping operators must have more than 50 per cent of their staff in qualifying activities, a provision which does not in effect apply to bus companies.

461. The first stated objective (see Cmnd. 2986, May, 1966) of S.E.T. has been to improve equity in the tax structure by taxing services as a *quid pro quo* for purchase and excise taxes on goods. It is not the concern of the Committee to judge its success in achieving this. It is sufficient to note that the Government has adopted the principle that indirect taxation should fall away at the frontier and that, as sales of manufactured exports are almost entirely

exempt from indirect taxes, the S.E.T. premiums to manufacturing amount to the provision of an additional advantage to them as compared with invisible services.

462. The second stated objective emphasizes the need to encourage economy in the use of labour by taxing labour-intensive, and therefore service industries, and to make more labour available for manufacturing industry. If efficiency is to be judged by the willingness of firms to vary their inputs of capital and labour, then all the evidence suggests that, in the banking, insurance, merchanting and finance sectors, no spur has been needed to economize in labour input. Broadly speaking, what seems to have happened in these sectors is that employment has remained fairly static but that firms have nevertheless been able to handle a greatly increased volume of business as a result of automation.

463. What is more immediately relevant is the recent deployment of the argument that S.E.T., by conferring a differential advantage to manufacturing industries, wherever sited, will concentrate support on those industries of most importance in the export market. This argument needs detailed scrutiny. The *prima facie* case for the S.E.T. as a means of encouraging exports looks quite a good one. This is because the relative proportion of manufactured goods exports is much higher than for the service industries other than insurance. The following table illustrates this point:

PROPORTION OF NET OUTPUT EXPORTED, 1954 AND 1963

		1963		1954
	Direct	Indirect	Total	Total
1. Total manufacturing	21	7	28	28
of which				
Engineering products	29	4	33	34
Metal manufacture	17	24	41	35
2. Services	13	6	19	18

Source: Derived from 1963 input-output table in *Economic Trends*, August 1966, p. xxxii.

464. This table also makes the important point that while the proportion of manufactured goods going to export is higher than for services, the proportion has not altered over the decade 1954-63. The "services" sector, on the other hand, slightly increased its proportion of net output exported and its indirect contribution is a higher proportion of its total percentage than in the case of manufacturing. In addition manufacturing industry has a relatively high import content compared with services. In 1963, for example, each £100 of net output in textiles and related products required £27 of imports and a figure of £20 is a reasonable average for each £100 of net output in all manufacturing. In contrast, each £100 net output in services required only £9 of imports.

465. These arguments suggest, therefore, that so far as balance of payments policy alone is concerned, there is a strong case for the same S.E.T. treatment for invisible trade as for visible. The question is how to achieve it. The Committee considered various ways of doing so. But the way S.E.T. is

constructed places a major obstacle in the path of any simple administrative device for achieving such a balance. The exemptions to S.E.T. are granted not according to the *type* and *destination* of output but according to the *type of employment*, i.e. broadly speaking as found in the Standard Industrial Classification used by the Ministry of Labour. In practice, therefore, visible trade is given a relative advantage by the tax not by reason of being in the exporting business but by reason of the type of employment. Accordingly it is clearly difficult to exempt (or to offer a premium to) the invisibles sector without making major changes in the present form of S.E.T. Even if the sole object of the tax were to help the balance of payments, a tax which tried to discriminate in favour of both visibles and invisibles on the basis of *employment* would be very difficult to administer. It is clearly impossible in many sectors which contribute towards invisible trade to attribute a particular proportion of employed to export business. It is conceivable that turnover or profit might be divided into foreign or domestic earnings and used as a basis of exemption. But in some parts of invisibles, even these could not be used because of the impossibility of identifying the nationality of the customer (especially in tourism).

466. Thus, in spite of S.E.T.'s positive and obvious disincentive to invisible exports, there remain two important barriers to any attempt (or argument) to provide exemption. The first is that the objectives of the tax involve other considerations, e.g. short-run internal stability and long-term growth, than the balance of payments alone. The second is that the structure of the tax denies the possibility of removing the relative disadvantages suffered by invisibles without major structural changes in the tax itself.

467. Yet the Committee remains convinced that a major tax which on balance imposes a burden on a sector that has produced a persistent payments surplus over the years and which provides a deliberate premium to a sector that invariably produces a payments deficit is in need of some adjustment. There are four possibilities:

    (a) One is to extend the exemption already afforded to sections of the transport and communications industry to other service industries. But, of course, if the exemption was extended to insurance, banking and finance, professional services of all kinds, hotel and catering services (as part of the tourist industry) this would leave the distributive trades as the sole sector paying S.E.T.

    (b) Another possibility is to extend the employment exemption on a narrow front. For example, it could be made to include the whole of order XIX[1] of the S.E.T. classification and the special provision for bus companies could be extended to other transport undertakings. In addition, the exemption could be extended to Order XXI, which covers insurance, banking and finance while other invisible sectors, such as tourism, could be given more specific tax stimuli in other ways.

    (c) The tax could be abolished.

1. Order XIX includes transport and communications.

243

(d) The tax could be made a flat rate polltax on everyone as in many other countries, thereby removing its discriminatory effect against invisible exporters.

468. The Export Rebate scheme is a form of tax relief persistently criticized by many earners of invisible income. As operated at present, it offers relief from vehicle excise duty, hydro-carbon oils duty and some elements of purchase taxes on inputs of exported goods. In order to qualify for Rebate, 20 per cent of the costs of production must be attributable to U.K. expenditure. The amount of relief varies according to the circumstances of individual industries and has ranged from 1 per cent to $3\frac{1}{4}$ per cent of the export value of goods. The weighted average relief comes out at about $1\frac{1}{4}$ per cent.

469. The fact that relief is based on money values of inputs would certainly make it easier to apply to certain classes of invisibles than would be the case with an employment-based tax such as S.E.T.

470. An important administrative condition is that it would have to be possible to identify overseas earnings. Clearly this condition cannot be easily fulfilled in some important classes, notably tourism. In other classes the reverse applies. It would clearly be comparatively simple for the export houses to provide evidence of overseas earnings, and for insurers to establish the quantities of foreign premiums earned. Therefore the export rebate could be extended to invisibles on an initially selective basis, e.g. to shipping and aviation concerns operating internationally, to export houses and to insurance premiums earned overseas.

RECOMMENDATION

471. The Committee recommends, therefore, that the Government (a) consider ways of mitigating the impact of the selective employment tax on those service trades earning foreign exchange, either by enabling them to receive matching refunds or by allowing S.E.T. to be rebated through the export rebate scheme, and (b) consider urgently the extension of the export rebate scheme to earners of invisible income.

BROADENING THE EXPORT DRIVE

472. Throughout its examination of government policy towards invisible earnings, the Committee has been concerned to discover how far official support, both fiscal and moral, has been given to visible exporters and how far the invisible trades have been overlooked. The Committee is far from satisfied that invisible exporters get as much help as they might in such matters as information about overseas markets, help in sales promotion from U.K. embassies and consulates, and publicity in trade fairs, etc. The Committee has recommended adjustments in this attitude at various points in this report. But one criticism has been raised persistently by invisible exporters: the way in which the recently introduced Queen's Award to Industry is confined to visible exports, to the exclusion of Britain's invisible exporters. The Committee has, therefore, examined this particular export promotion arrangement with some care.

473. The award scheme is based on the recommendations of a Committee chaired by the Duke of Edinburgh. These were set out in a report published in August, 1965[1]. The Government accepted these recommendations in full. The main points of the scheme and the criteria on which the awards are based are set out in the following extracts from the report:

> The purpose of the scheme is to recognize outstanding achievement by industry either in increasing exports or in technological innovation. We therefore recommend that the Award should cover achievement either in exports or in technology or in a combination of both. We conceive the Award as recognizing various aspects of industrial efficiency and we recommend that it should be related to the production of goods by any branch of British industry, including agriculture and horticulture. We suggest as an appropriate title The Queen's Award to Industry. . . .

> We recommend that Awards should be announced on a single date in each year. Her Majesty has consented to this date being her actual birthday, April 21. We suggest that the first announcement of Award winners might be made on April 21, 1966, and that the first Awards should run from this date. . . .

> We do not intend to exclude from consideration bodies whose activities conform with the terms of the scheme as a whole even though they are not industrial units in the conventional sense. We therefore recommend that units or agencies of central or local government with industrial functions, as well as research associations, educational institutions and bodies of a similar character should be eligible provided they can show they have contributed to industrial efficiency in the fields with which the scheme is concerned. . . .

> We recommend that the Award should be made for industrial efficiency, assessed in terms of achievements such as:
>
> (i) A substantial and sustained increase in total exports over a period of three years.
>
> (ii) A substantial and sustained increase in the percentage of total export sales to total business over a period of three years.
>
> (iii) A percentage of exports to total business which is considerably and consistently higher than the average for the applicant's sector of industry.
>
> (iv) A spectacular increase over a shorter period than three years where there is a reasonable prospect that the performance can be maintained.
>
> (v) A breakthrough in a particularly difficult market.
>
> (vi) The greatest value of export sales by any group or company in a given year.
>
> (vii) A significant advance in the application of advanced technology to a production or development process in British industry.

1. *The Queen's Award to Industry:* H.M.S.O. price 1s. 9d.

Recognition should only be accorded under this head if greater efficiency results from the process.

(viii) The production for sale of goods which incorporate new and advanced technological qualities.

In respect of (vii) and (viii) credit would be given for earnings from royalties and manufacturing licences, and fees from designs, particularly when received from abroad. . . .

Export Achievement should be based on visible exports, including where appropriate construction work by British companies overseas. . . .

We recommend that the objective of the scheme should be to further the practical application of scientific research and development. . . .

We recommend that the emphasis should be on current technological innovation; but technological achievement in the recent past should not be ruled out of consideration when it has a special relevance to today's technological development. . . .

We recommend that the working of the Award Scheme as presented in our Report should be reviewed after five years so that any modifications which practical experience of its operation had shown to be desirable could be introduced.

474. Thus the awards in terms of export achievement are confined to visible exports. In the light of the importance of invisibles to Britain's balance of payments, already established in earlier chapters, and in view of the criticisms of the Award made by invisible exporters, the Committee believes that there is a strong case for extending the criteria to include invisible exports.

RECOMMENDATION

475. The Committee recommends that the Queen's Award to Industry Scheme, due to be reviewed at the end of five years, should be modified to include invisible exporters *as soon as possible.*

CHAPTER XIX

THE USE OF STERLING

476. The recurrent foreign exchange crises of the past 20 years and the various proposals for changes in the international monetary system raise the question of how important the present international role of sterling is for invisible earnings. At present sterling plays a dual role—it is a currency in which a substantial part of world trade is invoiced, settled and financed, and it is also one of the world's two leading reserve currencies. It is obvious that the use of sterling in international trade is closely linked with invisible earnings, though the connection is closer for some forms of earnings than for others. It is not so immediately obvious however, that there is any close connection between sterling as a reserve currency and invisible earnings. The Committee felt it necessary, therefore, to consider the outlook for such earnings in the light of any change in these uses of sterling.

477. The first step was to consider any changes, both actual and potential, in sterling's roles as a trading currency and a reserve currency. The second was to examine how these changes might affect Britain's invisible earnings. TABLE 49 thus sets out the amount of the U.K.'s external liabilities to other countries in sterling (i.e. the pounds held by non-residents) at the end of each year from 1951 to 1958 and, thereafter, at the end of each quarter. The Bank of England introduced a new series of figures at the end of 1962. In the old series holdings were divided into "central bank and other official" funds and "other funds." The new one distinguishes between "central monetary institutions" and "others." These and other differences (described in the Bank of England's *Quarterly Bulletin* for June 1963) make accurate comparisons between pre- and post-December 1962 impossible. Despite this difficulty, however, a number of conclusions emerge.

478. In general, the holdings of central monetary institutions can be regarded as representing the role of sterling as a reserve currency, and those of others as representing its trading function. The distinction is a rough and ready one since both types of holder use sterling as an investment currency and since central banks hold some working balances, apart from what they would regard as reserves, while some private holdings may be for reserve rather than trading purposes. If it is accepted as a rough guide, however, it can be said that between 60 and 75 per cent of overseas owned sterling has been held as reserves. In the old series official holdings fell from about three quarters of the total in the early 'fifties to about two thirds in the early 'sixties. The new series indicates a slightly lower proportion of reserves. But it has not been in existence long enough for a clear trend to become apparent, even if it existed, and it has been distorted by the very large sums which the

Table 49

U.K. STERLING LIABILITIES AND THE BALANCE OF PAYMENTS
1951–1966

Period		Total	Sterling Liabilities at end of period—£ million				Balance of Payments during period—£ million	
			Central Monetary Institutions		Others		Current Account	Current and Long Term Capital
			O.S.A.	Rest	O.S.A.	Rest		
(1)		(2)	(3)	(4)	(5)	(6)	(7)	(8)
1951		3,577	2,252	659	333	333	−369	n.a.
1952		3,219	2,019	477	463	260	+163	+ 29
1953		3,493	2,203	474	512	304	+145	− 49
1954		3,703	2,260	460	562	421	+117	− 74
1955		3,576	2,266	438	498	374	−155	−277
1956		3,422	2,240	400	490	292	+208	+ 21
1957		3,273	2,126	383	482	282	+223	+117
1958		3,353	1,993	399	526	435	+336	+140
1959	1	3,337	2,034	350	540	413	+ 46	+ 11
	2	3,379	2,076	295	573	435	+ 83	+109
	3	3,443	2,097	306	580	460	+ 19	− 33
	4	3,507	2,165	325	539	478	− 12	−206
1960	1	3,490	2,154	335	514	487	− 26	− 80
	2	3,612	2,152	387	520	553	− 57	−124
	3	3,740	2,083	467	492	698	−122	−137
	4	3,883	2,029	499	449	906	− 70	−126
1961	1	3,714	1,985	568	454	707	− 4	+ 45
	2	3,696	2,097	535	500	564	− 12	− 61
	3	3,490	2,061	453	538	438	+ 7	+ 47
	4	3,546	2,097	440	534	475	+ 4	+ 32
1962	1	3,431	2,025	424	543	439	+ 34	+ 64
	2	3,516	2,098	394	585	439	+ 84	+ 61
	3	3,448	2,068	373	591	416	− 28	− 57
	4	{ 3,501	2,056	375	619	451 }	+ 11	− 65
		{ 3,772	1,769	451	908	692 }		
1963	1	3,778	1,803	412	951	612	+ 84	+ 20
	2	3,840	1,851	376	955	658	+ 70	+ 73
	3	3,946	1,836	379	1,020	711	− 43	− 72
	4	4,072	1,895	437	964	776	− 4	− 84
1964	1	4,223	1,934	474	1,034	781	− 52	−148
	2	4,305	2,023	428	998	856	− 57	−166
	3	4,395	2,006	438	1,057	894	−192	−251
	4	4,199	1,928	523	991	757	− 94	−198
1965	1	4,240	1,850	633	1,037	720	− 34	−122
	2	4,033	1,808	525	981	719	− 11	− 36
	3	4,166	1,739	702	990	735	−107	−203
	4	4,239	1,780	629	1,049	781	+ 34	+ 4
1966	1	4,200	1,825	506	1,077	792	− 35	−108
	2	4,329	1,881	516	1,191	741	− 76	− 67
	3	4,410	1,790	916	1,089	615	−112	−140
	4	4,464	1,743	922	1,128	671	+164	+128

Note: Sterling liabilities up to end-1962 are net and later ones gross.

Bank of England has borrowed from other central banks on several occasions since 1964. The main reasons for the decline of the proportion of reserves in the total seem to have been the downward trend in reserves held in sterling by the sterling area countries, and the rise in the holding of sterling as a trading currency with the relaxation of exchange controls.

479. The rise in the amount of trading sterling (or perhaps more accurately, private holdings of sterling) affected both sterling-area and non-sterling countries. The yearly average for both areas in the old series shows a rise in holdings of trading sterling from £735 million in 1951-53 to £1,145 million in the period 1960-62. The end-year figures for the new series also show a further expansion:

	£ million
1962	1,600
1963	1,740
1964	1,648
1965	1,830
1966	1,799

480. Thus it appears that trading sterling has formed a growing proportion of Britain's total sterling balances, reserve sterling a declining one. What has to be considered, in the light of current discussions about international liquidity, is how far changes in sterling's role as a reserve currency would affect trading sterling and Britain's invisible income. Although different ways of creating international liquidity have been suggested, none of the schemes under discussion within the Group of Ten or the International Monetary Fund contemplates that all sterling holdings of overseas central banks should be fully converted into gold, into balances with the I.M.F. or into some newly created international reserve unit. Even the extreme liquidity schemes put forward in recent years envisage that central banks would still keep working balances in sterling, and no one has suggested any interference with private holdings. There is no obvious reason why a reduction in the sterling holdings of overseas central banks should make any difference to the volume of private holdings, though this is a matter that plainly needs examination.

481. Some advocates of a new reserve system believe that a reduction in the volume of reserve sterling would remove an important source of instability, and so reduce the need for policy changes of the "stop-go" kind. Yet it seems likely that benefits of this kind would be strictly limited. In other words it is clear that a change in the international reserve system would help in so far as it contributed to the stability of sterling, and would be harmful in so far as it weakened the institutional links that help to bring trading and financial transactions to Britain. The Committee has no grounds for believing that either effect would be very strong.

482. The next question concerns the relations between invisible earnings and trading sterling. The latter, as we have established, has constituted a growing proportion of Britain's sterling liabilities. But it is also necessary to consider

how far this kind of sterling has been, and is being, used in international trade.

483. Many different estimates have been made from time to time about "the share of world trade financed in sterling." For a time the figure was invariably put at 50 per cent. More recent official figures have indicated a third.[1] But no details have been published. The Committee prepared its own estimates, which are set out in the appendix to this chapter. As is explained, they show the amount of trade invoiced and settled in sterling and are based on the following assumptions: that a constant 90 per cent of sterling area trade is settled in sterling; that 70 per cent of trade between the sterling area and the rest of the world is settled in sterling; and that between 5 and 10 per cent of non-sterling area trade is thus settled. On this basis the share of world trade settled in sterling was put at between 25½ and 29 per cent in 1965 compared with over 30 per cent in the 1950's. The absolute amount, of course, has continued to rise—from £12,000 million in 1960 to roughly £18,000 million in 1965, reflecting the buoyancy of world trade, as well as price increases.

484. "Invoicing and settlement" naturally imply rather less than "the financing" of world trade. Yet they remain important for the operations of the financial institutions of the City of London. They imply that the City's world-wide banking network is being used for the payment and settlement of trade even if not always for the financing and credit-backing. And, as Walter Bagehot[2] recognized nearly a century ago, it is the use of a financial centre as a "settling-house" that leads to other things, including the leaving of trading deposits. But while the absolute amount of world trade settled in sterling has risen, its share of world trade has continued to decline. At the same time two other developments have occurred. Both the City of London and foreign traders using its services have come to terms with the pound. They have turned to two ways of living with its crises. One is the growing use of the forward exchange market to provide cover against the exchange rate risk. The other is the use of other countries' currencies. While foreign sterling balances on private account have increased, it is highly likely that a growing share of them have been protected in the forward market. There are no official figures to confirm this, but the significant intervention of the Bank of England in the forward market (with the deliberate intention of protecting the gold reserves) has plainly provided foreign traders with cheap protection for their sterling commitments. Secondly, the use of dollar and other foreign deposits to finance some of the City's activities has grown rapidly in recent years.[3] The rise in foreign currency credits offered from London from £906 million in 1962 to £1,785 million in 1965 shows that this new form of financial credit (a direct reflection of the growing Euro-dollar market) is

1. E.g. the Bank of England's evidence to the Committee on Decimal Currency; the statement of Lord Longford in the House of Lords (November 9, 1966): "According to the Treasury we calculate that 30 per cent of the world's trade is still financed by sterling"; and the *D.E.A. Progress Report* for April, 1967 ("about 30 per cent").
2. As he wrote in *Lombard Street* (1873): "Now that London is the clearing house to foreign countries, London has a new liability to foreign countries. At whatever place many people have to make payments, at that place those people must keep money. A large deposit of foreign money in London is now necessary for the business of the world."
3. Most foreign deposits are "on-lent" in foreign currencies.

beginning to rival that from sterling itself. Postwar experience, particularly the recovery in the City's foreign earnings in the face of recurrent sterling crises and more especially the City's recent growing use of other currencies, strongly suggests that London will not only survive but will expand its activities and its profitability, irrespective of the currency in which payment is made. This would be a reflection of the inherited structure of domestic and overseas banking, an experience of trading in money abroad and a capacity for taking risks which cannot be evaluated statistically.

485. The Committee also considered how far different types of invisible income were affected by changes in the international role of sterling. Some were clearly much more involved than others. For this purpose six broad groups were considered: (1) transport, (2) travel, (3) investments, (4) insurance, (5) merchanting and (6) banking.

486. The first two, (1) and (2), depend for healthy growth on rising incomes and a rising level of trade in the world as a whole, and on freedom from restrictions, both physical and financial. To this extent they depend on an efficient system of international currencies and must be damaged by any failure of that system that either slows down the growth of income and trade or leads to restrictions. The comparative freedom of trade, communications, and payments within the sterling system has obviously helped, but a change need not necessarily imply more restrictions.

487. As far as shipping is concerned, it is considered that the use of sterling as a world currency probably has no *direct* effect either on the earnings of British shipowners or on those of shipping brokers, as even if sterling ceased to be a world currency, the broker's services on cross trade fixtures would result in his commision, for example, being paid in whatever currency was currently being used as a world currency, which would again benefit the U.K.'s invisible exports. However, the *indirect* effect on a broker's earnings through the use of sterling as a world currency can be most important and beneficial. One example is the foreign shipowner who fixes his vessels for cross trades with freights payable in sterling in London to the account of the shipowner's London brokers. This means the keeping of accounts for the foreign shipowner in the office of the London broker, which, over the years, inevitably leads to a strengthening of ties between the shipowner and his London broker, and the likelihood of further business coming via London. If sterling became purely a national currency leaving the U.S. dollar as the sole world currency these same fixtures might well be fixed with freights payable in New York in U.S. dollars to the account of the shipowner's New York agents, inevitably leading to a loosening of the ties between the ship-owner and his London broker, and giving an encouragement to the New York agent in his competitive efforts.

488. Britain's overseas investments (3) have been built up over many years and, apart from war or other disaster, the income from them can be expected to change only slowly. However, present policies, both in regard to direct and portfolio investment, must be adverse to the long-run growth of invest-ment income. In so far as a change in the position of sterling enabled the

government to dispense with such policies it would clearly be helpful. The growth of investment income is also helped by the absence of restrictions both on the process of investment and on the transfer of investment income in other countries. Here again, the comparative freedom that has existed within the sterling area has favoured the growth of investment and investment income there. Against this, however, it must be pointed out that the sterling system may have tended to divert British investment to the sterling area and away from other countries with higher growth rates and opportunities for more profitable employment of capital.

489. Insurance (4), like transport and shipping, depends on the general growth of income and trade, and on freedom of transfer of funds between countries. Given favourable conditions in these respects, British firms can operate in countries which do not use sterling either as a reserve or in the finance of trade—witness the large volume of American business. There is equally no evidence that the Swiss are in the slightest degree handicapped in world markets for insurance by the fact that their currency is seldom used in international trading transactions. There is, of course, an indirect connection between sterling and British insurance overseas, in that both the widespread use of sterling in international trade and the foundations of British insurance operations abroad coincided in the nineteenth century. But it is clear that British insurance business overseas is now dependent on the efficiency of the insurance companies and Lloyd's, and the way they conduct their business, both in London and in overseas markets, and not on the fact that sterling is an international currency. What needs to be added, however, is that their earnings depend to a large extent on a freedom of movement of funds. This was the basis of the insurance market in the past. It meant that risks could be spread; it meant that premiums could be invested widely in the most rewarding markets at home and abroad; and it also meant that, when claims arose, payments could be made promptly. The British insurance market is naturally prepared to follow statutory control of the investment of technical reserves. It strongly opposes any compulsory localization of free assets in overseas countries which would threaten its ability to meet exceptional losses in any part of the world from central reserves held in the United Kingdom.

490. Merchanting (5) and banking (6) earnings are closely linked in that trade handled by a British mercantile house is also likely to be financed in London. Both are very much more closely involved with the role of sterling as an international currency than are any of the other categories. The commodity merchants certainly use sterling but regard the following features as more important: (a) the convertibility of the pound. (They were severely hampered until 1948 and it was necessary for special commodity schemes to provide controlled convertibility before the markets could re-open.); and (b) that a large part of the commodities dealt in are grown or produced in the sterling area and that this area has a useful network of branches and financial links with London. The fact that such a high proportion of sterling area trade is settled in sterling does not, of course, imply that the use of sterling as a

reserve currency causes trade to be conducted in this way. It could more plausibly be argued that countries keep their reserves in sterling because they settle their transactions in sterling, though it is probably most realistic to think of both as having common causes in the historical, political and economic ties between the countries concerned.

491. There is clearly no reason why a transaction paid for in sterling need be financed by a credit from a British institution or handled by a British trader, though a high proportion may well be. London firms also provide finance for some trade which is not settled in sterling and some such trade is handled by British traders. More information on all these relationships is desirable, though there is no doubt that a large part of the invisible earnings of banking and merchanting are in respect of transactions settled in sterling, and anything which diminished the use of sterling as a trading currency would damage these earnings.

492. In considering the dependence of these individual activities on the use of sterling, it becomes clear that at least three sets of conditions are important for maintaining and increasing invisible earnings:

1. Freedom of convertibility between sterling and foreign currencies. This includes, of course, freedom from official controls but it also extends more widely, embracing stability in value and freedom from damaging crises of confidence, and the operating efficiency of the foreign exchange market. These things affect both the cost of spot transactions and of obtaining forward cover when required. A large part of British invisible earnings come from transactions which are settled in sterling, and so by-pass the foreign exchange market, but the willingness of overseas residents to accept payment in sterling depends ultimately on their confidence that they can, if they wish, convert their sterling holdings easily and cheaply into other currencies.

2. The efficiency and competitiveness of the various institutions, banks, insurance companies, merchants, shipping and airlines, etc., and of the markets in which they operate. The efficiency of these organizations determines Britain's competitive position in supplying the various services they provide, just as the efficiency of manufacturing industry determines competitiveness in visible trade.

3. The institutional links between British firms and their overseas customers. These range all the way from British ownership of banks and other organizations operating abroad to the ordinary "goodwill" generated by any mutually satisfactory trading relationship. Though this is something that cannot be quantified there is no doubt that it is important, and no doubt that it is easier to destroy links of this kind than to forge them.

493. To conclude, the Committee is conscious that far too little is known about the way in which changes in sterling might affect invisible earnings. It has, however, come to a few tentative conclusions, and combines them with recommendations for further detailed study.

253

494. 1. There is no necessary reason why a change in the present system of reserve currencies involving a reduction in the volume of reserve sterling should lead to any significant reduction in the use of sterling as a trading currency, or in invisible earnings.

2. In so far as such a change weakened institutional links or led other countries to impose restrictions on the conversion of their currencies into sterling, trading sterling would be damaged; and invisible income undermined; in so far as it lessened the frequency and severity of exchange crises, trading sterling would benefit. There is little reason to suppose that either of these effects would be large.

3. Several sectors of Britain's invisible earnings are more dependent on the use of a convertible currency than on the use of an international reserve currency. While all invisible earnings depend for their growth on currency convertibility, the direct impact of any decline in the use of sterling as a trading currency would fall almost entirely on the earnings of merchanting and banking.

4. The continued use of sterling as a trading currency depends to a significant extent on the services offered in the City of London and particularly on their efficiency and competitiveness.

RECOMMENDATIONS

495. The Committee recommends that the following questions deserve more detailed study:

1. If central banks kept their main reserve in a new international currency instead of in sterling, would this lead to a reduction in other sterling holdings, and in the use of sterling in trade?

2. What proportion of the trade at present *settled* in sterling is (*a*) handled by British merchant houses and (*b*) financed by credits obtained in Britain?

3. How far is the current business of the different financial and commercial institutions of the City of London dependent on the role of sterling as an international reserve currency?

The Committee recommends that, if thought appropriate, the Bank of England might initiate such studies in collaboration (particularly in relation to the third question)with City associations.

APPENDIX A: CHAPTER XIX

USE OF STERLING IN WORLD TRADE

For the purpose of working out world trade settled in sterling it is convenient to distinguish between three separate categories of trade:

(i) trade within the sterling area;

(ii) trade between the sterling area and the rest of the world; and

(iii) trade amongst countries outside the sterling area.

Exchange control records have never existed for trade between sterling area countries but the effect of exchange control regulations, reinforcing already existing commercial practice, makes it likely that most (say 90 per cent) of it is settled in sterling, with the balance settled in local sterling area currencies such as the rupee, etc.

The latest data for the second category of trade—between the sterling area and the rest of the world—relate to a few years ago when it was estimated that about 70 per cent of it was conducted in sterling.

The estimates for third category are the weakest point in the estimates as the data for this category are even more out of date. The latest figures available are for 1952—the last full year when detailed records were available of sterling transfers (for trade purposes) between non-sterling area countries, and of transactions in non-sterling area commodities carried out by non-sterling area countries through the London commodity markets. At that date these represented just over 5 per cent of the trade between those countries. This was, however, before sterling arbitrage was permitted, and with the greater freedom of trade and the coming of convertibility, it seems likely that the percentage will have increased substantially since that time—perhaps to as much as 10 per cent. It is possible that high London interest rates and the development of the Euro-dollar market in recent years will have led to a greater use of other currencies for settling trade between non-sterling area countries. On the other hand trade has increased between Communist countries and the rest of the world and sterling is known often to be used for this. In general this will have gone some way towards offsetting a decreased use of sterling in other directions. The present percentage use of sterling for this third category area of trade probably does not exceed 10 per cent, nor on the other hand is it likely to be less than 5 per cent—the level at which it stood in 1952.

On this basis estimates for the percentage of world trade settled in sterling in 1964 are shown below with provisional estimates for 1965.

(£ thousand million)

		Total Trade	Financed in Sterling %	Value
Trade within the sterling area	1964	4·3	90	3·9
	1965	4·4	90	4·0
Trade between the sterling area and the rest of the world	1964	14·2	70	9·9
	1965	15·3	70	10·7
Trade amongst countries outside the sterling area	1964	43·4	5–10	2·2–4·3
	1965	47·3	5–10	2·4–4·7
Total Trade	1964	61·9	26–29½	16·0–18·2
	1965	67·0	25½–29	17·1–19·4

The estimates show that the percentage of world trade settled in sterling is likely to have been slightly lower in 1965 than in 1964: about ½ per cent on the figures shown above.

CHAPTER XX

CONCLUSIONS

496. The Committee has deliberately appended specific conclusions and recommendations to individual chapters. As a result all that remains in this final chapter is to draw some general conclusions and to point the way ahead.

497. The first general assessment is essentially statistical. Of the six major invisible categories in the balance of payments, two are non-commercial—Government transactions and private transfers; both are in deficit, the former sizeably so. Of the four remaining items (investment income, other services, shipping and travel) the first two are in substantial surplus, the last but one marginally in surplus, the last in deficit. The consistency of overall performance should be noted. In terms of net gains or losses, all of these items, except shipping, remain now what they have always been. In terms of gross earnings the three items—investment income, other services, and shipping (with civil aviation)—emerge as the backbone of the invisible account. These three have always provided the surplus, not merely for the invisible balance but for the trade balance as a whole, and this function they still discharge today. The linked evolution of these three incomes since 1913 is worth considering. Assuming, as is legitimate, that investment yield outflows in 1913 were not above £30 million, then the following comparison emerges:

		£ million 1911–1913	1934–1938	1965
Shipping[1]:	Receipts	78	90	910
	Payments	15	85	881
	Balance	+63	+5	+29
Other Services:	Receipts	59	70[2]	583
	Payments	14	16	323
	Balance	+45	+54	+260
Investment Income:	Receipts	218[2]	200	989
	Payments	30	30	538
	Balance	+188	+170	+451
Total of the three items:	Receipts	355	360	2,482
	Payments	59	131	1,742
	Balance	+296	+229	+740

1. Including civil aviation in 1965.
2. Estimated.

498. The interplay of the three elements is clear. Investment income receipts fell from 60 per cent of total gross receipts in 1913 to 40 per cent in 1965. Shipping receipts, in spite of the change in the net position, actually rose to 40 per cent of the triple incomes. "Other services" receipts remained steady throughout at around 20 per cent of the total. This ranking however changes

when payments are taken into account and "net" figures are compared. Gross shipping payments moved from a level of a quarter of the total, to one of about half. "Other services" payments were reduced, from a quarter to less than a fifth. Payments on investment income fell from a half to less than a third. The effect of the net positions is significant. The net balance from investment income remained at about 60 per cent of the total, although gross payments grew far faster than receipts. Shipping actually had a tenfold increase in incomes, but payments increased even faster (over 50 times), causing the near elimination of the net surplus. "Other services," with a tenfold increase in earnings and a 23-fold increase in payments, still came out (in view of the low starting level of the latter) with a net surplus nearly six times greater than in 1913 and equal to 33 per cent of the total surplus. This about made up for the virtual disappearance of the shipping surplus as a share in the total. However, this left investment income, with a net balance more than doubled, still as the source of 65 per cent of the total surplus.

499. What of prospects from now on? The Committee did not find it possible, with the limited time and resources at its disposal, to undertake a detailed analysis of the prospects for invisible earnings over the next few years. But it took the opportunity to discuss the forecasts contained in the National Plan with government departments and with some invisible trades.

500. The starting point is paragraph 41 on page 76 of the National Plan. This states:

> "The net surplus on private invisible transactions averaged £404 million in 1955-59 and £514 million in 1960-64, reaching £561 million in 1964. It has been estimated at £680 million in 1970 at 1964 prices. This improvement on 1964 is the outcome of a wide range of factors operating on different parts of the account."

501. This forecast is then supported by certain assumptions about the expected behaviour of certain trades and services. The main assumptions were as follows:

> "In the transport sector, the shipping account has shown, in recent years, a small deficit, and civil aviation a moderate surplus. Greater productivity in the whole economy as well as in the industries concerned, together with a successful incomes and prices policy, can help to improve the performance of both these industries, especially to the extent that they seize the opportunities presented by growing overseas trade. Receipts and payments on shipping may therefore be expected to be roughly in balance, while the surplus on aviation should grow. Expenditure on travel services must be expected to rise at a high rate, although probably less fast than the very rapid expansion in the early years of this decade. On the other hand, an improved United Kingdom cost position can contribute to the growth of the British tourist industry and thus to a substantial improvement in our earnings. On balance, the deficit on the travel account is expected to continue to rise somewhat.

> "The already large surplus on 'other services'—a big miscellaneous

category—can be expected to grow further. An important part of this category are the financial services associated with 'the City'. It is clear that the United Kingdom has a well-established position in supplying the banking, merchanting and insurance facilities which are a fundamental part of the City's expertise and make a major contribution to the balance of payments. With increasing opportunities in a growing world economy, we can expect the large surplus on 'other services' to rise further.

"The development of interest, profits and dividends is extremely difficult to predict, since there are so many offsetting forces at work. A more competitive and more rapidly growing United Kingdom economy ought to attract overseas direct and portfolio investment, and thereby increase the income due to be paid abroad. On some existing foreign-owned assets in this country, moreover, the effect of the corporation tax seems likely to increase the amounts available to pay dividends abroad.

"On the receipts side, the rate of increase of our income is likely to be adversely affected by the slowing down in the growth of our stock of overseas assets due to the new exchange control measures and the corporation tax. None the less the net result, certainly within the plan period, seems likely to be a continuing, but limited, growth in our net income from abroad, since the earnings from our assets held overseas are so much larger than those from foreign assets in the United Kingdom. Interest received on inter-governmental loans made by the United Kingdom in the past (even although much of our aid will now be given in interest-free loans) and on trade credit are also likely to go on increasing."

502. The major change in economic prospects since the National Plan was first published in the summer of 1966 is the assumption of a slower growth in the national product. This is unlikely to have any marked impact on the underlying assumption that invisibles will show an increasingly favourable balance over the years up to 1970. On the one hand the Government's policies to contain its expenditure overseas are expected to continue. On the other hand the fiscal and exchange control changes introduced to deal with the financial crisis of July, 1966, are likely to curb earnings under the general heading of "interest, profits and dividends." Elsewhere invisible earnings may be expected to grow in line with original expectations. The expected slower growth in the national product and the lower level of incomes may help to improve the travel account and, perhaps, shipping by reducing U.K. demands for such services abroad. Beyond these shorter term factors, the outlook for the expansion of world trade and the possibility of Britain's entry into the Common Market are either difficult or impossible to assess. A more potent factor, in the view of the Committee, is the prospect of expanding invisible earnings by the recommendations set out in earlier chapters.

503. In broad terms four elements have impressed the Committee. They are:
    (*a*) Britain's continuous historical dependence on an invisible surplus for at least two centuries;
    (*b*) the post-war re-establishment of a sizeable invisible surplus in spite of the regular series of exchange crises;
    (*c*) the fact that gross invisible earnings have grown faster than visible exports (and re-exports) over the past decade (up 54 per cent between 1956-65 compared with 41 per cent for visible exports); and
    (*d*) the fact that the import content of invisible exports from the service trades is less than half that of visible exports from the manufacturing trades.

504. The post-war record is all the more impressive when it is realized that over this period visible exports have had continued support from the Government. Virtually every sector of the service trades giving evidence to the Committee contrasted the facilities and encouragements provided for visible exporters with the lack of support (and often understanding) given to invisible exporters. Export rebates, E.C.G.D. policies, the Queen's Award scheme, as well as continued exhortations, have contrasted sharply not only with the absence of support but with such tax burdens as the selective employment tax. In almost every case, as previous chapters have borne out, the difficulties in providing equal support for invisible exporters are real. On a number of occasions Government departments have expressed sympathy to invisible exporters but pleaded these difficulties. The Committee believes that, in the light of the evidence provided in this report, the time has come to realize the full contribution of invisibles, and their potential, and to tackle such difficulties. The service industries providing invisible income on such a large and encouraging scale are highly complex and so naturally are the difficulties in extending export incentives to them. The Committee believes that they should now be faced and tackled.

505. In saying this the Committee is convinced that the contribution of invisibles should be kept constantly in mind and with this objective makes the following recommendations:

RECOMMENDATIONS

506. The Committee recommends that the Bank of England and the Central Statistical Office should be invited to continue to organize regular inquiries into invisible earnings along the lines of those undertaken *ad hoc* by the Committee. The regular collection of such statistics, in the view of the Committee, is essential.

507. The Committee also recommends that some permanent organization should be responsible for keeping a continuing watch on the whole field of invisibles with a view to suggesting means of further promoting invisible earnings at home and abroad. Such a body could also undertake or sponsor the analysis of invisible earnings, including the co-ordination of such work as is already undertaken by individual service industries.

CHAPTER XXI

SUMMARY AND FULL RECOMMENDATIONS

1. SUMMARY

508. The Committee on Invisible Exports has spent over twelve months looking into Britain's invisible earnings and finding ways of making them grow faster. These are the earnings that the people of Britain produce every year by offering a whole variety of services (finance, shipping, entertainment, etc.) to customers abroad. They earn the country a significant and growing amount of foreign exchange. If Government transactions, which are normally included in invisible earnings in the official balance of payments figures, are excluded, the resultant private invisible earnings come to well over a third of Britain's total foreign income. In 1966 private invisible receipts were £2,823 million, compared with £5,110 million from exports and re-exports. (*Chapter I.*)

509. Even if invisible payments (the equivalent of visible imports) are taken into account, the net figure for invisibles remains in surplus. It has been in surplus for every year since the war, while visible trade (apart from the years 1956 and 1958) has been in persistent deficit. When the Committee investigated the same figures over a much longer period, pushing its comparisons back to the beginning of the nineteenth century, the same pattern emerged. It became clear that Britain, as far back as the statistical records went, had had a continuing deficit on visible account. Only seven out of the past 175 years had shown a visible trading surplus. (*Chapter II.*) And over the same extended period, Britain had had a continuous surplus on invisibles. Such earnings, from finance, commerce and other services, the Committee concluded, were an important and persistent feature of Britain's economy.

510. An attempt was made to see how important these earnings were in relation to other countries and to world trade in invisibles as a whole. The Committee's analysis (one of the first of its kind) showed that Britain, along with the United States, played a vital role in the world's invisible trade. (*Chapter III.*) The two countries together dominated the earnings, accounting for over 40 per cent of the total. Britain, in second place in the world league table, earned double the third country—Italy. And the world total was expanding well, rising faster than visible trade over the years 1952-64. A significant feature was that countries usually in surplus on invisibles, like Britain, tended to stay that way and countries in deficit persisted in deficit.

511. In examining different industries and professions earning invisible income, the Committee found that statistical information about several of them was either incomplete or unreliable. Suggestions are made in the report about possible improvements in the collection of figures. (*Chapter XIV.*)

In addition the Committee undertook a number of new investigations. In the City of London it started special inquiries into the invisible earnings of the banks (*Chapter IV*), the Stock Exchange (*Chapter VII*), the Baltic Exchange (*Chapter VIII*) and several commodity markets (*Chapter VI*). It received new information from Lloyd's Register of Shipping (*Chapter VIII*) and the export houses (*Chapter V*). It produced for the first time an official estimate of the invisible earnings of the insurance companies and Lloyd's. (*Chapter IX.*) And outside the City, other special inquiries (*Chapter XII*) provided details of the overseas earnings of Sotheby's, Christies, the casinos, management consultants, accountants, solicitors, surveyors, actuaries, etc., etc.

512. It was on the basis of this new information that the Committee also made an estimate of the invisible earnings of the City of London for 1965. (*Chapter XIII.*) The figure, made up of the earnings of banking, insurance, merchanting and several types of brokerage, amounted to between £205 million and £225 million. The Committee regarded this as a conservative estimate. It did not include the earnings from the portfolio investments of the insurance industry. It excluded the earnings of accountants and solicitors in the City. And 1965 was one of the worst years for insurance underwriting. The Committee recommended that such estimates of the City's earnings should be published annually in future.

513. The Committee pointed to several encouraging features of Britain's invisible earnings. They had been growing faster than visible exports. They had a smaller import content than ordinary visible exports. They produced a surplus big enough, year in year out, to offset the expected deficit on visible trade. Yet, in the view of the Committee, over the years invisible exporters had not been, and were not being given, as much encouragement as visible exporters. Most of the service trades earning invisible income suffered from the selective employment tax; and few of them benefited from the export rebate scheme. As the report states: "Virtually every sector of the service trades giving evidence to the Committee contrasted the facilities and encouragements provided for visible exporters with the lack of support (and often understanding) given to invisible exporters." (*Chapter XX.*)

514. Thus throughout the report, the Committee suggests ways in which individual service industries might be helped by the government and its agencies. It also suggests ways in which these industries might help themselves and calls for further studies (*Chapter XV*) and inquiries: into the operations of the banks' foreign business; into the technical obstacles in the international capital market; into the use of sterling by the City and the City's dependence on it. (*Chapter XIX.*) The Committee also suggests that the Government should give more help to the hotel industry to encourage earnings from tourism (*Chapter X*). It warns of some of the dangers to shipping and insurance arising from the policies of the developing countries at the next U.N.C.T.A.D. conference (*Chapter XVI*). It analyses how far Britain can consider giving incentives to invisible exporters, without transgressing any of her international obligations. (*Chapter XVII.*) It recommends that the selective employment tax and the export rebate scheme should be recon-

sidered in the light of the needs of invisible exporters. And the Committee recommends that the Queen's Award might be extended to invisible exporters "as soon as possible." (*Chapter XVIII.*)

515. The Committee finally hopes that its work will be continued and suggests that the Bank of England and the Central Statistical Office should take on the regular collection of similar figures and that there should be a permanent body to promote invisible exports. (*Chapter XX.*)

2. THE COMMITTEE'S RECOMMENDATIONS

The Committee recommends that. . . .

Invisibles in World Trade—Chapter III

. . . regular analyses of world trade in invisibles, along with Britain's role in it, should be carried out and published by the Central Statistical Office aided by the Bank of England.

Banks—Chapter IV

. . . the leading banking associations arrange an inquiry into the operation of the banks' overseas business and into the comparative rates and facilities offered by Britain and other nations.

. . . the Bank of England and the leading banking associations examine exchange control regulations with the specific purpose of removing restrictions which are hindering the banks' role as major parts of an international financial market and whose removal would not undermine the pound.

. . . the Treasury and the Bank of England consider whether Government departments make enough use of Britain's overseas banking network.

. . . the Confederation of British Industry and the Association of British Chambers of Commerce be asked whether member firms operating overseas, make full use of British banking facilities abroad and, if not, why not.

Export Houses —Chapter V

. . . the British National Export Council should study the question of how far the present system of visible export missions can be extended in their present form, where appropriate, to invisible exporters. Under this scheme help is available through the British National Export Council for export missions which meet certain requirements, such as a minimum number within the mission, market and product approved in advance by Board of Trade officials, sponsored by a non-profit-making body, report to be made public, etc.

. . . the Export Credit Guarantees Department should consider how far it could extend the facilities it provides on External Trade Policies as a direct stimulus to the earning of invisible income. Such a move would not, it is clear, help British visible exports; but in the light of the importance of invisible income to Britain's payments balance, the Committee believes that a general re-consideration of E.C.G.D. policies to reflect an invisible export drive as well as the accepted visible export drive is now necessary.

. . . the contribution of the export houses needs to be evaluated more closely in statistical terms than has been done so far. Since, as is shown in the Committee's examination of the commissions on exports and imports in Appendix B (*Chapter V*), there is a strong case for an official survey of these commissions and of the values shown in customs documents, the Committee recommends that such an official examination might be combined and co-ordinated with a more detailed survey by the British Export Houses Association of the earnings of their members.

Commodities—Chapter VI

. . . in order to provide more frequent (statistical) "benchmarks" the British Federation of Commodity Associations should consider, after discussions with the Bank of England, what regularity would be acceptable to members and at the same time most fruitful to the official statisticians.

Stock Exchange and Capital Market—Chapter VII

. . . the Bank of England, Accepting Houses Committee, the Issuing Houses Committee and the Council of the London Stock Exchange undertake a specific inquiry to examine the technical obstacles standing in the way of further earnings from the arranging of such international issues through London.

Transport (Shipping)—Chapter VIII

. . . more of the information already collected should now be published. In particular this might be done for the earnings of liners, tramps and tankers separately. It is suggested that talks might take place between the Central Statistical Office and the Chamber of Shipping about the kind of breakdown that might be provided without disclosing confidential information about individual firms.

. . . efforts be made to get shipping statistics available earlier, although the Committee recognizes that there are practical difficulties involved and earlier figures might produce inaccuracies. The results of the Chamber of Shipping surveys (both the annual samples and the periodical full-scale inquiries) are not available until some time after the end of the year to which they refer. This is a clear handicap in the preparation of quarterly figures. Any progress that can be made without throwing an unreasonable amount of extra work on the shipping companies would be welcome.

. . . the Baltic Exchange, in collaboration with the Bank of England and the Central Statistical Office, should consider undertaking an inquiry into members' invisible earnings on a regular basis in future.

Insurance—Chapter IX

. . . following talks between the Board of Trade, the British Insurance Association, Lloyd's and the Corporation of Insurance Brokers, efforts should be made to fill the statistical deficiencies relating to the insurance industry's portfolio investment, the foreign earnings of life insurance companies overseas and "home-foreign" underwriting business (other than marine) transacted in the U.K.

... an estimate of the insurance industry's foreign earnings should be published annually in future.

... the insurance companies and Lloyd's should continue to study ways and means of improving their underwriting results in North America.

... the insurance companies and Lloyd's should be given government support abroad:

(a) in cases where insurance control regulations require the immobilization of funds in any country beyond those required to establish normal technical reserves and where companies are required to maintain funds and no suitable avenues of investment exist.

(b) in cases where discriminatory legislation imposes greater restrictions upon British companies and Lloyd's than upon national companies.

Travel—Chapter X

... separate figures for international fare payments, at present included under transport, should be prepared and published by the Board of Trade. This would allow the British Travel Association and others involved with the potential of travel to the British economy to know their significance. The Committee, however, is *not* persuaded that the form of the balance of payments should be altered in order to add the fare payments to the "travel" account.

... the Board of Trade should consider estimating the spending of foreign travellers on goods etc., not at present included in the "travel" account in the balance of payments. Such figures would be of prime significance in assessing Britain's travel potential and in comparing Britain's experience with that of other countries. Again no change in the present form of the balance of payments accounts need be contemplated.

... the Government should significantly increase its financial help to the hotel industry. The Committee's view on the selective employment tax and the export rebate scheme are set out in Chapter XVIII.

Overseas Investment—Chapter XI

... a detailed study be made of the role of the United Kingdom in the international flow of capital—direct, portfolio and "other"—and of the impact of this, and of the returns flowing from it, on the U.K.'s balance of payments.

... in the belief that obstructions to both the inflow and outflow of portfolio investment are likely to undermine earnings of invisible income, the Government should consider policies aimed at eliminating or reducing such obstructions, for example:

(i) The removal of stamp duty.

(ii) An increase in the number of fixed interest securities free of tax at source to non-residents.

(iii) The negotiation of further double taxation relief agreements with the minimum possible rate of withholding tax.

(iv) Introduction of shares of no par value.

(v) Bearer share issues by U.K. companies.

(vi) Removal or adjustment in the case of Investment trusts of the 25 per cent surrender of exchange to the Treasury arising from sales of foreign securities.

(vii) Adjustment of death duty provisions relating to the foreign ownership of U.K. securities.

City's Earnings—Chapter XIII

The Committee suggests that in future corresponding estimates of the "City's" earnings should be made and published annually by the Bank of England or the Central Statistical Office, separately from the official balance of payments statistics.

Statistical Conclusions—Chapter XIV

. . . that the detailed correlations between invisible earnings and invisible payments should be closely analysed, where possible, sector by sector, either by individual trade associations or by the appropriate government department.

. . . that the Central Statistical Office, along with the appropriate government departments, should undertake a specific inquiry into the feasibility of producing monthly estimates of invisible earnings and payments, and, if thought appropriate, should publish its findings.

. . . every effort should be made, within the resources of government departments and of the industries concerned, to improve the quarterly estimates of invisible earnings and payments.

. . . that the Board of Trade should consider the form of its monthly press release relating to visible trade, with a view to including the following improvements:

(*a*) It is recommended that the table published monthly in the press release should in future include columns showing private invisible trade figures, Government spending and Britain's total payments position. An example of this is set out in TABLE 45.

(*b*) It is recommended that, after the first sentence setting out the latest monthly visible trade figures in the press release, a reference to invisibles should be included, along the following lines: "In addition to visible trade, net invisible earnings produce a regular surplus, which, in the year to (say) June 30, 1966, averaged £11 million a month."

. . . that the Central Statistical Office should consider whether it could produce a monthly moving average of invisible transactions (taking into account the latest quarterly figures) so that the suggested monthly reference to invisibles might be brought close to recent experience.

Efficiency of City—Chapter XV

. . . that further practical studies should be encouraged into the efficiency of the main service trades earning invisible income.

. . . individual trade associations in the City should consider some criterion for measuring the efficiency of their members.

. . . City associations should consider both a joint effort to promote their combined services in overseas markets on a continuing basis, and an examination of the City's future role *vis-à-vis* other financial and commercial centres abroad.

Policies of Developing Countries—Chapter XVI

. . . Britain's main invisible trades concerned with U.N.C.T.A.D. should liaise more closely among themselves in order to formulate a more coherent policy. There is a clear need for a continuing analysis outside the Government departments of the policies of the developing countries in general and of U.N.C.T.A.D. policies in particular, as they are likely to affect Britain's invisible earnings.

Tax and Other Obstacles—Chapter XVIII

. . . the Government:

(a) consider ways of mitigating the impact of the selective employment tax on those service trades earning foreign exchange, either by enabling them to receive matching refunds or by allowing S.E.T. to be rebated through the export rebate scheme.

(b) consider urgently the extension of the export rebate scheme to earners of invisible income.

. . . the Queen's Award to Industry Scheme, due to be reviewed at the end of five years, should be modified to include invisible exporters *as soon as possible*.

Sterling—Chapter XIX

. . . the following questions deserve more detailed study:

(1) If central banks kept their main reserve in a new international currency instead of in sterling, would this lead to a reduction in other sterling holdings, and in the use of sterling in trade?

(2) What proportion of the trade at present *settled* in sterling is (a) handled by British merchant houses and (b) financed by credits obtained in Britain?

(3) How far is the current business of the different financial and commercial institutions of the City of London dependent on the role of sterling as an international reserve currency?

. . . if appropriate, the Bank of England might initiate such studies in collaboration (particularly in relation to the third question) with City associations.

Conclusions—Chapter XX

. . . the Bank of England and the Central Statistical Office should be invited to continue to organize regular inquiries into invisible earnings along the lines of those undertaken *ad hoc* by the Committee. The regular collection of such statistics, in the view of the Committee, is essential.

. . . some permanent organisation should be responsible for keeping a continuing watch on the whole field of invisibles with a view to suggesting means of further promoting invisible earnings at home and abroad. Such a body could also undertake or sponsor the analysis of invisible earnings, including the co-ordination of such work as is already undertaken by individual service industries.